THE FUNCTION OF NEWSPAPERS IN SOCIETY

A Global Perspective

Edited by
Shannon E. Martin and David A. Copeland

Foreword by
John C. Merrill

Westport, Connecticut
London

Library of Congress Cataloging-in-Publication Data

The function of newspapers in society : a global perspective / edited by Shannon E. Martin and David A. Copeland ; foreword by John C. Merrill.
    p. cm.
    Includes bibliographical references and index.
    ISBN 0–275–97398–0 (alk. paper)
    1. Newspapers—History.   I. Martin, Shannon E.   II. Copeland, David A., 1951–
PN4731.F74   2003
070.1′72′09—dc21   2002029765

British Library Cataloguing in Publication Data is available.

Library of Congress Catalog Card Number: 2002029765
ISBN: 0–275–97398–0

First published in 2003

Praeger Publishers, 88 Post Road West, Westport, CT 06881
An imprint of Greenwood Publishing Group, Inc.
www.praeger.com

Printed in the United States of America

The paper used in this book complies with the
Permanent Paper Standard issued by the National
Information Standards Organization (Z39.48–1984).

10 9 8 7 6 5 4 3 2

Contents

Foreword

John C. Merrill

At last, we have a book that shines a spotlight on newspapers, and what is more, on newspapers around the world. Most such anthologies, in my opinion, have tried to cover too much of the various media, trends, and philosophers in the vast field of mass communication. This book resists such a broad sweep and focuses on "newspapers" or what are generally called newspapers in various parts of the world.

In addition, it provides a much-needed historical setting for the newspaper press of the various world regions. This is an important feature that adds significant value to this volume. Just what is a "newspaper"? The various contributors discuss this. I have puzzled over the meaning of "newspaper" for many years and am not sure I understand it yet. But this book helps. I do know that perhaps the term "newspaper" is really a misnomer today, for at least 80 percent of a newspaper's space is given over to non-news, such as editorials, features, pictures, puzzles, advice to the lovelorn, gossip, conjecture, letters, and so on. And, of course, there is the substantial amount of space devoted to advertising. Maybe these periodicals should just be called "papers" or something more appropriate.

Be this as it may, what we generally call newspapers do carry some news—and this is true in every country, and has been true in every age of the printing press. The contributors to this book have merged descriptive discourse with historical context, and they are all to be commended. All the major areas of the world have been covered, and the variety of newspapers have been highlighted. Little more can be expected of a book of this nature and size. In Chapter 10, two of the authors even deal with newspapers in the twenty-first century, discoursing on the directions and types of periodical reading material that will face our children and grandchildren. It is a good book and one that I, long interested in global newspaper journalism, am glad to see published.

Introduction

Shannon E. Martin

James Gordon Bennett, founder and editor of the *New York Herald*, declared in 1850 that "newspapers—the circulators of intelligence merely—must submit to destiny, and go out of existence" because of the overwhelming success and adoption of the telegraph as a means of delivering the news.[1] He was not the only prophet of the newspaper industry's doom, but he was surely among the earliest.

Near the end of the twentieth century, the phrase "newspapers are dead" could be found among many special topics media panels organized at meetings around the globe.[2] Ted Turner was reported, as early as 1986, to have said that newspapers had no future. "The day will come when we'll have a tree ethic and we won't be able to waste them," Turner said, making reference to the use of tree pulp for publishing newspapers that are then thrown away by the ton, day after day, only to clog the landfills and waste disposal systems around the world.[3]

Rich Meislin, editor of the *New York Times Digital* denied, however, that newspapers were dead. "When the Web first started, people said newspapers are dead because readers will go to the direct source of the news. But no one wants to spend that much time gathering information every day."[4] Gary F. Sherlock, then a Gannett publisher, was reported in 1997 as believing that "the claim that daily newspapers are dead is a tired old story."[5] But *InfoWorld Electric* declared it was true in a headline over an article by Marc Ferranti posted March 19, 1998, "Newspapers Are Dead—Long Live Newspapers!"[6]

There were some among the media and information technology industries that stubbornly would not accept *Info/World*'s claim as a fact. The *Zeitgeist Gazette* headlined a brief in the September 7, 1999, issue with "Not Dead Yet." The article reported: "The information technology writers are at it again, commandeering acres of newspaper space to confidently proclaim that newspapers are dead. This has been going on for generations. First it was radio..., then television, then the Internet. Now—according to Samantha Amjadali's unquestioning splash in the Computer section of the *Oz*—it's e-ink and plastic paper."[7] And as the twenty-first century dawned, Roger Schank, a computer scientist and cognitive psychologist at Northwestern University, chose the Internet as the most important invention of the recent past. He supported his vote by noting all the conveniences brought about by the Internet, and then added, "Newspapers? Not dead yet," though he did go on to speculate that their demise was likely.[8]

As recently as 2001, however, editors found evidence immediately after the September 11 New York City World Trade Towers and Washington, D.C., Pentagon attacks that the general readership still flocked to the newspaper stands when they wanted "to hold the news in their hands."[9] Every major daily newspaper in the United States reported publishing extra copies and special editions to meet the demands of readers who wanted what only newspapers seemed able to supply in the immediate and protracted aftermath of the tragedy—a format that made the dizzying swirl of events stand still long enough for a thorough looking over.

When prognosticators announce that newspapers are dead, what do they mean? There is obviously some difference of opinion among those inside the industry as well as those observing societies' habits and choices. Do they mean that the term "newspaper" is no longer a useful concept, or do they mean that the news in a format of ink on paper is about to cease?

Bennett made a distinction between the newspaper and its contents when he wrote that, while newspapers may be doomed by the invention of the telegraph, "[j]ournalism, which possesses intellect, mind and originality, will not suffer. The public mind will be stimulated to greater activity by the rapid circulation of news.... Thus the intellectual, philosophic and original journalist will have a greater, a more excited, and more thoughtful audience than ever."[10] Are newspapers in fact merely a commercial product sold quickly and tossed aside as soon as a newer edition is available? Or are they a component of a vigorous society that thrives on intelligence and information delivery, that saves portions as mementos, and that refers to newspapers, either with denigration or eulogy, as an extension of the government?[11]

How can there be so many views about, and so much interest in, newspapers if they are but another passing convenience for society? If we review the roles that newspapers have provided in societies around the world, might we better understand the concept, and why that thing we call a newspaper today seems to be found in all parts of the globe and throughout history? How can it be that the death knell for newspapers has rung for decades and yet we find newspapers still available everywhere we go? For example, Publishers Electronic Printing Concept (PEPC) announced that it had begun installing kiosks or "presspoints" around the world where, for a fee, sixty-five newspapers from thirty-five countries can be selected, reviewed, and printed as a full edition.[12] Even the concept "newspaper" seems to have an indefatigable life. University and semiprofessional theater groups as recently as 2002 are restaging plays called "living newspapers" that were originally performed in the 1930s and presented coast to coast.[13]

The aim of this book—a collection of chapters that report the history of newspapers within particular geographic regions—is to give the reader an opportunity to look across cultural uses of newspapers so that a larger view of the functions they serve can be assessed. Though all parts of the world are not represented among the chapters, the authors here hope that the somewhat wider view provided within a single cover will make it possible for historians, media scholars, and industry insiders to more easily recognize the fundamental characteristics of newspapers. With this clearer understanding of those elements that, combined, we now call a newspaper, we can thoughtfully work toward providing, more effectively and efficiently, a news product to any society that wants and needs the day's intelligence in a stable format that is easy to recognize and understand.

The chapters that follow begin with a more thorough review of what has been identified at various times throughout human history as a newspaper. Chapter 1 intends to provide a framework for understanding the more specifically detailed histories of newspapers within geographic regions of the world.

Chapter 2 then begins the regional histories with a look at the Arab world and its development of newspapers in a postcolonial era. While much of that history is of relatively recent and modern newspapers, the Nile Valley is one of the oldest locations for newspaper-like social products.

Chapter 3 takes the entire African continent in a review that focuses on the political role of newspapers across the many cultures and nations there. This review focuses on the political types and uses of newspapers among those countries.

Chapter 4 moves to the Asian cultures of Japan, Korea, and China. These countries, though in close proximity to one another, have very different uses for newspapers. And though these cultures are among the oldest in the world that used paper and printing techniques, their development of community newspapers is somewhat recent.

Chapter 5 reports on the Pacific Rim and its widely varying societies. The newspapers in this region, however, do share one characteristic—that of developing and enhancing self-identity.

Chapter 6 tells the more familiar story of early European countries and their uses for newspaper-like products. This chapter highlights the developments in technology and use that many of us easily recognize as precursors to modern newspapers.

Chapter 7 brings to full view those European advances in the post-sixteenth-century period that were exported to so many parts of the world during rapid colonization.

Chapter 8 provides an inclusive review of newspaper history in the Americas and the wide range of uses for news products in the lands thought to be untouched by civilization until the colonials arrived.

Chapter 9 summarizes the newspaper trends often reported in the twentieth century. And Chapter 10 speculates on the fundamental uses of a newspaper of the twenty-first century.

The Conclusion then is offered as a selection of those characteristics that seem to carry across cultures and times so that the scholar and practitioner might easily survey the life and breadth of newspapers as they have been and speculate about their future.

The contributing editors would like to thank the chapter authors for their willingness to participate in this project. Their cooperation about deadlines and manuscript formats helped the process of manuscript collection along to completion. We would also like to thank our many institutional colleagues who helped by listening to long conversations in pursuit of the project's goals, and who probably allowed us more than our share of community resources. There are also scholars and newspaper practitioners who inspired us to think outside the normal rubric of historical research. We would like to thank them individually because we probably did not show enough appreciation for their guidance when it was given. These include Donald L. Shaw and Margaret A. Blanchard at the University of North Carolina, Chapel Hill, William David Sloan at the University of Alabama, Bill F. Chamberlin at the University of Florida, and John Merrill at the University of Missouri.

Our families, too, deserve more than the usual thanks. Robert J. and Mary K. Rossi were seemingly tireless in listening to us talk through the project over the course of several years. Zachary and Jacob Rosenbarger were uncomplaining when their school or cycling events went unattended so that deadlines on the book could be met. Craig Martin was generous in sharing his ancient languages knowledge with us. And Edwin Martin and Robin Copeland lost nearly as much sleep over the project as the contributing editors, and yet remained a kind and willing companion. There are of course dozens of others who might also be named, but we hope that instead they will enjoy the book itself as a thanks for a job well done.

NOTES

1. Isaac Clark Pray, *Memoirs of James Gordon Bennett and His Times* (New York: Stringer and Townsend, 1855), p. 363.

2. For example, see Jane Black, "No, the Net Isn't Annihilating Newspapers," *BusinessWeek*, 1 February 2001, at http://www.businessweek.com/bwdaily/dnflash/feb2001/nf2001021_527.htm (viewed March 2002); Charles Rappleye, "Cracking the Church-State Wall, Cover Stories/Newspapers," *Columbia Journalism Review* (January–February 1998), at http://www.cjr.org/year/98/1/church.asp (viewed March 2002); Mark Gross, "Publishing Strategies Conference Keynote," Seybold Seminars, San Francisco, California, 1999, transcript; Pat Borninski, "Journalism Leaders Say 'Yes' to Sophisticated Audiences of the Future," *WSU Campus News*, 16 April 1998.

3. "Notebook," *Communications Daily*, 31 October 1986, p. 13.

4. Cited in "Media in Transition," MIT Communication Forum, 30 November 2000, at http://media-in-transition.mit.edu/forums/journalism_2000/summary.html (viewed March 2002).

5. Cited in Robert Nixon, "Print Media Rest in Peace?" *Fairfield County Weekly*, 1997, at http://www.fairfieldweekly.com/articles/dailyside.html (viewed March 2002).

6. Marc Ferranti, "Newspapers Are Dead—Long Live Newspapers!" *InfoWorld Electric*, 19 March 1998, at http://ww1.infoworld.com/cgi-bin/displayStory.pl?980319.eh paper.htm (viewed March 2002).

7. *Zeitgeist Gazette* Archive, 7 September 1999, at http://www.zeitgaz.com/au/ archive/990907/print.htm (viewed March 2002).

8. Roger Schank, *Edge*, 29 October 2001, at http://www.edge.org/documents/ Invention.html (viewed March 2002).

9. Susan Ellerbach, "Extra! Extra! Extra!" *Coffee with Clark*, aired 20–21 October 2001, at http://www.kcscfm.com/Clark/10201021.html (viewed March 2002).

10. Pray, *James Gordon Bennett*, pp. 363–4.

11. For an exploration of the connection between U.S. newspaper design and format, see Kevin Barnhurst and John Nerone, *The Form of News* (New York: Guilford, 2001).

12. "PEPC Worldwide, Printing a Swiss Daily at Thailand's Latest Presspoint," *Editor and Publisher*, 4 March 2002, p. 15.

13. Jane Mathews, *The Federal Theatre 1935–1939* (Princeton, NJ: Princeton University Press, 1967), at http://memory.loc.gov/ammem/fedtp/ftbrwn03.html (viewed March 2002).

Chapter 1

Newspaper History Traditions

Shannon E. Martin

The physical presentation of most newspapers in the twentieth century was very similar to those of the eighteenth and nineteenth centuries—type on a large sheet of paper that could be, and often was, folded to facilitate carrying or storing. But during the 1980s and 1990s, several newspaper companies and some university labs experimented with the form of newspapers. These experimental versions were delivered digitally to computer notebooks or downloaded onto plasma-like handheld panels. In these prototypes, there were no large sheets of paper, and the typeface consisted of 0s and 1s that could be altered to suit the reader's preference. While there was not widespread adoption of these models by the end of the century, there was intuitive understanding by many that the intention of these new products was simply to provide a better newspaper to modern readers.

There were some, however, who wondered if these new prototypes were newspapers at all. Perhaps these news products were just newspapers in a progressive format, but maybe they were different enough to be considered a new medium altogether. There was no fixed format, for instance, so readers of the same "newspaper" might see three stories on their computer or notebook screens at a time, while others might see seven. Though the content of the text itself might remain the same from screen print to screen print, the breaks and jumps might be different from printer output to printer output. While many of these elements seem minor, they matter a great deal among some industry insiders, legal practitioners, and researchers.[1] When and how some particular group of readers learn something noteworthy or how much they might have seen at a quick glance is of particular importance not only to the newspaper industry, but also in legal cases, sociology studies, and opinion poll data. In order to appreciate the richness of what, at first blush, appears to be a relatively narrow question—Is any news product that claims to be a newspaper actually a newspaper?—a review of the history of the form of those news products called newspapers is the first task.

DEFINING THE NEWSPAPER

What is a newspaper? Historians during the twentieth century seemed to have settled on a definition that was succinctly rendered in a 1930 *Journalism Quarterly* article by Eric W. Allen.[2] Allen's definition of a newspaper was actually adapted from Otto Groth's *Die Zeitung—Ein System des Zeitungskunde* published in 1928.[3] The definition requires seven components, or consists of seven characteristics. It is this definition of newspapers that is most often used by modern historians. Allen and Groth said a true newspaper must be periodic, mechanically reproduced, and available to all who pay for it. In addition, the content must be varied, general, timely, and organized.[4]

This definition appears to have been generally adopted by most of the scholars who are interested in tracing the progress of news publications. Some examples of these studies include, for example, Joseph Frank's *The Beginnings of the English Newspaper, 1620–1660*, and Michael Harris and Alan Lee's edited volume *The Press in English Society from the Seventeenth to Nineteenth Centuries*, as well as *Newspaper History: From the 17th Century to the Present Day*, edited by George Boyce, James Curran, and Pauline Wingate.[5] Frank sets out very clearly what he intends to include as a newspaper. He says newspapers are printed, not handwritten, published regularly, at frequent intervals, and focus on current events.[6] The general introduction to *The Press in English Society* admits to some inconsistency among the contributing authors about what constitutes a newspaper, as differentiated from other periodicals.[7] But the general outlines are easily inferred: that newspapers are published regularly and feature the political concerns of the day. And Boyce, Curran, and Wingate, in their *Newspaper History*, simply and straightforwardly note 1621 as the starting point for newspaper history.[8] That date has become the accepted launch for the first publications that meet the definition of a newspaper as described by Allen.

There are many texts that look at the development of newspapers within the publishing industry, while others examine the influence of newspapers at a particular point in history. These works are clear about segregating publications that did or did not meet the accepted twentieth-century criteria of newspapers. For example, Charles E. Clark's *The Public Prints: The Newspaper in Anglo-American Culture, 1665–1740* goes to some lengths in explaining the difference between newspapers and other forms of news publication.[9] These differences include not only the printing format, but also who commissioned the publication and the intended audience. And Leslie Shepard's *The History of Street Literature* includes discussion and examples of seventeenth-century news sheets or news pamphlets.[10] These were publications on a particular topic, often satirical and hard for the general public to read. But because they were published sporadically and may not have included a wide range of news topics, these publications are usually excluded from newspaper history and, instead, are considered part of broader category of street literature. There are also some texts that explore the specific content of newspapers within a particular political environment. These works include those like Jeremy D. Popkin's "Journals: The New Face of News" in *Revolution in Print: The Press in France, 1775–1800* and David A. Copeland's *Colonial American Newspapers: Character and Content.*[11] Each of these authors provides many examples of newspapers published during the era cited in the titles, and neither worries the reader with long explanations about what a newspaper is. The characteristics are widely known and therefore assumed to be understood; they are those explicitly named by Allen and Groth.

This closely defined list of criteria for describing a newspaper, however, excludes many texts that carried news for the expressed purpose of informing a constituency about events. Examples can be easily found from the time of the Roman Empire as well as during the Chinese Han and T'ang dynasties.[12] There are even those who assert that the Cro-Magnon cave dwellers, Archaic period cultures in the Americas, and Fifth Dynasty kings of Egypt 4,000 years ago were posting news items on the stone walls and pillars of their communities.[13] These examples, however, fall short of the Allen definition because they were not mechanically reproduced and were somewhat limited in their availability. In the case of the Roman diurnals, or journals, the news was, by decree, written and posted in a public place. The text was then copied many times by scribe houses for wider distribution. These copies were then hand-delivered to subscribers or those who had paid for particular editions. These reports were usually called news letters, but given the technology of the time were very similar to modern newspapers in most respects.[14]

Lucy Maynard Salmon reports in her 1976 book *The Newspaper and the Historian* that for the purposes of her research, news formats included single news-carrying items like placards, broadsides, posters, circulars, handbills, and walls.[15] But she spends some time discussing the various forms of news texts in order to establish the function served by them and of the more recent format called newspapers throughout the history of humankind. An example of the more expansive use of the concept "newspaper" is offered in the following quote among Salmon's pages: "In the small Bohemian town the newspaper is a crier who summons the people by a vigorous roll on this drum, and when the curious townsfolk are assembled he proceeds to impart the latest news to them."[16]

Salmon goes on to compare the newspaper, or these news-carrying texts, and their evolving form and content to the experience one has with museums of natural science and history or public libraries. "The museum [and the newspaper] today seeks whatever represents normal life in its own native locality and with infinite pains its collections are arranged in the manner natural to them in their own habitat."[17] And from this Salmon observes that "the newspaper in all of these stages of its development is but recording the spirit of the times as it has been disclosed in other and corresponding activities. Like them also it gives evidence of the changes in purpose and in method that are already on the way."[18]

And so, one might ask if the criteria identified by Allen and Groth at the start of the twentieth century for "newspapers" is sacrosanct, or was it really more of a convenience for academic research and discussion purposes. It seems that at least some historians gave voice to the idea that newspapers fill a social role, and the modern newspaper is an evolving artifact of a social need to learn and distribute news. The evidence of this social function that the modern newspaper fills, and the shifting and changing item used to meet that function, can be found most easily among the more common uses of the term "newspaper" across the many centuries of organized society, rather than strictly adhering to the modern definitional parameters of the newspaper given by scholars in the twentieth century.

NEWSPAPERS

No matter where we go around the world, among the most common questions we ask one another is: What's the news? Though researchers may have wondered at that expression, and what it might mean to various cultures and societies, most scholars agree that as a species we are curious about the world around us and that we ask ourselves for evidence of the new or different or unexpected every chance we get. The awareness of our need for news is not a twentieth-century idea. The English playwright Ben Jonson offered a satire, reportedly successful among theatergoers in 1626, titled *The Staple of Newes*. So it is not a recent phenomenon that people want and seek the news of the day, and playgoers in Jonson's day deemed this behavior a fit topic for popular comedy.

Mitchell Stephens in his 1988 book *A History of News: From the Drum to the Satellite* states that news-seeking behavior among human beings crosses all cultural boundaries because it is a behavior hardwired into us. News, he says, provides social awareness and security.[19] Sociologists Harvey Molotch and Marilyn Lester claim that our interest in news is an "invariant need for accounts of the unobserved." Our curiosity for these accounts was a survival mechanism, an early warning system "of potential threats and potential rewards." The need for news transcends the particulars of content or a focus on specific kinds of items. It is, these researchers believe, a generalized need to be aware of the world around us.[20]

Another historian suggests that the tradition of news grows out of self-governance political systems. Sian Lewis, in his 1996 book *News and Society in the Greek Polis*, finds that news held a special political value in the Greek city states during the second and third centuries B.C. He reports that news, as it was provided through systematic reports, strengthened a shared set of cultural values within a community. He finds that it legitimized the authority of the community by reporting community actions that were deemed suitable or appropriate, as well as deviant or illegal behavior.[21] This sort of news, or purposeful information transfer, reinforced the community members' understanding of the law, of the punishments for breaking the law, and of accounts of the extraordinary that reaffirmed community understanding of the ordinary or what qualified as the usual.

Authoritative news accounts were also part of the Chinese government as early as the second century B.C. Anthony Smith reports that the imperial court created a network of information gathering to both send and receive news through local postmasters.[22] And that by the sixth century A.D., there was an official newspaper circulated among the government, with special editions for the general court and the imperial court. The circulation of this newspaper was later expanded to the wider intelligentsia and by the fourteenth century could be read by many accepted into polite society.

It seems, then, that there is a recognized human need for news that is evident at least as early as the Greek city states, and that at least by the Chinese dynasties, there were organized networks to facilitate formal news gathering and distribution. When cultures developed a written language and materials to inscribe, however, the seeds of a newspaper were born. The need for news and the means of consistently spreading it were at hand, but historians place the inauguration at various times and places.

There is evidence that societies found many ways of communicating news beyond face-to-face spoken reports. Among the earliest sorts of examples are the pictographs found in North America. These are about 4,000 years old and include symbols and signs scratched into the rock face at easily readable locations. Some of these are clearly like bulletin boards. The notation runs conveniently juxtaposed, like dialogue. Examples can be found from northern California into South America.[23] Some of these sites are so strikingly like news forums that they are referred to as "newspaper rocks" and are found, so named, among national parks' literature for Blanding, Utah, and the Painted Desert of Arizona. When a parks service researcher was asked about the naming of these petroglyph areas, she said there was no science involved. "They just look like communication tools that express the human condition at the time of their making. The term 'newspaper' seemed to fit the descriptive need."[24]

Richard Jebb's essays on Greek life and the means of swaying public opinion report that there was evidence of written news texts as early as the fourth century and that these were used as a way to persuade fellow citizens with the authority of the facts at hand. "Every possessor of a copy was a centre from which the ideas would reach the members of his own circle."[25] Another Mediterranean area example of early news posting is found throughout the Roman Empire under the reign of Julius Caesar. Gaston Boissier wrote at the turn of the twentieth century that his research about Roman life suggested Romans had several means of telling each other about the news of other parts of the world. It was critical for Roman citizens to be well informed because each member was responsible for participating in the decision-making by the community. To facilitate the general population knowing about government activity and the greater victories of himself, Julius Caesar required in 59 B.C. that the actions of the Senate be distributed in written form. This posting of news became the *Acta Senatus et Populi*. And Cicero, during the same time, asked in his letters to friends about the *Actis Diurna*, which apparently was something like a daily gazette that was broadly distributed with foreign as well as local news in it, and produced by scribes in a letter-like format. Boissier reminds his readers, too, that during this time many of the important texts or decrees were also carved in stone or clay in order to withstand diminished presentation or memory over time.[26] Clearly, some news texts were meant to be kept and some were disposable.

It seems clear then from these brief historical examples that social organizations look for formal ways of spreading news to influence opinion or establish power, as well as to reinforce social values and condone the actions of government. The success of news dissemination, however, seems to have depended, at least in part, on the stability of the news presentation format and the ease with which it could be accessed—or how available it was to the general reading constituency. The growth and expansion of a news-hungry society may not have been that news was available, but rather how easily the news came to it and how easily and accurately news could be passed along. Mechanical printing that fixed the text in a stable format increased the likelihood that each copy of the news items was the same and that it was in a format easily transported. Word of mouth, big stones, clay tablets, and handwritten letters were not as convenient or replicable as something like a modern newspaper, and it may be that this news form developed and flourished because it best served the function of news dissemination at the time. That development of printing that we now call publishing evolved as typography and technology came together. Later chapters in this book report the history of newspaper publishing in detail across many continents and centuries. But before we explore the particulars of newspaper publishing within a specific culture, we need to review the more elemental history of the printing process.

PUBLISHING

Any comprehensive history of written news or newspapers requires an exploration of the evolution of the printing process as well as an examination of the ways of communication of news. There are many interesting texts on the history of printing as it developed in Europe and separately in China and the Far East. In Charles A. MacIntosh's *Popular Outlines of the Press: Ancient and*

Modern, the distinction is drawn between the use of stamps for embossing and "legitimate" printing. He claims that the latter practice—legitimate printing—is the use of moveable type for words, as opposed to blocks or seals used for impressions of more purely artistic expression.[27] He reports that the first authentic information among European countries connecting the art of printing from blocks or woodcuts is for playing cards in the Venetian republic of 1441, discovered among records belonging to the Company of Painters at Venice, a legitimate printing project.[28] The first move from animal skin used for handwritten work to fiber-based paper printing is reported to be when manuscripts were produced on cotton in 1050.[29] And linen paper was introduced in England in 1320, bearing the watermark of Joyhn Cranden, the prior of Ely.[30]

Karl Bücher reports that in the twelfth and thirteenth centuries there were organized news letters among the monasteries and universities of the Germans. In the fourteenth and fifteenth centuries, the word "zeitung," usually translated as newspaper, was used to identify "postlike, organization of local messenger bureauxs for the epistolary intercourse of traders and of municipal authorities."[31] Bücher also suggests that letters, circulars, and newspapers served the same social function—communicating news—and employed writing to do it. They have, he says, only one difference among them: who the intended reader is. Letters, he says, are addressed "to individuals, circulars to several specified persons and newspapers to many unspecified persons."[32] Another early version of newspapers is said to be the Venetian gazettes of the 1530s. "Gazette" is sometimes said to refer to the cost of the daily news product, a small Venetian coin, or to refer to the Greek word for treasury, and thus, a news treasury.[33]

Smith provides an abbreviated list of early news publications and offers a distinction between most of them and what he considers to be legitimate newspapers. "The crucial distinction between such publications and the phenomenon of the newspaper is that in the latter a continuing relationship is set up between the reader, printer and the originator of the information. As the publisher of one of the English corantos of the 1620s explained it:...'[I]f the Printer have not the wherewithal to afford satisfaction, yet will the Readers come and ask every day for the new Newes.'"[34] Smith goes on to recount the stages of news publication development before it arrived at the modern daily newspaper format. These stages, he says, include single-story and single-issue publications, then publications in a series but not in regular intervals, then in weekly accounts of the news, and then larger bound sets of news pages, sometimes called news books.[35]

There is some debate about the first English-language newspaper. Matthias A. Shaaber devotes an entire book to the study of those publications leading up to the first newspapers in England.[36] His research dates those publications that resemble newspapers, but are not considered to meet the exact definition of twentieth-century scholars, to be from 1476 to 1622. He also reports that in the seventeenth century the use of the term "paper" meant a single sheet. Sheets could be folded into eight pages, and so a news sheet or newspaper might have been a single sheet of paper but folded into several pages so that it had a smaller presentation or delivery format.[37]

Scholars variously cite the *Weekely Newes* in 1622, the *Oxford Gazette* in 1665, or the *Daily Courant* of 1702 as the original English-language newspaper.[38] Some of the distinction is based on the English stationers' records that noted, "A Currant of generall newes. Dated the 14th of may last," and entered in 1622.[39] Others are more concerned with the exactness of the terminology and the news product's format itself.[40] And still others consider the point at which regular and number publications occurred on a daily basis as the inauguration of newspapers.[41]

The debate about the first English-language newspaper is mentioned here only as an illustration of the difference of opinion that is probably found in all cultural histories and analysis. There is enough evidence to suggest, without too much disagreement, that news conveyance is an integral part of every successful culture. But the particulars of how, when, where, why, and in what format those news messages were passed around or posted is still a point of research and understanding. The further refinement of newspapers as a long-standing means of conveyance, though not disputed on the whole, is much debated in the details, which should be clear from the preceding discussion. The aim of this chapter is to provide a foundation for examining the finer details of newspaper history in many parts of the world and for questioning the assumptions drawn about what constitutes a newspaper as defined by scholars nearly a century ago.

Many newspapers, either self-described or commonly designated, at the beginning of the twenty-first century no longer fit the precise definition of newspapers as described by Goth and Allen. And yet they seem to function and serve their readership in ways that meet their respective community's standard for a newspaper. Any of several encyclopedias' or dictionaries' entries for "newspaper" identify characteristics of news, advertisements, and being printed and published regularly as the core components.[42] Legal scholars in the United States, however, can provide at least fifty unique definitions for the term "newspaper," each tied to a particular state and its laws within the union. Even though there are many similarities among these definitions, there are also a wide range of details, such as size, subscription rates, geographic distribution requirements, availability, and publisher ownership, that are distinct from state to state.[43] *Black's Law Dictionary*, a U.S. legal standard, says a newspaper is "a publication, usually in sheet form, intended for general circulation, and published regularly at short intervals, containing information and editorials on current events and news of general interest."[44] In comparison, *Butterworths New Zealand Dictionary* says a newspaper is "any paper containing public news or observations on public news which is printed for sale or distribution and is published periodically at intervals not exceeding 40 days; but does not include any paper containing only matter wholly of a commercial nature."[45] Evidently, the range of definitions and variations on particular characteristics used to describe newspapers is such that consensus is difficult. Though most people would probably claim that they "know it when they see it," newspapers are not as obviously identifiable as we might wish. What all this loose confusion should tell us is that since the birth of newspapers is nebulous, perhaps so, too, is their death.

Salmon observes that the strength of newspapers as a historical artifact is their adaptability to and reflection of their immediate environment. She quotes Theophraste Renaudot, the founder of the *Gazette de France,* who proclaimed in 1631, "History is the record of things accomplished. A *Gazette* is the reflection of feelings and rumours of the time which may or may not be true."[46] She goes on to say, "The newspaper thus did not spring full armed from the head of Zeus, but as far back as human history can be traced it had its beginnings in the various expedients that provided partial equivalents for gratifying a desire for news, as well as the early awakenings of a desire for an expression of public opinion."[47]

There is much evidence that news products or conduits serving the needs of news-hungry cultures preceded the modern newspaper and the twentieth-century description of it. Sometimes this need was expressed as a desire to enjoy public opinion, sometimes it was the necessity to maintain order and social identity that made news sheets, postings, or broadcasts a part of everyday life.

There is also much evidence that the newspaper found its modern form because of the kinds of inventions available for its needs and uses among an increasingly literate society, rather than the idea that the newspapers generated the need for news. As cultures evolve in the particulars of their composition and progress, it is reasonable to expect the form of newspapers to evolve, too. So, if society recognizes its need and desire for news, and it retains the concept of a newspaper, it will surely have to accept the fact of an evolving format for this durable news conduit.

The next eight chapters report the history of newspaper use among cultures around the world. The work is intended to prepare the reader for a new look at the form and function of newspapers in all societies, no matter their place in time or geography. The penultimate and concluding chapters will revisit the history of newspapers in broad outline and discuss some of the ideas offered among scholars about the future of newspapers as both a particular form and a nebulous concept meeting longstanding social functions.

NOTES

1. For example, see Shannon E. Martin and Kathleen A. Hansen, *Newspapers of Record in a Digital Age: From Hot Type to Hot Link* (Westport, CT: Praeger, 1998).

2. Eric W. Allen, "International Origins of the Newspaper," *Journalism Quarterly* 7, no. 4 (1930): 308–19.

3. Otto Groth, *Die Zeitung—Ein System des Zeitungskunde (Journalistik)* (Mannheim: J. Bensheimer, 1928–1930), p. 1:21.

4. Allen, "International Origins of the Newspaper," p. 311.

5. Joseph Frank, *The Beginnings of the English Newspaper, 1620–1660* (Cambridge, MA: Harvard University Press, 1961); Michael Harris and Alan Lee, eds., *The Press in English Society from the Seventeenth to Nineteenth Centuries* (Rutherford, NJ: Fairleigh Dickinson University Press, 1986); George Boyce, James Curran, and Pauline Wingate, eds., *Newspaper History: From the 17th Century to the Present Day* (Beverly Hills, CA: Sage, 1978).

6. Frank, *Beginnings of the English Newspaper*, pp. 1–2.

7. Harris and Lee, *Press in English Society*, pp. 13–15.

8. Boyce, Curran, and Wingate, *Newspaper History*, p. 407.

9. Charles E. Clark, *The Public Prints: The Newspaper in Anglo-American Culture, 1665–1740* (New York: Oxford University Press, 1994).

10. Leslie Shepard, *The History of Street Literature* (Detroit: Book Tower, 1973).

11. Jeremy D. Popkin, "Journals: The New Face of News," in *Revolution in Print: The Press in France, 1775–1800*, ed. Robert Darnton and Daniel Roche (Berkeley: University of California Press, 1989); David A Copeland, *Colonial American Newspapers: Character and Content* (Newark: University of Delaware Press, 1997).

12. Anthony Smith, *The Newspaper: An International History* (London: Thames and Hudson, 1979).

13. Daughters of Eve; Dennis Slifer, *Signs of Life: Rock Art of the Upper Rio Grande* (Santa Fe, NM: Ancient City, 1998); James Henry Breasted, *A History of Egypt: From the Earliest Times to the Persian Conquest* (New York: Scribner's, 1942), see for example p. 109.

14. Gaston Boissier, *Tacitus and Other Roman Studies*, trans. W. G. Hutchison (New York: Putman's, 1906), pp. 208–29.

15. Lucy Maynard Salmon, *The Newspaper and the Historian* (New York: Octagon, 1976).

16. L. S. Kirtland, "Obstacle Race in Central Europe," *Travel* 37 (May 1921): 5–10, 34, cited in Salmon, *Newspaper and the Historian*, p. 8.

17. Salmon, *Newspaper and the Historian*, p. 35.

18. Salmon, *Newspaper and the Historian*, p. 36.

19. Mitchell Stephens, "The Need for News—A Social Sense," in *A History of News: From the Drum to the Satellite* (New York: Penguin, 1988).

20. Harvey Molotch and Marilyn Lester, "News As Purposive Behavior: On the Strategic Use of Routine Events, Accidents and Scandals," *American Sociological Review* 39 (February 1974): 101–12.

21. Sian Lewis, *News and Society in the Greek Polis* (Chapel Hill: University of North Carolina Press, 1996).

22. Smith, *Newspaper*, p. 14.

23. For example, see Slifer, *Signs of Life*; Lance Trask, *Ancient Billboards: The Rock Art of the Lower Jemez Mountains* (Santa Fe, NM: Santa Fe National Forest and University of New Mexico Maxwell Museum, 1992).

24. Gretchen Ward, cultural resource specialist on the archeology staff in Albuquerque, New Mexico, telephone conversation with author, June 2001.

25. Richard Jebb, *Essays and Addresses* (Cambridge: University of Cambridge Press, 1907), pp. 145–48.

26. Gaston Boissier, *Tacitus and other Roman Studies*, trans. W. G. Hutchison (New York: Putnam's, 1906).

27. Charles A. MacIntosh, *Popular Outlines of the Press: Ancient and Modern* (London: Wertheim, MacIntosh and Hunt, 1859), pp. 1–28.

28. MacIntosh, *Popular Outlines of the Press*, p. 8.

29. MacIntosh, *Popular Outlines of the Press*, p. 21.

30. MacIntosh, *Popular Outlines of the Press*, p. 24.

31. Karl Bücher, *Industrial Evolution*, trans. S. Morley Wickett (New York: Kelley, 1968), p. 221.

32. Bücher, *Industrial Evolution*, p. 217.

33. J. B. Williams, *A History of English Journalism to the Foundation of the Gazette* (New York: Longmans, 1908), p. 7.

34. Smith, *Newspaper*, p. 9.

35. Smith, *Newspaper*, pp. 9–11.

36. Matthias A. Shaaber, *Some Forerunners of the Newspaper in England: 1476–1622* (Philadelphia: University of Pennsylvania Press, 1929).

37. Shaaber, *Some Forerunners*, p. 3; Williams, *History of English Journalism*, p. 9.

38. For example, see Marjorie Wilkerson, *News and Newspapers* (London: Batsford, 1970); Joad Raymond, *The Invention of the Newspaper: English Newsbooks: 1641–1649* (Oxford: Clarendon, 1996); Williams, *History of English Journalism*; and Shaaber, *Some Forerunners*, p. 3.

39. Shaaber, *Some Forerunners*, p. 3 n. 2.

40. Williams, *History of English Journalism*, p. 8.

41. Boyce, Curran, and Wingate, *Newspaper History*, p. 407.

42. For example, see Britannica.com (viewed April 12, 2002); *Oxford English Dictionary*, 8th ed. (Oxford: Oxford University Press, 1991); *Webster's New Universal Unabridged Dictionary* (New York: Barnes and Noble, 1992).

43. Shannon E. Martin and Kathleen Hansen, "Examining the Virtual Publication As a Newspaper of Record," *Communication Law and Policy* 1, no. 4 (Autumn 1996): 579–94.

44. *Black's Law Dictionary*, 6th ed. (St. Paul, MN: West, 1990).

45. Peter Spiller, *Butterworths New Zealand Law Dictionary* (Wellington: Butterworths, 1995).

46. Salmon, *Newspaper and the Historian*, p. 10.

47. Salmon, *Newspaper and the Historian*, p. 10.

Chapter 2

Arab Cultures and Newspapers

William A. Rugh

The focus of this chapter is on print media in the Arab world. The Arab countries examined here are Algeria, Bahrain, Egypt, Iraq, Jordan, Kuwait, Lebanon, Libya, Morocco, Oman, Palestine, Qatar, Saudi Arabia, Sudan, Syria, Tunisia, the United Arab Emirates (UAE), and Yemen. Each Arab country is unique in several ways, yet they share some common characteristics and some generalizations can be made about the region and about the press that functions in that region.[1]

The vast majority of the populations in these eighteen countries fit the definition of Arab used here, namely peoples who consider their mother tongue to be Arabic.[2] All of these peoples understand Arabic even though they may also speak English, French, or other languages fluently and often. The majority of the people are Muslim, and most of them are Sunnis. Most have a sense of a commonly shared cultural heritage and destiny, and pan-Arab nationalism has a strong appeal throughout the region. Moreover, despite differences in wealth, they are all living in the developing world characterized by substantial economic and even political change with rapid modernization as a shared goal.

At the same time, there are significant differences among these eighteen countries. They are spread across a large geographic area, from Morocco on the Atlantic Ocean, to Iraq and Kuwait on the Persian Gulf, and climates vary from moderate Mediterranean to harsh desert. Some, particularly the seven states bordering the Persian Gulf, have substantial petroleum resources, while others are quite poor. Population densities also vary considerably. As a consequence of these two variables, per capita incomes vary widely, from Kuwait, which has one of the highest in the world, to Yemen, which has one of the lowest.

These geographic and economic differences have an impact on the press in the region. On the most basic level, the economic and population differences affect the "density" of media and media access, that is, the number of newspapers, radios, and television receivers compared with the number of inhabitants in each country. Table 2.1 gives an idea of the variations across the region.

The impact of these economic and population factors is, however, secondary to the most important variable that influences the structure and function of print media. This variable is the political system that prevails in each Arab individual country, which provides the context in which the press must operate. A fundamental assumption of this chapter, therefore, is that the print media in the Arab countries cannot be understood separately from the political environments in each of these countries, which shape, restrict, and nurture or curtail the media in many ways. The press, in short, is part of the political process and is rooted in the political culture of each country.

The legal and constitutional systems that relate to the press in the Arab world vary from country to country. Yet, some generalizations can be made that apply essentially throughout the region. First, the constitutions or laws usually make some reference to freedom of speech and of the press, even though these freedoms are circumscribed in law and in practice. Typically, the press is not permitted to attack the head of state, the royal family, or even the heads of state of friendly countries. Also, typically there are legal prohibitions against publishing anything that undermines state security, and often this is not defined in any detail so it is left to the courts or, in some cases, to the arbitrary decision of the executive branch to interpret that prohibition. In addition, criticism of the armed forces, attacks on religion, incitement to violence, and publication of material regarded as immoral are usually prohibited by statute. In some countries, libel laws protecting public officials are quite strict, and it may not even be possible to defend against a libel suit by demonstrating that published accusations are true. Beyond that, a few Arab countries have provisions in the law that are so broad that they allow essentially for arbitrary arrest of journalists or closure of newspapers that offend the regime.

Every Arab country has an official news agency, controlled by the government, that puts out news and information that is sanctioned by the government. These services are used by editors and journalists as sources for official statements, and they serve as guidance mechanisms on what official policy happens to be on issues of the day. For the many journalists who practice self-censorship, the official news agency gives them clear indications as to what they can and cannot say, without having to receive formal instructions from the ministry of information.

This chapter will review the historical development of Arab print media, describe its salient characteristics, make some generalizations that are possible to make, and then present a typology of subtypes that currently prevail in the Arab region, mentioning some variations that occur across the region.

Table 2.1
Media Density Table

	Daily newspapers			Receivers (in 1000s)		Receivers per 1000 inhabit.		pop'n (Mill.)
	titles	total copies (1000)	copies per 1000 inh.	Radio	TV	Radio	TV	
Algeria	6	1080	38	7100	3100	242	105	29
Bahrain	4	67	117	338	275	580	472	0.6
Egypt	17	2400	38	20500	7700	317	119	65
Iraq	4	407	20	4850	1750	229	83	21
Jordan	4	250	42	1660	500	271	82	6
Kuwait	8	637	377	1175	875	678	505	1.7
Lebanon	15	435	141	2850	1180	907	375	3
Libya	4	71	14	1350	730	259	140	5
Morocco	22	704	27	6640	3100	247	115	27
Oman	4	63	28	1400	1600	607	694	2.3
Qatar	5	90	161	256	230	450	404	0.6
Saudi Arabia	13	1105	59	6250	5100	321	262	19
Sudan	5	737	27	7550	2380	272	86	28
Syria	8	287	20	4150	1050	278	70	15
Tunisia	8	280	31	2060	920	224	100	9
UAE	7	384	170	820	310	355	134	2
Yemen	3	230	15	1050	470	64	29	16

Note: Newspaper data are as of 1996; radio, television, and population data are as of 1997. Reliable data are not available for Palestine (the West Bank and Gaza).

Source: UN Educational, Scientific, and Cultural Organization, *UNESCO Statistical Yearbook 1999* (Paris: UN Educational, Scientific, and Cultural Organization, 2000), http://www.uis.unesc.org (viewed 2001).

THE BEGINNING OF ARAB PRINT MEDIA

Arab journalism has a history that is nearly two centuries old. The first truly Arab newspaper, that is, a periodical carrying news and written by Arab writers for Arab readers, was *Jurnal al Iraq*. This publication appeared in Baghdad in 1816 and was printed in both Arabic and Turkish, reflecting the fact that Baghdad was then part of the Ottoman Empire. It was issued by the Iraqi government, and its intended readership was the government bureaucracy, the army, and the educated elite.[3] Over the following years, other Arab newspapers emerged in other major Arab cities throughout the region. In 1827, the Egyptian government started publishing *Jurnal al Khadyu*, and the following year it started *al Waqa'a al Masriya*. In 1847, the Algerian government started publishing *al Mubashir* in Algiers as an official biweekly. A newspaper appeared in Beirut starting in 1858. In 1861, the Tunisian authorities launched the newspaper *al Ra'id al Tunisi*. In 1865, the Syrian government began the paper *Suriya* in Damascus, and in the following year, the Libyan government started *Trablus al Maghrib*. By 1879, the Yemeni government was issuing the paper *Sanaa*, and by the end of the century, the Sudanese government was issuing the paper *al Sudania*. As early as 1873, a daily paper was being published in Beirut. Most of these papers were nondailies, but all of them were vehicles for the dissemination of news and information approved by the government that issued them. In addition, however, they typically also carried literature, such as short stories and even poetry.[4]

The vast majority of nineteenth-century Arab newspapers were controlled by governmental authorities. Much of the Arab world was under Ottoman rule at the time, and the Ottomans and their Arab representatives were influential in determining the content of the print media. Only a few private individuals and families in Egypt, Syria/Lebanon, and Morocco managed to enter the publishing field. In 1858, Khalil Khuri came out with his newspaper *Hadiqat al Akhbar* in Beirut. The privately owned newspapers *Wadi al Nil* and *Al Ahram* began appearing in Egypt in 1867 and 1876, respectively, and the private paper *Al Maghrib* started in Morocco in 1889. But these were exceptions.

Beirut became one of the major centers of journalism for the Arab world because of higher literacy rates and the priority that the Lebanese gave to education. Between 1870 and 1900, about forty newspapers and periodicals appeared there, including the first Arab daily, which began in 1973. The first newspapers were written by and for intellectuals who had connections with Europe—mainly France—and their early publications were influenced in style and content by French journalism. Also, their liberal ideas sometimes got them into trouble with the Ottoman authorities. Ottoman censorship especially during the reign of sultan Abdal Hamid (1876–1909) caused some Lebanese journalists to flee to Egypt, where they established newspapers with fewer restrictions. Then the more liberal press law of 1909 allowed the Lebanese press to become more involved in the Arab nationalist movement.

But in the following years, the authorities restricted the press and punished liberal journalists.

Although Arab newspapers emerged in Syria and Iraq during the second half of the nineteenth century, Arab publishers were restricted in what they could print by strict regulations of the Ottoman rulers, enforced by local authorities. After 1908, these restrictions were eased somewhat because of pressure from the Young Turks for reform, and thus Arab newspapers proliferated during the next decade. Young Arab writers and politicians, many of them educated in colleges in the region, started their own newspapers and expressed ideas of Arab nationalism on their pages.

Saudi Arabia is an example of a different type of development of the Arab press. Ottoman influence over the Arabian Peninsula was very limited and literacy there was quite low, so indigenous Arab journalism was modest and really started at the beginning of the twentieth century. It primarily took the form of nondaily newspapers that were published in the Hijaz, in the western part of the peninsula, after 1908. In the early days, moreover, these papers were produced and managed by resident foreigners from Syria and elsewhere in the Arab world. Between 1909 and 1925, the Hijaz was under the rather loose control of the Hashemites government of Sherif Hussain in Mecca, acting on behalf of a remote Ottoman sultan, as Abdal Aziz al Saud was expanding his control in the central and eastern parts of the peninsula. The Hijazi newspapers were not uniform in content, with some supporting Hussain's rule and others criticizing it. Then in 1924 when the al Saud captured Mecca and unified the country, the Hijaz press flourished under the leadership of Hijazi intellectuals, but the content became less political and focused on literary matters. By the 1940s, modern papers with an emphasis on news began to emerge. Newspapers that still exist as dailies first appeared during this period. For example, *al Madina* has been published since 1937, *al Bilad* since 1946, *al Nadwa* since 1958, *al Yawm* since 1959, and *Ukaz* since 1960.

In the late 1950s, the Saudi press became more active and somewhat more diverse as the country experienced a surge of modernization from growing oil revenues. The kingdom attracted not only new business, but also writers and journalists, some of whom began to criticize aspects of government and public life. When the press went too far, for example, by reporting on rivalries within the royal family, the government took steps to restrict its scope of freedom, without directly taking control of the print media. After King Faisal ascended the throne and brought greater political stability to Saudi politics, the press became quieter.

THE PRESS IN THE COLONIAL ERA

European colonial rule that dominated much of the Arab world (except for the Arabian Peninsula) in the middle of the twentieth century also continued the practice of substantial government involvement in the press, despite the fact that the British and French colonial rulers were well acquainted with private press ownership at home.

French colonialism stretched from Lebanon and Syria across North Africa to Tunisia, Algeria, and Morocco. When Lebanon was under a French mandate (1920–1946), more newspapers appeared and many were politically involved, although the French imposed controls on the press. During the French mandate in Syria (1920–1946), Arab journalism grew somewhat, although the French used their authority to encourage only publications that supported their policies. By 1929 and into the 1930s, editors were calling for independence from France, and the French authorities periodically suspended opposition papers or arrested editors. In 1943, Lebanon became nominally independent, but France retained some powers and did not relinquish authority to regulate the press until 1946 when French troops finally withdrew. The Lebanese National Covenant of 1943, an unwritten agreement to balance the major religious and political groups, set the rules, and a diverse press reflecting a variety of different parties and religious sects emerged. In the decade after World War II, the Lebanese press was relatively strong, and some editors were able to criticize the government for corruption, election fraud, and other shortcomings. The government sought to restrict press attacks, but journalists resisted controls better than in most other Arab states. During the 1950s, the number of newspapers and the role of the press increased as politicians found newspapers useful in their political battles.

In Tunisia, when it was governed by a French protectorate (1881–1956), the French controlled the content of print media, but Tunisian writers and intellectuals did develop an indigenous Arab press within limits. The French also imposed tight controls during World War II and until 1947, but then continued some restrictions afterwards.

Algeria, in the second half of the nineteenth century and the first half of the twentieth, was under such firm control of the French, who administered it as a department of France, that it did not permit any significant development of Arab journalism. Newspapers that emerged were controlled by Europeans and tended to ignore Arab news. Even after World War II and up to independence in 1962, all the daily papers and most of the others in Algeria were published by the French and in French. Arab nationalists were able to print a few weeklies for a while, but these were suppressed in the mid-1950s when the independence movement heated up. An underground Arab press did develop, and it emerged into the open at the time of independence. By 1963, and after a brief period, the regime of newly independent Algeria declared itself a one-party state and this led in effect to the nationalization of the press so that all newspapers were then supportive of government policies.

British colonialism, at the same time, stretched from the Persian Gulf through Iraq and Palestine to Egypt and the Sudan, and this too, substantially influenced the Arab press. In Egypt, Arab newspapers had begun to appear in the nineteenth century, first as governmental publications, and then private individuals started newspapers in the cultural renaissance of the 1860s and 1870s. After 1882, newspapers backed by political parties became very active, and some newspapers even helped spawn parties. British colonial administrators were less tolerant of opposition parties than of opposition newspapers, so the latter tended to grow faster, although what the British allowed to be published was circumscribed. In the first half of the twentieth century, and except for censorship during World War II, the British authorities did allow newspapers to criticize policies, expose corruption, and express diverse editorial views.

In the Sudan, the press started late because of low literacy rates and a weak economy. In 1898, the Anglo-Egyptian condominium was established over the Sudan that lasted until 1956. In 1903, a biweekly paper *al Sudan* was published in Sudan by three Syrian journalists who also owned the famous Cairo daily *al Muqattam* (so *al Sudan* was seen as linked with foreign interests). In 1919, the first Sudanese-owned newspaper, *Hadarat al Sudan,* appeared. Editorially, it supported the British administration and opposed the condominium with Egypt. After 1924, the colonial administration increased restrictions on the press, and for the next decade, Sudanese newspapers focused more on literary material than political. In 1935, the first Sudanese daily, *al Nil,* started, and it showed some independence by expressing popular dissatisfaction with the 1936 Anglo-Egyptian treaty.

Amman had only two low-circulation weeklies prior to 1948 when Israel was established, but in 1948 Arab editors and journalists fled to Amman and began to expand print media there. During the next decade, dailies and new nondailies were established and political writers became active. Libya had no Arab-owned newspapers before independence in 1951, so the Libyan journalists worked for British-owned papers. And in Iraq, during the British mandate (1920–1932), Arab journalists were somewhat freer than their counterparts in Syria under the French, but the British, too, used their authority to limit the freedom of the press within certain bounds.

PRINT MEDIA IN THE INDEPENDENT ARAB STATES

After World War II, as Arab self-determination grew with the end of colonialism and the rise of Arab nationalism, the new Arab leaders recognized that controlling the press was politically useful in establishing and maintaining their authority. At that time, Arab governments tended to seek to increase their influence and control over the press as they found themselves in competition with each other and with opposition elements in their own countries. The electronic media became particularly interesting targets of ambitious political elements at this time, as radio expanded its reach and television was starting to become popular. As a consequence, Arab governments, almost without exception, took steps to control all radio and television as official monopolies. But they also were interested in the print media for similar political reasons, and during the second half of the twentieth century, they made considerable efforts to ensure that the newspapers and magazines read by their populations were supportive of them and their policies. These efforts varied from direct intervention and overt coercion to subtler methods (different approaches are described later on), but generally the purpose was to make use of the press for political ends.

The Arab governments that took steps to influence the media justified their actions in various ways. A common theme for newly established Arab governments was that they were the true representatives of the people in developing an independent nation, free from outside control, and the government had to make use of all available weapons, including the press, in order to defend the nation against dangerous foreign elements such as neocolonialism which they said threatened this independence. As the Arab-Israeli conflict heated up in the late 1940s, Arab governments tended to assert that in order to combat the perceived Zionist threat to Arab nationalism, they had to ensure that the media were sufficiently following an anti-Zionist, pan-Arab policy. Invoking patriotism and mobilizing for war with Israel, the Arab governments thus described their new states as engaged in a serious struggle for existence that, they said, required not only sacrifices by the public, but also special measures involving the press.

Until recently, the development of a strong private Arab press also was retarded by low literacy rates and by economic circumstances. Literacy, and education generally, were historically limited to the Arab middle classes, which were quite small, making the print media audiences few in number and, therefore, not an incentive to the development of large private newspapers. Literacy rates grew substantially in the latter part of the twentieth century, yet even highly literate Arabs often prefer oral communication over written. This is partly because of cultural reasons that are related to the prestige of oral traditions. For example, as new communication technologies developed in the 1990s, popularity of the cell phone grew rapidly while use of the Internet was much slower to develop.[5]

As for economic circumstances, the Arab independent private sector has always been relatively weak and has not been attracted to investing in the press. Some Arab countries did become significantly wealthy in the second half of the twentieth century, but they did so primarily because of the export of petroleum, which was government-owned and -controlled. Commercial advertising has been much less robust than in the West, so the press has limited commercial potential, and private individuals have lacked the interest or resources to invest in print media. As a result, when private newspapers did appear, they faced economic difficulties that they generally resolved by seeking a financial patron, either a government, a political party, or a politically ambitious individual or family, which affected the editorial content of the publication. Financing by governments took several forms, including direct payments, advertising, and newsprint subsidies. Foreign governments, in some cases, even made clandestine payments to selected newspapers that editorially supported their interests. Thus, patronization of newspapers became common, and publication on the basis of a straightforward commercial calculation was rare.

For the reasons mentioned above, it also was characteristic of Arab print media to concentrate in the largest cities in the Arab world. They were much less likely to be published or even distributed in provincial areas, while in cities such as Cairo and Beirut, multiple newspapers appeared side by side and competed for readership.

Ownership of newspapers varies considerably. In some Arab countries, all print media are owned by the government or its agents. In others, the government does not own or directly control any publications as they are all in the hands of private individuals, groups, or political parties. The electronic media, in contrast, are owned and controlled almost everywhere in the Arab world directly by the state as a public monopoly. The difference is, essentially, that the governments in the Arab world regard radio and television as important politically because they reach virtually the entire population, so that they insist on direct control of all electronic means of communication. The print media in most Arab countries are less strictly controlled mostly because they reach only the literate members of society, as well as fewer individuals, and are somewhat less potent political instruments.

PRESS TYPES

Arab print media at the beginning of the twenty-first century can be divided for purposes of analysis into four different types: mobilization, loyalist, diverse, and transitional.[6]

Mobilization Press

The press in four countries—Iraq, Libya, Syria, and Sudan—falls into the mobilization category. In each of these countries, the press is uniform on content because all print media are directly owned and tightly controlled by the government. Journalists are government employees and are in no sense independent. The regime does not allow the media to express any criticism of or dissent from official policy or of the top leadership. In fact, the regime uses the press as a tool to mobilize the public behind its views and policy positions.

This type of press fits well into the political system prevailing in these four countries. The regimes in power thoroughly dominate the political process, and the only public discussion of policy or controversial issues that they allow must be supportive of their views. No public criticism or dissent is allowed, and no opposition political parties or groups are permitted to exist openly. The regimes not only prevent the press from becoming a channel for dissent, but they also actively use the press for political advocacy.

In Iraq, independence from colonial rule came in 1932, and during the next three decades (1932–1963), there was intense party political activity, the press reflected a broad political spectrum, and newspaper turnover was rapid. In the 1945–1955 period, half the papers were in opposition to the government. In 1954, in Iraq the government of Nuri Said suspended some party newspapers that opposed him. During 1958–1963, under Abdalkarim Qasim the regime gave Communist writers greater scope and encouragement. By 1962, there were twenty papers in Baghdad, one-third Communist and the rest of various political orientations.

In November 1963, Colonel Abdul Salam Arif seized power in Iraq, formed the Arab Socialist Union, and declared it was the only legal political organization. He ended the party press that had been active for three decades. In April 1964, he promulgated a new press law that gave the government power to censor newspapers critical of the government.

The preamble to the 1967 press law in Iraq stated that the private press had to be abolished because of the so-called "current battle the Arab nation is waging against imperialism, Zionism and reaction."[7] Iraq also has a national front with nominally independent parties, but they are in fact not critical of the regime in any way. The Bath Party publishes *al Thawra*, and the government publishes *al Jumhuria*.

Since 1991, the northern region of Iraq has been under Kurdish administration independent of the central government in Baghdad, and this has profoundly affected the press there. Many independent newspapers have emerged there, all of them critical of Baghdad, and they even contain some criticism of Kurdish authorities in the north. Moreover, the north is under de facto political sway of two rival parties: the Kurdistan Democratic Party of Masoud Barzani and the Patriotic Union of Kurdistan of Jalal Talabani, which control separate sectors and prohibit distribution of each other's papers in their respective zones.

In Syria, in the first decade after independence (1946–1958), there also was considerable political party activity that was reflected in the press. Most editors had close ties with individual political parties, interest groups, influential families, and even foreign embassies. In 1949, however, when General Husni al-Zaim came to power in Syria, he suspended eleven of the nineteen Damascus papers, including the leading dailies that had opposed him.[8] Governmental controls increased after that.

In 1958 when Syria and Egypt merged into the United Arab Republic (UAR), at the peak of pan-Arab nationalist sentiment and Gamal Nasser's power, political parties and their newspapers were banned in Syria as they had been in Egypt, and the regime-sponsored National Union was declared the only legal political organization. The UAR government imposed press censorship on Syria and sponsored its own newspapers. The December 1961 military coup in Damascus led to Syria's withdrawal from the UAR, but the previous political parties and their papers did not reemerge because the Syrian regime monopolized power and the press, preventing any groups or papers that challenged its authority and continuing the censorship. The Bath coup of March 1963 led to Bath rule but the political leadership still does not allow diversity or significant opposition.

In the 1970s, Syrian parties again reemerged but their newspapers did not. These parties were not genuine opposition groups but were members of the national front, and as such, they did not oppose Bath Party policy. Hafez al-Assad was in power 1970–2000 and was succeeded by his son Bashar al-Assad. Bashar talked of press freedom, and there have been some small signs of liberalization, such as letters to the editors criticizing government policies and the constant praise of the president has been mitigated. But fundamentally, the system is the same.

Starting in 1976, Syria maintained a large military presence in Lebanon ostensibly to help keep order, and its presence had an impact on the Lebanese press. Some Lebanese newspapers supported Syria while others did not, although many were cautious about being too critical of Syrian intervention.

In Libya, the press under monarchy experienced a more liberal phase between 1951 and 1969. A spectrum of different newspapers reflected a variety of interest groups (but no political parties) that the monarchy tolerated, in addition to the progovernment papers. Editorially, opinion in the press included conservative and religious, as well as anti-Communist, Nasserite, and antigovernment viewpoints. In 1969 after Colonel Mu'ammar al-Qaddafi seized power from the monarchy, he prohibited political parties and independent newspapers from emerging, but he started his own newspaper, *al Thawrah*, to explain his ideas to the public. It disappeared in 1972 but a new government daily paper *al Fajr al Jadid* then appeared. Private newspapers were allowed to continue, but they did not receive the government subsidies that the government papers did.

In 1972, the Libyan government staged trials against "corruption of public opinion," canceling the licenses of ten papers, including the last of the private dailies. The proregime dailies have dominated the press since then, and all publications are controlled by official organs of government.

In the Sudan, the press went through three phases of some freedom and diversity (1953–1958, 1964–1969, and 1985–1989). In 1956 when the Sudan became independent, it had sixteen partisan papers including nine dailies. The regime of General Ibrahim Abboud (1958–1964) banned all political parties and their newspapers and started his own paper *al Thawrah*. Private papers continued, but they were nonpartisan, restricted, and kept in line by censorship and by periodic suspension of papers that disagreed with Abboud's policy.

In 1964, Abboud was overthrown and some press independence reemerged along with party activity. In May 1969, Colonel Jaafar Numairy came to power in a coup and within a month his authoritarian regime banned all political activity other than by his Revolutionary Council. He ended the party-backed press and restricted the rest of the press, which was private. In 1985, Numairy was overthrown in a civilian revolution and press freedom increased; some old papers reappeared and new ones emerged. Between 1985 and 1989, the three-coalition governments gradually increased restrictions on the press.

In 1989 in the Sudan, a military coup overthrew the democratically elected government and brought Lieutenant General Omar Hassan al-Bashir to power with his National Salvation Revolution Command Council. He suspended the 1985 constitution, disbanded all political parties, and abrogated press freedom. The press has since then remained under strict regime control.

Loyalist Press

The press in six Arab countries—Bahrain, Oman, Palestine, Qatar, Saudi Arabia, and the UAE—fall into the loyalist category. For the most part, the print media are privately owned, but in content they are quite loyal to the regime in power. There are few substantive differences among newspapers. The law contains provisions restricting press freedom, while in effect encouraging support for the government, and these provisions are enforced. Laws on the books tend to encourage editors and writers to be supportive of the regime. But these laws do not have to be enforced often because journalists tend to practice self-censorship. They know what the sensitive issues are and are willing to be careful in dealing with them.

The political environment in these countries supports the loyalist press. These countries have political systems that can generally be described as authoritarian. The systems have changed very little over time, and the leaderships in most cases (all but Palestine) are in the hands of hereditary rulers who base their legitimacy on many years of dominance by their families. Although it is true that in four of these countries (Kuwait, Palestine, Bahrain, and Qatar) some limited elections have taken place, no political parties are permitted to exist and expressions of popular will are strictly circumscribed.

Newspapers first appeared in the Persian Gulf later than in other Arab countries because of low literacy rates and because some of the area remained under British domination until 1971, when the UAE, Bahrain, Oman, and Qatar became fully independent. A few newspapers had emerged by then, but they were all nondailies, such as Bahrain's *Jaridit al Bahrain* in the 1940s, Qatar's weekly *Gulf News* in 1969, and six nondailies in the Trucial States in the 1960s. The first dailies appeared about the time of independence: in the UAE in 1970, Oman in 1971, Qatar in 1975, and Bahrain in 1976.

Many of the Persian Gulf papers depended on nongulf journalists, especially Lebanese, Jordanians, and Palestinians. Petroleum wealth suddenly grew rapidly in the gulf in the 1970s, promoting the establishment of new newspapers there, but because the gulf states had been slower to develop print media, they lacked cadres of trained journalists. They therefore attracted Arab journalists from countries that had longer experience with the press, paying them high salaries to move temporarily to the gulf to get the new media started. The movement of journalists to the oil-rich states also was facilitated by financial and other difficulties they had encountered practicing their profession at home.

In Bahrain, there was a briefly elected parliament (1973–1975). This was reflected in the press, which was freer and more outspoken on political issues. But when the government decided that the debate was going too far and in August 1975 suspended the parliament, the press quieted down considerably.

As for the Palestinian press, it is a relatively recent phenomenon because of political circumstances. Palestine was ruled by the Ottomans 1517–1917 and the British 1917–1948, then occupied by Israel and Jordan. Israel also occupied the West Bank, East Jerusalem, and Gaza in 1967. Palestinian newspapers emerged in the 1960s, but they were usually published outside of Palestine. In 1964, when the Palestinian Authority (PA) took control of Gaza and parts of the West Bank, indigenous Palestinian newspapers emerged there, but the PA exerted some restrictions on the press, periodically suspending publications and detaining journalists.

Transitional Press

A third category in the typology of Arab press exists in four Arab countries, namely Egypt, Jordan, Tunisia, and Algeria. They differ from each other somewhat, but they also share basic characteristics. The term "transitional" is used because in all four cases the press system itself has changed significantly during the 1990s and appears to be evolving still, although it is not entirely clear to anyone what the eventual outcome will be.[9] That is, the press system is frequently debated in public within each of these countries, and different elements have contrasting views about how the print media should be organized. The largest-circulation print media are controlled directly by the government, while some smaller ones are owned and controlled by private individuals, groups, and/or political parties. The latter types of publication have some latitude to criticize the government and their style is distinctly different from the government publications. The government, however, uses a variety of means to try to restrict them, but these means are almost always based on existing law and follow legal procedures in the courts. Such court cases are fairly common. The government also uses economic leverage to try to encourage support for its policies by nongovernmental print media, whose editors also practice self-censorship.

The political system in these countries is conducive to the transitional type of press system. The government is rather dominant in the political system, as reflected in the fact that it controls the major print media. Yet, opposition political parties are legal and active, and elections are held on a regular basis, providing an environment that allows some criticism of the regime, and this criticism can be expressed through some of the press. And the press system itself is a subject of the debate because its constitutional status is not entirely settled.

In Egypt, the military officers who led the successful coup against the Egyptian monarchy in 1952 within two years had deliberately and completely taken over the press. They promptly established their own publishing house and daily newspaper, *al Gumhuria,* for the specific purpose of making their policies well known to and supported by the public. They abolished all existing political parties and groups and their newspapers, and they created a new political organization that was the only legal one. Although at first they left the nonparty private papers alone, the steps they took to monopolize the political process made clear to the remaining independent editors and journalists that the print media should all support the policies of the new leaders.

In 1960, one year before the Nasser regime nationalized major sections of the economy, it in effect nationalized the rest of the press, consolidating its control over all publishing houses, including the two major ones, *al Ahram* and *Akhbar al Yawm.*

During the 1950s and 1960s, Cairo's *al Ahram* became the leading daily newspaper in the Arab world primarily because its editor in chief, Muhammad Hassanain Haykal, was personally close to President Nasser, who was the most prominent political figure in the region. Nasser attracted attention throughout the Arab world because of his vigorous advocacy of pan-Arab interests, and it was assumed that when Haykal wrote his column on Fridays in *al Ahram,* he was revealing Nasser's thinking. The newspaper's Friday circulation increased dramatically and it was widely read. Haykal inspired a generation of Egyptian and other journalists, and he also expanded the *al Ahram* publishing house to include influential periodicals and to support Egypt's most prominent literary figures including Naguib Mahfouz. After Nasser's death in 1970, Haykal's influence began to decline and in 1974 he left *al Ahram,* while *al Akhbar* and *al Gumhuria,* the two other major Egyptian dailies, became competitive with *al Ahram* in circulation and prominence.

In the last quarter of the twentieth century, Nasser's successors Anwar Sadat and Husni Mubarak allowed some political party newspapers to emerge, and with the exception of the daily *al Wafd,* they were only small-circulation weeklies. These party papers had some impact on the public political debate, and also the national papers—which remained indirectly under the control of the government—occasionally expressed criticism of the actions of government officials. During this period, the government has from time to time allowed some liberalization of the press, but it also has periodically sought to restrict press freedoms, to a great extent, by taking action in the courts against individual editors, journalists, and newspapers. Yet, the national press, which is read by the vast majority of the public, in its overall posture during the last third of the twentieth century has been supportive of the general lines of official policy.

In Algeria, there was a brief period in 1990 and 1991 when the government allowed party and private newspapers to appear, but then the regime canceled the parliamentary elections and enacted emergency laws that eliminated opposition newspapers once again. Later in the 1990s, the government eased its restrictions on the press somewhat and allowed more freedom of expression, but strict limits remained.

In Tunisia, Habib Bourguiba who dominated Tunisian politics from independence in 1956 until 1987, had a special interest in the press. He wrote in preindependence newspapers and founded one of his own. He regarded the print media as a potent political weapon. As president, he allowed some party press to function but periodically restricted or closed newspapers for what they wrote. Bourguiba's one-party state was gradually replaced by a multiparty system beginning in the 1970s, but it was not until the late 1980s, after Bourguiba, that the government substantially eased restrictions on the press. A decade later the security situation allowed further relaxation of governmental controls, and newspapers were able to express opposition views more freely.

In Jordan, Amman had only two low-circulation weeklies prior to 1948 when Israel was established, but in 1948 Arab editors and journalists fled to Amman and began to expand print media there. During the next decade, dailies and new nondailies were established and political writers became active. The Jordanian government periodically sought to restrict press freedoms, especially in times of emergency such as the summer and fall of 1970 when Palestinian groups challenged the monarchy and after the Intifada began in 1987. The government backed some newspapers while others remained in private hands. In the 1990s, the government eased restrictions on the press and new party newspapers appeared. But from time to time the authorities suspended papers or took action against journalists.

Diverse Press

Finally, in four countries—Lebanon, Kuwait, Morocco, and Yemen—the press system at the end of the twentieth century was characterized by a degree of diversity not found elsewhere in the region. Some of the print media are controlled by the government, but many are not, and many of the ones that are not regularly criticize government policy. Government influence over the press is exercised through the media it happens to control and otherwise through legal means by enforcing the law through the courts. The political environment in these four countries makes such a system possible, since opposition groups or parties are legal and active, and some kind of elections are held on a fairly regular basis.

In Lebanon, for three decades between independence and the beginning of the civil war (1946–1975), the print media were the most diverse, lively, and free of any in the Arab world. In these early days, the main rivals to Cairo's *al Ahram* for attention in the region came from Beirut, where the newspaper *al Nahar* and a few other dailies gained audiences beyond the borders of Lebanon because of the quality of their reporting and editorials. Then the Lebanese civil war, which began in 1975 and lasted nearly fifteen years, affected the press in several ways. The carefully balanced political system established by the

National Covenant of 1943 came apart as factions, with outside support, used violence to express their frustrations and anger, and unregulated militias controlled much of the country. Partisan newspapers reflected this superheated atmosphere, becoming more strident and uncompromising, and because of divisions along geographic lines, distribution of newspapers became more restricted to their respective zones of influence and support. The number of newspapers also declined during the civil war. Of the twenty-one most widely read Lebanese dailies that existed in 1975, nine were gone by 1979, and the others were considerably below their 1975 circulation levels.

By the end of the civil war, however, the Lebanese press had maintained its characteristic diversity and multiplicity of viewpoints, and many of the newspapers represented editorial lines that clearly and predictably reflected policies of political factions or religious sects. The government had fewer means with which to repress unwanted views, although it did from time to time suspend newspapers or take action against journalists.

In Kuwait, journalism began to emerge strongly in the 1960s after the country became independent in 1961. Kuwait's daily newspapers have tended to represent somewhat different editorial positions over the years. Some were family-owned papers, and some were established by groups of Kuwaiti businessmen. During the 1970s, Kuwait developed a vigorous and active press, producing several daily newspapers and a number of nondailies despite its small population. Several papers also gained readership elsewhere in the Arab world. By the mid-1980s, seven Kuwaiti dailies were distributing nearly 300,000 copies at home, and there were more than a dozen other Kuwaiti publications even though the population of the country was less than 2 million.

Morocco developed a relatively lively press after it gained its independence in 1956. By the mid-1980s, it had eleven daily newspapers with a total circulation of nearly 300,000 copies and dozens of other publications. These newspapers are in private hands and represent a spectrum of political views, including those of the Moroccan government. Political parties own or support both dailies and nondailies.

In Yemen, the press was dominated by the regime until the early 1990s when the system was radically changed, allowing political parties to exist and grow and they contested competitive elections. Many party newspapers as well as others appeared and represented a spectrum of opinion that continued into the twenty-first century.

NOTES

1. A fuller, more detailed study of Arab media is available in William A. Rugh, *The Arab Press: News Media and Political Process in the Arab World*, 3rd ed. (Syracuse, NY: Syracuse University Press, forthcoming).

2. There are other definitions of "Arab," but this is the simplest and most useful.

3. In 1798, the newspaper *Courier de l'Egypte* appeared in Egypt, but it was published by Napoléon Bonaparte on imported French presses and intended to inform French expeditionary forces then occupying the country.

4. Sami Aziz, *al Tatawwur al Sahafah fi al 'Alam al 'Arabi* (*The Development of the Press in the Arab World*) (Cairo: al Ma'had al Qawmi li al Sahafiyin al 'Arab, 1969, mimeographed), pp. 2–3.

5. Of course, use of the Internet was also retarded relative to the cell phone because the former usually required knowledge of English, but the comparison still has validity.

6. A detailed discussion of this typology can be found in Rugh, *Arab Press* Syracuse, NY: Syracuse University Press, 1987, pp. 31–112.

7. Law no.155, Baghdad Radio, 3 December 1967, 1500 GMT.

8. *New York Times*, 4 March 1942.

9. The third edition of the *Arab Press* discusses the transitional type in detail. When the second edition of the book was published in 1987, the transitional category did not exist, so Egypt and Algeria were categorized as mobilization types, while Tunisia and Jordan were loyalist.

Chapter 3

African Cultures and Newspapers

W. Joseph Campbell

THE POLITICAL ROLE OF NEWSPAPERS IN AFRICA: FOUR TYPOLOGIES

The 1990s were bleak years for the press in Nigeria, where newspapers had long before established a reputation as among the most assertive, challenging, and freewheeling in Africa. For most of the decade, military regimes held power in Nigeria, and they punished the press relentlessly.

Repression came "in many styles and patterns," states Dapo Olorunyomi, a prominent Nigerian editor. The regime's methods included:

detention without trial, imprisonment without due process, constant security and police visitation to newspaper houses, frequent "invitations" to journalists and editors for security questioning, proscription of critical newspapers and journals, arson against opposition newspapers, assassinations or attempts, death threats against investigative journalists or courageous newspaper commentators, massive product seizure so as to bankrupt newspapers, harassment and intimidation of vendors selling anti-government newspapers ... counterfeiting opposition newspapers to discredit them, smear campaigns against journalists, bribery and infiltration of media ranks to stain their credibility.[1]

While devastating, those measures failed to extinguish the inventive and militant spirit of Nigerian journalists. A number of them defied the military authorities and took to what they called "guerrilla journalism." It was a covert and decentralized kind of newsgathering that sought to outwit the regime and keep alive political dissent and resistance. Olorunyomi's weekly publication, the *News*, was banned in May 1993. But soon afterward a clandestine replacement, *Tempo*, emerged from the underground and appeared week after week for several months. The guerrilla journalism that gave rise to *Tempo* was, Olorunyomi writes, "a dynamic, on-the-wheel experience.... Places like stadiums and theaters became the 'newsrooms,'"[2] where editors and reporters eluded the authorities to plan and design forthcoming issues. Correspondents, moreover, would "write their stories in longhand and leave them" at designated drops, such as at cemetery graves or amid roadside litter.[3] Once collected, the reports were edited in secret and then smuggled to a press. Cellular telephones and laptop computers eventually became tools of guerrilla journalists, making them even more elusive.[4]

However bold, resourceful, and unconventional, guerrilla journalism was not an unbroken success. Press runs were seized. Journalists—and their families[5]—were arrested or jailed.[6] But "guerrilla journalism" undoubtedly helped Nigeria's press endure the harsh military interregnum, which gave way at the end of the decade to an elected civilian government. More broadly, guerrilla journalism represented a dramatic if unorthodox example of the activist, even militant role that often have defined newspapers, both clandestine and above ground, in Africa.

Newspapers were introduced to Africa by European colonialists some 200 years ago[7] and have since become inextricably linked to the uneven, often messy, and long-running processes of political change across the continent.[8] While the function and imperative of African newspapers have been decidedly political, the precise nature of that role has been elastic and has varied markedly over the decades, reflecting in some respects the size and complexity of Africa. The continent is home to more than 50 independent states, some 2,000 spoken languages, and untold thousands of newspapers—a diverse tableau that makes generalizations precarious. Nonetheless, the varying political character of African newspapers can be captured and classified as four distinct typologies. Like all broad taxonomies, the typologies cannot define the press in every African state in every era. But the typologies are valuable nonetheless in illuminating and clarifying the multiple functions of newspapers in African societies over time. The typologies are:

- Vanguard, in which newspapers have been agents at the forefront of political change. The vanguard political role was most dramatically evident during the late colonial era, from the 1940s to early 1960s. Many newspapers pursued the goals of African nationalism, agitating for reforms and, ultimately, political independence. Several newspapers were also in the vanguard of the antiapartheid movement in South Africa, directing attention to the abuses of white-minority rule.

- Subservient, in which newspapers have been more docile political instruments, usually the captive media of authoritarian regimes. During the 1970s and 1980s, many state-controlled newspapers were exponents and practitioners of what was widely called "development journalism," an experiment of sorts in which the power of the press ostensibly was to be tapped to stimulate nation-building and economic development. In practice, "development journalism" was little more than a pretext for regime control of domestic news media.

- Reinforcing, in which newspapers independent of state control have emerged to become conspicuous contributors to the process of political change and democratization.

The typology became evident during the late 1980s and early 1990s as newspapers in their critical scrutiny of power-wielding authority effectively promoted respect for, and understanding of, democratic practices and values. Newspapers in Zambia and Benin were notable cases where nonofficial newspapers have acted to expand political debate and discussion and to help keep the process of democratic reform on track.

• Clandestine, in which newspapers and other forms of printed communication such as tracts and leaflets are prepared and distributed surreptitiously, presenting low-level yet persistently irritating challenges to state authority. Clandestine publications in some cases have been the precursors to above-ground, nonofficial newspapers. The clandestine typology has the closest links to the loose, oral-based, informal networks of political communication traditions that have characterized many African urban societies. These networks are known in French-speaking Africa as *radio trottoir* (pavement radio).

Each of the four typologies will be discussed in some detail in this chapter. First, however, it is important to address two enduring misconceptions about newspapers in Africa—namely, that they are the essential instruments of, and for, the political elite[9] and that they are frail components of African societies.

To some extent, African newspapers *are* elite-oriented, circulating as they do principally in urban areas where they are accessible to the affluent (who can afford them) and the literate. While this elite orientation may seem evident, the versatility of newspapers is usually not so readily recognized.

Newspapers in African society are perhaps best understood as important links in a chain of communication, "in which reading is only part of the chain."[10] The chain of communication in Africa is predominantly oral, but it is also flexible and can absorb newspaper reports readily. African journalists often have described the sight of literate people reading newspapers to those who cannot read. The sight is not uncommon in Africa.[11] Kenneth Best, who in the 1980s established independent newspapers in Liberia and the Gambia, speaks of illiterate market women in the Gambia buying copies of his newspaper and placing them under their wares. At night, the women took the newspapers home where their children read to them.[12] In Niamey, Niger, Ibrahim Hamidou, the publisher of the French-language weekly *Tribune du Peuple*, describes how the contents of his newspaper invariably circulated by word of mouth. "The day the paper comes out," he states, "virtually everyone in the city knows what's in it."[13] Privately owned radio stations—which proliferated in many African countries during the 1990s—have served as another means to link newspapers and Africa's oral traditions. In Mali, radio programs devoted to reviewing articles published in that country's independent newspapers reportedly stir "more anguish in political circles than the original written versions."[14]

Perhaps because they have become important links in Africa's chain of communication, newspapers collectively have proven remarkably resilient in the face of an array of economic constraints and regime hostility. Over the years, untold thousands of newspapers have failed from want of resources or have been forced to close by authoritarian leaders. Because this vulnerability is so overt, it has been

a focal point of scholarly and popular studies for more than thirty years. It is
striking indeed how routinely and centrally the litany of limitations[15]—the
limited financial resources, the limited advertising base, the limited pool of potential readers, and the limited professional training[16]—has figured in scholarly
works. But newspapers in Africa—and the "ethos of independent journalism"[17]
that sustains them—have been more dynamic and malleable than commonly
recognized. It is more revealing and nuanced to consider the collective *resiliency* of African newspapers, their tendency to emerge and proliferate and
take on political roles with even the slightest easing of restrictions and censorship.[18] This phenomenon was perhaps most noticeable and sustained in the varied political reform movements that emerged across Africa in the late 1980s
and 1990s. During that time, newspapers independent of state control emerged
in unprecedented numbers in Africa. Over the years, then, the press in Africa
has proven to be deceptively dynamic—fragile and vulnerable to repression,
but also gritty and resilient, and infused with potential to evolve and expand. A
measure of this resiliency is embedded in each of the four typologies that have
characterized newspapers in African societies. The respective typologies will be
discussed in turn.

THE PRESS AS VANGUARD

The most celebrated and perhaps most assertive role that African newspapers
have filled has been that of the vanguard, of militant advocates ahead of their
time, pressing for political change, notably during the period of anticolonial nationalism. While it would be mistaken to say that newspapers were decisive
variables in Africa's prolonged struggle for self-rule,[19] they were salient features of numerous and disparate nationalist movements. The vanguard role of
the press can be seen in newspapers in Egypt during the early twentieth century[20] and took hold in earnest in West Africa beginning in the 1920s and 1930s.
In many instances, these newspapers emerged *before* the legalization of African
political parties, which ultimately became "the organizational weapon[s] of
nationalism."[21]

Notable among the West African newspapers that anticipated political parties
were those published in the French colony Dahomey (known since the 1970s as
Benin). Beginning in the 1920s, a small number of weekly, French-language
newspapers emerged to call attention to the abuses and hardships of colonial
rule.[22] Their publishers typically had been schooled or lived in France and were
usually dexterous enough to avoid or blunt open confrontations with French
authorities. These newspapers were fundamentally an elite press, written by
and for a literate minority, many of whom had descended from former slaves
returned from Brazil. The Dahomean elite for the most part accepted, and even
incorporated, cultural values of the French. But in their outspokenness, their
newspapers were unrivaled elsewhere in French-ruled Africa.[23] Few of these

survived very long, suffering economic hardships and chronic material short-ages. But they undeniably established a tradition of combative journalism that was to reemerge in Benin in the late twentieth century.[24]

The combativeness of colonial-era African journalism also characterized newspapers in English-speaking West Africa, where some nationalist leaders first came to prominence as editors and publishers of newspapers. Among them was Nnamdi Azikiwe, who has been described as "one of the most compelling personalities of the African nationalist movement"[25] and who in 1937 founded the *West African Pilot*.

The newspaper, the first in a chain Azikiwe established in Nigeria, was un-mistakably a political organ and served as "one of the principle formers" of the nationalist sentiment in West Africa.[26] "Pride in the African was a constant theme" of Azikiwe's *Pilot*, writes Frank Barton, a veteran analyst of the press in sub-Saharan Africa. "Every new lawyer, every new doctor, every new graduate was a triumph. And the political message was direct; why were people of this status still second-class citizens in their own country?"[27]

Azikiwe and his newspaper endured frequent confrontations with the British, Nigeria's colonial rulers, who regarded him "the biggest danger of the lot" of Nigerian nationalists.[28] Activist journalism propelled his political career, during which he was president of Nigeria in 1963–1966.

Kwame Nkrumah of Ghana was another prominent African nationalist who understood the value of newspapers as political vanguards—but in the end sub-verted them as tools for his own adulation. He established the *Evening News*, a "tub-thumping pamphlet" that grew in significance during the 1940s and early 1950s as Nkrumah's "star rose as the brightest African nationalist on the con-tinent."[29] For a time, the *Evening News* published editions in several of Ghana's indigenous languages as well as in French and in Hausa, the dominant language of northern Nigeria.[30] Although its reach was remarkable, the newspaper cre-ated "a mystique around Nkrumah which elevated him almost to the level of a god."[31] A cult of personality characterized Nkrumah's stormy and increasingly radical political career,[32] which culminated in his becoming the first president of Ghana in 1957. He was toppled in a coup in 1966.

Although the press as vanguard often was crucial in their emergence, African nationalists once in power often showed little tolerance for aggressive, outspo-ken newspapers. Nkrumah proved autocratic as president. He muzzled the op-position press and allowed only sycophantic coverage in proregime newspapers. The irony of such turns of events was not lost on observers of Africa's press. Barton, for example, notes: "When the Nkrumahs, the Kenyattas, the Nyereres, the Kaundas and the scores of other African leaders took control of their na-tions from colonialists, they considered that they had enough trouble getting their news ships of state launched without any of the ships' company arguing with the captain. And more significantly still, all those African leaders and most of the others had in one way or the other used the press in their fight against colonialism."[33]

With the advent of political independence across much of sub-Saharan Africa in the late 1950s and 1960s, the vanguard press of African nationalism was largely "discarded as having served its purpose."[34]

In South Africa, however, the vanguard typology characterized the role of several English-language newspapers that figured significantly in the long-running struggle against apartheid, or white-minority rule. The *Rand Daily Mail*, a Johannesburg daily, gained international prominence during the 1960s and 1970s as it "hammered away at apartheid and the need to bridge the racial barriers of South Africa."[35] Another South African newspaper that exposed the abuses of apartheid rule was the *Daily Dispatch* of East London.

The editors of both the *Daily Mail* and *Daily Dispatch* eventually were forced to leave the country after clashing with state authorities over their newspaper's reporting. Laurence Gandar of the *Daily Mail* was tried in the mid-1960s after the newspaper published a series of articles describing abuses of black inmates in South African prisons. Gandar was fined a nominal sum, given a suspended sentenced, and eventually left the country.[36] Donald Woods of the *Daily Dispatch* was a friend of Steve Biko, a leader of South Africa's Black Consciousness movement who died in police detention in 1977. Woods directed a campaign in his newspaper, challenging official accounts that Biko had killed himself. The Biko story took on international dimensions, "doing ever more damage to South Africa's tattered image."[37] South African authorities banned Woods from journalism, effectively silencing him. He fled to Britain in 1978.[38]

As the cases of Gandar and Woods suggest, the vanguard role of the press can be hazardous for journalists—especially for those on the front lines. South Africa's best-known photojournalist was Peter Magubane, who endured physical attacks and other hardships in covering some of the worst violence in South Africa, including riots in 1976 in the Johannesburg suburb Soweto.

"My nose was fractured by the police in 1976," Magubane recalled years later, after the white-minority regime had yielded power. "I was detained for 586 days in solitary confinement. I was shot 17 times below the waist with buckshot. I was banned for five years. They tried to kill me."[39] But he added: "I knew I could use my camera to tell the world how apartheid operated. That was one of my missions, to show the world how black people were treated in their own country."[40]

THE SUBSERVIENT PRESS

To be sure, not all newspapers in white-ruled South Africa figured in the vanguard against apartheid.[41] Press pluralism, in Africa or elsewhere, rarely has meant that newspapers are of one voice. As Barton notes, it is a mistake to regard South Africa's English-language press as having been monolithic in opposing white-minority rule.[42] Many titles filled a role perhaps more familiar for newspapers in Africa—that of reflecting interests of power-wielding authorities.

Indeed, scholars and other analysts of the press in Africa have often called attention to the compliant or subservient roles of newspapers in many African countries. As suggested by Nkrumah's intolerance of dissenting views in Ghana, postcolonial African leaders often insisted on the subservience of newspapers. Barton writes that "as political freedom came to the Continent, so did press freedom disappear."[43]

In many countries, the subservience of the press was deemed necessary to the task of nation-building after decades of inhibiting rule by European colonialists. The subservience of the press was even conceptualized as "development journalism"—a model that gained wide approval among African leaders in the 1970s and 1980s. Development journalism defied ready definition; it was once described as "an amorphous and curious mixture of ideas, rhetoric, influences, and grievances."[44]

The appeal of development journalism was enhanced by the fairly frequent criticism in UN bodies at the time that searching critical, Western-style journalism was a handmaiden to cultural imperialism.[45] Western news organizations, notably the international wire services such as the Associated Press, Agence France-Presse, and Reuters, were seen as excessively focused on the turmoil and political conflict in African states. The purported failings of Western journalism were central to debates within the UN Educational, Scientific, and Cultural Organization (UNESCO) during the 1970s on developing what was ambitiously called the New World Information and Communication Order. Amid the controversy—which prompted the United States and Britain to quit UNESCO—the concept of "development journalism" took hold.[46]

In reality, though, development journalism proved little more than a guise for strict state control of newspapers and of the broadcast media. African leaders who adhered to development journalism tolerated only state- or party-controlled newspapers, which they turned into one-dimensional forums for self-aggrandizement and self-congratulation. As one international communication scholar writes, "In practice . . . development news consisted of endless puffery of government leaders and the nation's progress, even where there wasn't much."[47] It was a distorted, deceptive, and subservient style of journalism that allowed neither competition nor dissent.

Côte d'Ivoire, a former French colony known also as the Ivory Coast, was one of the many African states that pursued development journalism.[48] The country was ruled for thirty-three years by the deceptively ruthless autocrat Félix Houphouët-Boigny. He insisted that the Ivorian journalist be "an agent of development, a citizen engaged at the sides of his brothers in the struggle for dignity and well-being."[49] In practice, the press in Côte d'Ivoire became a forum for paying daily tribute to the *sagesse* of Houphouët-Boigny, who styled himself "le Vieux," the Wise Old Man of West Africa.

Houphouët-Boigny's "thought for the day" appeared regularly on the front page of the obsequious state-run newspaper *Fraternité Matin*, which closely covered the leader's comings and goings. His return from one of his many visits to Europe invariably was front-page news. Visiting heads of state were customarily described as paying homage to le Vieux and to seek his guidance. Until the closing years of his rule, Houphouët-Boigny allowed no place in Ivorian newspapers for criticism or close analysis of his policies or personality.[50] Instead, the image projected in the Ivorian news media was glowing but misleading, one steeped in the "endless puffery" of the head of state.

The conceptual premise of development journalism was that the presumed power of the press could be harnessed to promote economic growth and national unity. The press, states Jomo Kenyatta, the first ruler of independent Kenya, should "positively promote national development and growing self-respect since in Africa it can have a tremendous influence on nation-building."[51] But evidence accumulated that development journalism was having no such effect. Economic growth stalled across in sub-Saharan Africa during the 1980s, the continent's so-called lost decade.

In extreme cases, a captive, uncritical press had proved dangerous, as in Ethiopia during the early 1970s. At the time, the country was ruled by the emperor Haile Selassie, an autocrat whose regime imposed on the domestic news media no fewer than two dozen forbidden topics, or "taboos." Among the taboos was reporting on the famine that devastated parts of the country in 1973.[52] Had the domestic press covered the crisis, thousands of lives may have been saved because "news of the disaster would have been picked up much more quickly by the outside world and aid would have been [more quickly] available."[53]

Given its stifling nature, development journalism was embraced willingly or enthusiastically by few journalists. Instead, journalists tended to chafe at the model's inherent subservience. Given the chance, they spurned development journalism. For many African journalists, that chance came in the late 1980s and 1990s with the wave of political reform and democratization that swept sub-Saharan Africa.

THE PRESS AS REINFORCING CHANGE AGENT

The much-deplored fading of independent newspapers after the emergence of self-rule in Africa was not a permanent condition. In late 1980s and early 1990s, as a wave of political reforms and democratization swept sub-Saharan Africa, hundreds of newspapers emerged to promote and encourage political change. These newspapers almost without exception were independent of direct state control or influence, and their role was one of reinforcing agent for change. As John A. Wiseman writes, "In assessing the role of the indigenous media in the struggle for democracy it is necessary to see it as both a dependent and independent variable; as effect and as cause. The proliferation of pro-democracy newspapers free from government control, for example, can be seen as resulting from the new political space created in the struggle for democracy. Once in existence, however, [the newspapers] can be seen as a significant component of the struggle."[54]

Wiseman offers the case of Zambia as an example of emergent, independent newspapers acting first as a dependent variable and then as an independent variable in the process of political change. Strict government press controls were lowered in the early 1990s, in response to growing political opposition to nearly thirty years of rule by Kenneth Kaunda. Independent newspapers were allowed to appear and their reporting effectively promoted Zambia's transition to political pluralism. Kaunda's ruling party was voted from power in 1991.[55] Newspaper exposés that described abuses and corruption in Kaunda's regime undoubtedly contributed to his repudiation.[56]

The case of Benin also illustrates the dynamic of emergent, nonofficial newspapers acting as both dependent and independent variables—first in securing a toehold and then expanding the realm of political debate and discussion. The appearance in 1988 of nonofficial newspapers such as *La Gazette du Golfe* and *Tam Tam Express* signaled the coming collapse of Benin's nominally Marxist regime. *La Gazette du Golfe* and *Tam Tam Express* were soon joined by other papers published independently of state control. Collectively, their reporting about the regime's corruption and human rights abuses helped diminish its legitimacy.[57]

The Marxist regime fell in 1990 and was replaced the next year by a government chosen in fair and free elections—then a rarity in sub-Saharan Africa. The swift and astonishing turn of events gave rise to a tendency among journalists in Benin to overstate the contributions of independent newspapers in the country's democratization. For example, Ismaël Y. Soumanou, the founder of *La Gazette du Golfe*, asserts, "It is we who built this democracy."[58]

While tempting, such mediacentric characterizations tend to overlook broader and more powerful forces that better explain Africa's movement toward democratic rule in the 1990s—forces that included the widespread economic decline of the 1980s and the general failure of authoritarian regimes.[59] Nonetheless, the emergent, nonofficial newspapers were very much contributing or reinforcing agents to resurgent democratization. Their essential role has been a critical one in helping to promote understanding of, and respect for, democratic values and to help keep the process of political reform on track. Independent newspapers have been instrumental in exposing elected leaders as dubious democrats—as was the case in Benin in the mid-1990s. There, close and critical coverage of Nicéphore Soglo, the president elected in 1991, contributed to his repudiation by a narrow margin at the polls in 1996.[60] It was Benin's second successive presidential election in which voters had turned out the incumbent, an outcome unprecedented on mainland Africa.

As president, Soglo invited criticism with his high-handed treatment of the Beninese parliament. He announced cabinet changes without first consulting with the speaker of parliament, as the constitution required, and he declared the government budget adopted by decree in 1994.[61] In their coverage of these and other political controversies, Benin's independent newspapers, notably the daily *Le Matin,* withstood intense pressure from Soglo and his supporters to soften or otherwise modify their reporting. Journalists were frequently exposed to the president's wrath and intimidating criticism, which served further to undermine his democratic credentials.[62]

Benin's independent newspapers cannot be considered fateful variables in Soglo's electoral repudiation. He nearly won reelection despite much critical and unfavorable reporting. But the reporting threw into relief Soglo's authoritarian streak and demonstrated his inclination to run roughshod over democratic institutions and processes. In the end, he failed to abide by what Larry Diamond calls "the democratic rules of the game."[63] Such contributions by newspapers in Africa are scarcely insignificant—or even exceptional. In the closing years of the twentieth century, the critical reporting in independent newspapers in Senegal and Ghana helped prepare for the unprecedented election in those countries of opposition candidates for president.

THE CLANDESTINE PRESS

The independent newspapers that began appearing across Africa in the late 1980s and early 1990s simply "did not spring from a vacuum."[64] As Richard Sandbrook observes, independent newspapers in some countries "inherited a tradition of protest with its roots in the anti-colonial struggle,"[65] as in Benin and Ghana. In other countries, the wellspring for independent-minded newspapers was experience in clandestine journalism—their roots were in the tracts, leaflets, and other types of informal publications that represented an alternate means of political communication in authoritarian states.

Clandestine journalism in Africa is seldom so celebrated or well described as was the experiences of guerrilla journalism in Nigeria during the 1990s. The literature is thin about underground journalism and how the clandestine experience can give rise to above-ground independent newspapers. It is scarcely surprising that such alternate forms of communication were to be found, however, in Africa's authoritarian states. Such regimes, Nancy Bermeo notes, inevitably leave "small free spaces" for the circulation of dissenting views and other clandestine conduct. "It is in those circles of society where state constraint is loosest that dictatorships so often find their greatest challenge."[66] In those "small free spaces" in Côte d'Ivoire during the 1970s and early 1980s, clandestine tracts circulated, often to the anger and discomfiture of state authorities.

The political effects of clandestine tracts were at times quite striking and revealed the Ivorian regime's extreme sensitivity and hostility to unregulated dissent. And by reacting so vigorously and angrily, the regime unwittingly gave the tracts far wider attention than they otherwise would have received. An example came in August 1978, when antiregime leaflets were distributed across

Abidjan, the country's largest city. Some of the tracts, which blamed state authorities for failing to contain spiraling living costs, were inserted inside copies of the state-run daily *Fraternité Matin*.[67] The appearance of the tracts and their assertive, challenging content stunned Ivorian authorities. They responded with a stern warning published in *Fraternité Matin* beneath the banner headline: "Non Aux Tracts!" (No to Tracts!).[68]

Over time, clandestine criticism of Côte d'Ivoire's single-party regime became ever more pointed and direct. By the early 1980s, clandestine tracts "not only invited Ivorians to express openly their disenchantment with the government, but also went as far as to call for the resignation of the President."[69] Moreover, tracts accusing senior Ivorian officials of keeping money in Swiss banks provoked the country's leader, Houphouët-Boigny, to make one of the most startling and candid personal disclosures of his long political career.[70] It came in an impromptu television speech in April 1983, during a wave of strikes and demonstrations organized by secondary school teachers. On the television, Houphouët-Boigny acknowledged keeping "billions" in Swiss bank accounts, asserting, "I have money overseas. But it is not money of the Côte d'Ivoire. What serious man in this world does not place a part of his money in Switzerland? It's the bank of the world. And I, myself, would be crazy to sacrifice the future of my children with the actions of the crazies here [in Côte d'Ivoire] without thinking of their future."[71]

While usually handwritten or typed, some clandestine tracts were given titles and clear ties to political dissidents. In 1985, for example, there appeared a tract called *Le Patriote*, which fashioned itself "the newspaper of the oppressed and voiceless" peoples.[72] *Le Patriote* was linked to a then-clandestine political movement called the Front Populaire Ivoirien (FPI; Ivorian Popular Front) that emerged as a leading opposition party in the 1990s.[73]

Economic austerity measures and the regime's stranglehold on power sparked a political crisis in early 1990 in Côte d'Ivoire. Violent protests flared in the country's largest cities, Abidjan and Bouaké. Yet, *Fraternité Matin* assiduously avoided reporting about the disruption. The void in reporting was filled by what were called "informal"[74] clandestine newspapers, which included a typewritten tract called *Le Papillon*[75] as well as underground pamphlets of the FPI. When Houphouët-Boigny moved to end the crisis by legalizing opposition political parties, the clandestine newspapers emerged above ground in profusion. The proliferation of nonofficial newspapers came to be called "the springtime of the press" in Côte d'Ivoire.[76]

The clandestine experience has not only been a staging ground for aboveground, opposition-oriented journalism in Africa. It also has represented the closest conceptual link to the informal, word-of-mouth information networks that are known in French-speaking Africa as *radio trottoir*, which has been colorfully described as political "discourse in camouflage."[77] It has also been called the "language of political derision,"[78] little of which is complimentary to power-wielding authorities. Indeed, *radio trottoir* thrives "on scandal in the sense of malicious news, and rarely has anything good to say about any prominent person or politician."[79] Like clandestine newspapers, *radio trottoir* seeks "to bypass state monopolies on information."[80] In many ways, above-ground, independent newspapers that emerged in Africa since the early 1990s also have fulfilled this vital role.

CONCLUSION

Africa is a vast continent, a continent of extremes and contradictions. It is therefore not surprising that the years at the end of twentieth century and the start of the twenty-first can be seen as both promising and dismaying for Africa's newspapers. Despite the profusion of independent newspapers in Benin, Cameroon, Côte d'Ivoire, Congo, Ghana, Mali, Senegal, and Zambia, among other countries, the resiliency of Africa's newspapers in many respects seemed tested as never before. The Committee to Protect Journalists, a New York–based media advocacy organization, noted in 2001 that governments "across Africa used obsolete, often century-old laws to suppress news about their shortcomings, shutting down newspapers and jailing journalists for such vaguely defined offenses as criminal defamation, distributing false news, endangering state security, and espionage."[81]

In some places, journalists were the specific targets of ruthless rebel movements. In Sierra Leone, the Revolutionary United Front rebels killed thirteen journalists from 1997 to 2000.[82] Ten were slain in early 1999 alone. No African country kept more journalists in jail at the start of the twenty-first century than Ethiopia, where seven were imprisoned. Four of them had been held since 1997.[83] In Zimbabwe, the regime pursued its attacks against the country's independent-minded journalists and, notably, against the lone nonofficial daily newspaper, the *Daily News* in Harare. The newspaper, which "often expressed vocal opposition to the government,"[84] was bombed in January 2001 and its printing plant was destroyed. But thanks to other printers in Harare, the *Daily News* appeared the following day and did not miss an issue.

Despite the many hazards facing journalists and their newspapers in many places in Africa, the broader trend in newspapering was toward daily periodicity and greater competition. At the turn of the twenty-first century, daily newspapers in Africa were more numerous than ever. Benin was home to more than a dozen dailies. Algeria had more than thirty dailies, "many of them stridently critical of state policy."[85] And in Nigeria, Africa's most populous country, guerrilla journalism was a phenomenon of the past. At least twenty daily newspapers were on sale at newsstands early in 2001, testimony, declared the *New York Times,* to "the victory of a vibrant culture over military repression."[86]

NOTES

1. Dapo Olorunyomi, "Defiant Publishing in Nigeria," *Media Studies Journal* 10, no. 4 (Fall 1996): 69.

2. Olorunyomi, "Defiant Publishing," pp. 72–73.

3. Christina Lamb, "Editors Defy Nigerian Reign of Fear," *Sunday Times* (London), 24 December 1995.

4. Lamb, "Editors Defy Nigerian Reign of Fear."

5. Olorunyomi also writes that *Tempo* "set an example of defiant publishing under a ruthless dictatorship, but the costs were enormous. The government was unable to catch up with me so my wife and three-month-old baby were arrested in 1993." See Olorunyomi, "Defiant Publishing," p. 73.

6. See "Nigeria: 'Permanent Transition,'" Human Rights Watch Report (September 1996), at http://hrw.org/reports/1996/Nigeria.htm (Accessed December 30, 2001). The report states: "The independent press in Nigeria has been forced to adopt a mode of operation referred to as 'guerrilla journalism,' its editors and journalists often operating underground and constantly on guard against the possibility of arrest. Despite these precautions, journalists are regularly picked up and held for questioning." As many as fifteen Nigerian journalists were in prison before military rule ended in the late 1990s.

7. The first newspaper in sub-Saharan Africa, the *Cape Town Gazette,* was published in South Africa in 1800. See Rosalynde Ainslie, *The Press in Africa: Communications Past and Present* (London: Gollancz, 1966), p. 38.

8. Observers of the African press often have noted that newspapers there contained what Ainslie describes as "an exceptionally high proportion of political news." See Ainslie, *Press in Africa,* p. 18.

9. For example, Kwame Karikari writes that "both the state-owned and privately owned independent papers represent different and sometimes contending sections of the political and economic elite." See Kwame Karikari, "Africa: The Press and Democracy," *Race and Class* 34, no. 3 (1993): 56–57.

10. John A. Wiseman, *The New Struggle for Democracy in Africa* (Aldershot, UK: Avebury, 1996), p. 56.

11. Wiseman writes: "Most people [in Africa] cannot read newspapers but, equally, most people know somebody who can." See also Alpha Oumar Konaré, "Independent Newspapers Enjoy a Whiff of Freedom from Dakar to Kinshasa," *IPI Report* (May 1991): 21. Konaré, who later was elected president of Mali, describes "illiterate people buying newspapers and paying literate people to read them out loud." See Wiseman, *New Struggle for Democracy in Africa,* p. 56.

12. Kenneth Best, interview with author, Chapel Hill, N.C., November 1996.

13. Ibrahim Hamidou, interview with author, Arlington, Va., July 1998.

14. "Media: Private Radio Troubles in Ghana," *Africa Research Bulletin* (1–28 February 1995): 11769.

15. See, among others, William A. Hachten, *Muffled Drums: The News Media in Africa* (Ames: Iowa State University Press, 1971), pp. 7–16, 24–28, 271–76; Frank Barton, *The Press of Africa: Persecution and Perseverance* (London: Macmillan, 1979), pp. 1–11; Martin Ochs, *The African Press* (Cairo: American University in Cairo, 1986), pp. 123–24.

16. The literature is particularly detailed about shortcomings in professional development of African journalists. See, among others, Ainslie, *Press in Africa,* pp. 227–30; Hachten, *Muffled Drums,* pp. 132–40.

17. See Vicky Randall, "The Media and Democratisation in the Third World," *Third World Quarterly* 14, no. 3 (September 1993): 632.

18. To be sure, this phenomenon is not peculiar to Africa. Easing of restrictions has led to the sudden flowering of newspapers in many other settings, including Asia, Latin America, and the former Soviet Union.

19. Indeed, many factors beyond Africa contributed to the end of European colonial rule. These factors included the exhaustion of Europe's colonial powers after World War II, the emergence of self-rule in the Indian subcontinent, the establishment of the United Nations, and the rise of competing, postwar superpowers at least nominally opposed to colonialism. For a brief but useful discussion of the rise of self-rule in Africa, see Ieuan Ll. Griffiths, *The Atlas of African Affairs*, 2nd ed. (London: Routledge, 1994), pp. 56–61.

20. James J. Napoli and Hussein Y. Amin, "Press Freedom in Egypt," in *Press Freedom and Communication in Africa*, ed. Festus Eribo and William Jong-Ebot (Trenton, NJ: Africa World, 1997), p. 190.

21. Crawford Young, *The African Colonial State in Comparative Perspective* (New Haven, CT: Yale University Press, 1994), p. 238.

22. See W. Joseph Campbell, *The Emergent Independent Press in Benin and Côte d'Ivoire: From Voice of the State to Advocate of Democracy* (Westport, CT: Praeger, 1998), pp. 31–40; see also, W. Joseph Campbell, "The Uncertain State of Press Freedom in West Africa: The Contrasting Cases of Benin and Ivory Coast," *African Rural and Urban Studies* 4, no. 1 (1997): 24–26.

23. Campbell, *Emergent Independent Press*, p. 31.

24. Campbell, *Emergent Independent Press*, pp. 44–46.

25. Ainslie, *Press in Africa*, p. 33.

26. Ainslie, *Press in Africa*, p. 35.

27. Barton, *Press of Africa*, p. 26.

28. Cited in Martin Meredith, *The First Dance of Freedom: Black Africa in the Postwar Era* (New York: Harper and Row, 1984), p. 86.

29. Barton, *Press of Africa*, p. 35.

30. Barton, *Press of Africa*, p. 35.

31. Barton, *Press of Africa*, p. 24.

32. Meredith writes that by the early 1960s, "the personality cult which surrounded Nkrumah ... reached grotesque proportions. He assumed grand titles," such as "Man of Destiny," "Star of Africa," and "His High Dedication." See Meredith, *First Dance of Freedom*, p. 188.

33. Barton, *Press of Africa*, p. 3. In addition to Ghana's Nkrumah, the references were to Jomo Kenyatta of Kenya, Julius Nyerere of Tanzania, and Kenneth Kaunda of Zambia, all of whom were leaders of their respective countries at independence.

34. Barton, *Press of Africa*, p. 6.

35. Barton, *Press of Africa*, p. 204.

36. See Barton, *Press of Africa*, pp. 203–6.

37. Barton, *Press of Africa*, pp. 214–15.

38. Barton, *Press of Africa*, pp. 215–16.

39. Jerelyn Eddings, "Camera Invaluable Tool in Exposing Government Abuses, S. African Photojournalist Says," Freedom Forum Online, 16 October 1998, at http://www. freedomforum.org/templates/document.asp?documentID=4833 (Accesed December, 30 2001).

40. Eddings, "Camera Invaluable Tool."

41. Barton, *Press of Africa*, p. 211.

42. Barton, *Press of Africa*, p. 211.

43. Barton, *Press of Africa*, p. ix.

44. William A. Hachten, *The World News Prism: Changing Media of International Communication*, 3rd ed. (Ames: Iowa State University Press, 1992), p. 34.

45. See Robert L. Stevenson, *Global Communication in the Twenty-First Century* (New York: Longman, 1994), p. 13.

46. See Hachten, *World News Prism*, pp. 34–35.

47. Stevenson, *Global Communication*, p. 13.

48. See Campbell, *Emergent Independent Press*, pp. 75–76.

49. Cited in Auguste Miremont, "La presse ivorienne: Une mission noble," *Fraternité Matin* (Abidjan, Côte d'Ivoire), 22–23 May 1983, p. 1.

50. Campbell, *Emergent Independent Press*, pp. 76–77.

51. Cited in Jerry Komia Domatob and Stephen William Hall, "Development Journalism in Black Africa," *Gazette* 31, no. 1 (1983): 10.

52. See Barton, *Press of Africa*, pp. 258–61.

53. Barton, *Press of Africa*, p. 260.

54. Wiseman, *New Struggle for Democracy in Africa*, p. 55. Randall offers a similar observation: "Though the national media themselves rarely played a 'triggering role' [in democratic openings], they could widen awareness of issues. . . . By deepening and accelerating political communication in this way, they significantly added to the pressures on the authorities." See Randall, "Media and Democratisation in the Third World," p. 636.

55. See Wiseman, *New Struggle for Democracy in Africa*, pp. 56–57.

56. See Richard Carver and Dan Swanson, "Africa's Press of Freedom: *Le Messager*," *The Nation* (New York) 254, no. 6 (17 February 1992): 192.

57. Chris Allen writes: "The [Marxist] regime's residual legitimacy . . . was eradicated, at least in urban Benin, by the news of the scandals, spread by an increasingly free and confident press." See Chris Allen, "Restructuring an Authoritarian State: 'Democratic Renewal' in Benin," *Review of African Political Economy* 54 (July 1992): 47.

58. Cited in Théophile E. Vittin, "Crise, renouveau démocratique et mutations du paysage médiatique au Bénin," *Afrique 2000* 9 (May 1992): 48.

59. See Larry Diamond, "International and Domestic Factors in Africa's Trend toward Democracy," in *Window on Africa: Democratization and Media Exposure*, ed. Festus Eribo et al. (Greenville, NC: East Carolina University Press, 1993), p. 18.

60. Campbell, *Emergent Independent Press*, pp. 58–62.

61. Campbell, *Emergent Independent Press*, p. 59.

62. Campbell, *Emergent Independent Press*, p. 62.

63. Larry Diamond, "Introduction: Political Culture and Democracy," in *Political Culture and Democracy in Developing Countries*, ed. Larry Diamond (Boulder, CO: Rienner, 1993), pp. 13–14.

64. Richard Sandbrook, "Transitions without Consolidation; Democratization in Six African Cases," *Third World Quarterly* 17, no. 1 (1996): 82.

65. Sandbrook, "Transitions without Consolidation," p. 82.

66. Nancy Bermeo, "Democracy and the Lessons of Dictatorship," *Comparative Politics* 24 (April 1992): 287.

67. See Amin Maalouf, "A la une: Côte d'Ivoire, le malaise," *Jeune Afrique,* 6 September 1978, p. 23.

68. "Dernier avertissement du Bureau Politique: Non Aux Tracts!" *Fraternité Matin,* 16 August 1978, p. 1.

69. Cyril Kofie Daddieh, "The Management of Educational Crises in Côte d'Ivoire," *Journal of Modern African Studies* 26, no. 4 (December 1988): 643.

70. Daddieh, "Management of Educational Crises," p. 657.

71. "Grève des enseignants du secondaire," *Fraternité Matin,* 27 April 1983, p. 19.

72. Diégou Bailly, *La réinstauration du multipartisme en Côte d'Ivoire: Ou la double mort d'Houphouët-Boigny* (Paris: Harmattan, 1995), p. 181.

73. Laurent Gbagbo, the leader of the FPI, became the country's president following disputed elections in 2000.

74. The term was invoked by Bailly, *La réinstauration du multipartisme,* p. 180.

75. Bailly, *La réinstauration du multipartisme,* pp. 181, 191–92.

76. See Campbell, *Emergent Independent Press,* p. 91.

77. See Lye M. Yoka, "Radio-trottoir: Le discours en camouflage," *Le Mois en Afrique* (October–November 1984): 154–60.

78. Comi Toulabor, "Jeu de mots, jeu de villains," in *Le politique par le bas en Afrique noire: Contributions à une problématique de la démocratie,* ed. Jean-François Bayart, Achille Mbembe, and Comi Toulabor (Paris: Karthala, 1992), p. 127.

79. Stephen Ellis, "Tuning in to Pavement Radio," *African Affairs* 88, no. 352 (July 1989): 322.

80. Naomi Chazan, "Between Liberalism and Statism: African Political Cultures and Democracy," in *Political Culture and Democracy in Developing Countries,* ed. Larry Diamond (Boulder, CO: Rienner, 1992), p. 90.

81. Yves Sorokobi, "Overview: Africa," in *Attacks on the Press in 2000* (New York: Committee to Protect Journalists, 2001), p. 82.

82. "Sierra Leone," in *Attacks on the Press in 2000* (New York: Committee to Protect Journalists, 2001), p. 118.

83. "Ethiopia," in *Attacks on the Press in 2000* (New York: Committee to Protect Journalists, 2001), pp. 102–3.

84. "Zimbabwe," in *Attacks on the Press in 2000* (New York: Committee to Protect Journalists, 2001), p. 128.

85. "Algeria," in *Attacks on the Press in 2000* (New York: Committee to Protect Journalists, 2001), p. 252.

86. Norimitsu Onishi, "Nigeria's Press Bounces Back from Military Rule," *New York Times,* 21 February 2001, p. A3.

Chapter 4

Asian Cultures and Newspapers

Bradley Hamm

Newspapers in modern China, Japan, and Korea do not emerge directly from their nineteenth-century foundations. They were drastically reshaped in the twentieth century by political conflict, war, occupation, communism, and social and economic revolutions. And today, for as close as their homelands are in physical proximity—just across the seas from each other—the philosophical and economic distance among the media in these three East Asian countries is remarkable.

T. J. S. George argues simply: "In Asian countries, historical factors have brought about different realities in different societies."[1] The histories of the press in China, Japan, and Korea both overlap and diverge sharply in the course of a century. Today, the different realities are apparent. The historical factors are well worth study.

In Japan, the constitution bans censorship. The literacy rate is virtually 100 percent. Leading newspapers have the largest circulations in the world. And the annual Freedom House surveys of press freedom consistently rank Japan first among all Asian nations.

In China, the media in the last half of the twentieth century were tools of the Communist Party. China ranks only above Myanmar and North Korea on the press freedom surveys in Asia. China and North Korea are the first two countries listed by an international communications scholar as "trouble spots around the globe" for communications freedom.[2] With the world's largest population, well over 1 billion people, China's newspaper circulation falls below 50 million. By comparison, Japan, with less than one-tenth the population of China, sells millions more newspapers each day.

In Korea, the century has seen the split between the north and the south, and with the split comes two vastly different media worlds. South Korea's press ranks among the most free in Asia (third behind Japan and Taiwan); in North Korea, press freedom is ranked as nonexistent—the lowest score of any Asian country.[3] South Korea's press freedom developed further after the overthrow of Chun Doo-Hwan's regime in 1987; in North Korea, control remains as tight as ever. The penalty for negative communication about the government can be execution.

To understand the present, and perhaps the future, of the Chinese, Japanese, and Korean press, it is essential to understand the first one hundred years of newspapers and the emergence of modern societies in these nations. Newspapers were so important in the development of the countries that the leaders felt it essential to exert full control over what was said and who was allowed to say it. As John C. Merrill said about press freedom in the 1990s: "Control, then, is the common—not the exceptional—state of things in the world."[4] Control, whether by internal or external forces, is a central theme to Asian media history over the past century. This chapter examines the periods of freedom, external and internal control, and the societal influences experienced by the press in China, Japan, and Korea.

REFLECTIONS OF CULTURE

Asian media, as products of their societies, reflect the goals and values inherent within those cultures. Therefore, the fundamental ideas about free speech and the search for truth, as expressed by European writers John Locke in *Areopagitica* and John Stuart Mill in *On Liberty*, may be cast in a different light in societies or religions that emphasize harmony. While some Asian countries allowed limited press freedom in the late 1800s, a guiding principle in determining regulations was the superior importance of the group, not the individual.

In Japan, for example, in development of the constitution and press laws, W. G. Beasley notes that "an emphasis on social harmony remained, appealing greatly to men who saw what they were doing in the tradition of Confucian thought and in the context of national strength. To the Meiji leaders, political dissent was seditious, because it weakened the state."[5]

The *Asahi Shimbun*, ranked by Merrill to be among the world's greatest newspapers, declared on filing an application to begin publication that its goal was to teach "social justice" to the common people, young and old, men and women, and promised "easy reading" that would be accessible even to children.[6]

Anne Cooper-Chen expands on the issue of Asian cultural values and harmony, compiling a list of ten specific factors that characterize Japanese society and therefore affect the *masu komi* (mass communication), including the country's insularity/uniqueness, homogeneity, and emphasis on harmony. Similar lists may be compiled for Korea and China, and certainly the tradition of Confucian thought is an important thread.[7]

Early journalism research comparing Asian media seemed to focus on Confucianism. The Confucian concept of social harmony and conciliation was cited as one of the three strands of legal thought shared by South Korea and Japan, particularly in regard to libel law.[8]

Likewise, John D. Mitchell argues that while China and Japan shared common cultural roots regarding the role of Confucianism and family, the use of mass media as agents of socialization differed greatly. Chinese media, he states, had as its primary goal the struggle of remaking the Chinese citizen through criticism and (learned) self-criticism. Mass media in Japan "tend to reinforce existing values, existing concepts of the rules of the game and majority concepts of what it means to be Japanese."[9]

In Korea, Confucianism, with its emphasis on duty and respect to authority, "has contributed greatly to the general acceptance of numerous governmental restrictions on the press." But Kyn Ho Youm argues that Confucianism is no more important in the way Koreans view their press than the nonreligious factors and the historical, legal, and political realities over the past century.[10]

Besides Confucianism, China, Japan, and Korea shared a basic writing system based on thousands of Chinese characters. Each country developed its own meanings and pronunciations for similar characters, but newspapers in these countries faced an enormous printing barrier unlike those faced in the Western world: how to typeset thousands of characters with intricate markings.

For the citizens to be literate required an exceptional educational system and in some sense that they shared in a national community. It is far easier—though still remarkable—to develop a heightened sense of community in the islands of Japan or in South Korea than it is in China. With 1.3 billion people, China's media face an enormous challenge in communicating. Whether Mandarin or Cantonese, or any of the more than fifty other languages, the Chinese people speak and write in diverse ways.

HISTORICAL ORIGINS

The newspaper history of East Asia is remarkable. The Chinese developed paper 2,000 years ago. The Koreans learned from the Chinese, then passed along paper-making techniques to the Japanese. As Buddhism spread from China to other Asian countries, so, too, did the Chinese writing. Printing and language were adapted by each country to forms that suited their own wants and needs.

China developed wood-block printing techniques in the 900s, and the Koreans worked on movable type well before Gutenberg. The Asian countries were rich in the tradition of media success. They advertised in the storefronts, pasted message posters on the walls, taught through plays and wood-block pictures, and used traveling performers to deliver news in creative ways.

The publishing output was so strong that shogun leaders in Japan during the Tokugawa era had had enough of the "information revolution" by the late eighteenth century. They tried censorship and punished or killed violators. Then, in 1790, they declared in a new decree: "[Since] books had long been published, no more are necessary; so there ought to be no more new books."[11]

Attitudes about free speech and free press, great newspapers and great books, and the importance of a literate and informed society have changed throughout the past two hundred years in ways that could hardly be imagined.

Perhaps modern-style newspapers were developed late in East Asia, by comparison to the West, but few could doubt the role of Asian innovators in publishing. The Chinese developed the *Peking Gazette,* the first printed news sheet for which there is a record, more than a thousand years ago. Still, an English missionary is credited with starting the first "modern" Chinese newspaper in 1815. Many Westerners published newspapers in China in the 1800s since trade and information were important to the Western world's desire for influence and control in Asia.

The Western influence is important historically, but one other surprisingly strong factor in the way newspapers developed in China, Japan, and Korea is the Japanese military. As historians can readily see, Japan's military from the late 1800s to the mid-1900s caused enormous change in the lives of average citizens in its own country and among its neighbors. Japanese military control led to the loss of hundreds of newspapers; just as importantly, the control sparked a free speech desire that created some of the most important early newspapers in Korea and China.

While foreigners published several hundred newspapers throughout the mid-1800s, the first Chinese newspaper run by the Chinese, *Zhaowen Xinbao,* was started in 1873. The best model for early Chinese newspapers, though, is probably the publications used to spread ideas after China's defeat in the Sino-Japanese War. The newspapers were revolutionary and run by intellectuals. The press argued for revolution and reform. They were, in many ways, just like their early Korean counterparts.

The first Korean newspaper, *Hansung Sunbo,* was started in 1883. It was a governmental publication and opponents destroyed the press equipment a year later. Merrill argues that the "first *real* Korean paper" was begun in 1896; all others, he argues, were official government gazettes.[12] The *Toknip Shinmun (Independence Press)* was published in response to the colonial rule by Japan.

Like in China, the Korean press wanted revolution and reform. According to Merrill, "It might be said that the early Korean press in its revolutionary tendencies (against Japan) could be compared to the American press of the eighteenth century."[13] Unfortunately for the Koreans, their press history was mostly aborted by the Japanese-forced annexation starting in 1910. By any measure, the Korean newspaper period was a small blip—hardly enough time to see what the public wanted, needed, or bought. The reading public in Korea experienced less than two decades of newspaper reporting in its own country before the industry was derailed.

The first Japanese newspaper, *Yokohama Mainichi Shimbun,* was started in 1871. The Japanese periodical press developed during the Meiji era, the reign of Emperor Meiji from 1868 to 1912. Just as importantly, the nation's constitution and basic press codes grew from the first years of the Meiji era. While the press was restricted, even its existence reflected the remarkable change in direction for Japanese society after the overthrow of the Tokugawa.

Links between China, Japan, and Korea in the late 1800s through the mid-1900s are based on language, religion, and food on one hand and aggression, violence, bitterness, and control on the other. Yet, there were brief periods, or attempts, of freedom. The aggression and control of land is intertwined with the repression of speech and control of newspapers.

The tale is not all negative. In fact, newspapers are credited by one scholar as creating a modern citizenry in Japan.[14] Literacy rates increased, newspapers provided information and views, and citizens became better informed about their communities, countries, and the world. As Westerners discovered, and some would say exploited, the Asian nations, they introduced Western newspapers.

Even in the face of domination by Japanese military, Chinese and Korean leaders tried to rely on the media to unite and inform their communities. When the Japanese banned Korean-language newspapers within Korea in the early 1900s, issuing only Japanese-language newspapers, citizens imported newspapers in their language from other countries. It was a heroic effort.

A common thread, then, for the first half of the twentieth century was the influence of the Japanese on newspapers in the three countries because they often determined freedom for their own journalists as well as journalists in other countries. It is difficult to imagine—and a testament to the remarkable change in Asian life in the past century—that the country with the largest newspapers in the world grew from a history where its military eliminated hundreds of newspapers throughout Asia.

DEVELOPING ASIAN NEWSPAPERS AND SOCIETY, 1880–1945

During most of the Tokugawa rule (1600–1868), Japan kept its borders and society closed to foreigners, and citizens were controlled in nearly every element of their lives. Leaders prevented Western ideas and people, such as Christian missionaries, from influencing the commoners. And they prevented opponents of the government to form alliances with outside military forces. Free speech and free press were not valued, supported, or expected.

The overthrow of the Tokugawa led to the transition from premodern to modern Japanese society.[15] Newspapers expanded as the country emerged from its self-imposed blockade on the outside world. Many observers are aware that Japan transformed itself—business, politics, and society—after World War II.

An equal transformation occurred after Admiral Matthew Perry ordered Japan to open its doors in 1854. But the catalyst for internal change was not the Western world, but an internal hunger for information and a new society. Newspapers fed the change.

James L. Huffman believes that "[n]o institution did more to create a modern citizenry than the Meiji newspaper press." Meiji newspapers were "a collection of highly diverse, private voices that provided increasing numbers of readers—many millions in fact, by the end of Meiji—with both a fresh daily picture of the world and a changing sense of their own place in that world." Newspapers provided a place for commoner protests to take on public significance, Huffman argues, and, just as importantly, the press was shaped dramatically by the wants and needs of the emerging political consciousness of Japanese people in the Meiji era.[16]

While newspapers were owned by elites, the Japanese commoners, known as minshu, created a "mass" reading public. To appeal to the masses, publishers changed the newspapers from dense political discussions to more appealing news stories and features. "From the people flowed circulation fees and a definition of what kind of journalism was commercially acceptable; from the papers came a fresh view of the world and a new sense of what it meant to participate in the public life of a nation," Huffman states. "The newspapers, in other words, turned the people into citizens; the people turned the papers into mass media."[17]

Newspapers were not free. But compared with the past 200 years, this press world was new to the Japanese. People could read and journalists could write. They shared stories about Japan and the world. Before, people who tried to disseminate information, news, or Western ideas in Japan could be punished by death.

The first censorship regulation was issued in 1673. Writers needed prior permission to discuss any public matters. A series of ordinances over the next 200 years reinforced the strict view that free expression had little place in the Tokugawa world controlled by the samurai class. So what happened to the samurai who were out of work, out of power, and out of favor in the post-Tokugawa area? They became the early journalists of the Meiji era.[18]

JAPANESE CONTROL OF NEWSPAPERS IN KOREA

The Korean media might have emerged just as strongly in the late 1800s and early 1900s if not for the Japanese occupation. Like the Japanese, the Koreans kept themselves isolated from the outside world for more than 200 years. The main reason was simple: Korea had been invaded repeatedly throughout its history. But by the late 1800s, Korea was open to participating with the outside world. Unfortunately, history repeated itself.

After the establishment of Korea's first private, independent newspaper in 1896, many other new publishers followed with weekly and daily newspapers.

The papers were published in Korean, and they were opposed to intervention by Japan. But the newspapers had a short life.

Japan forcibly annexed Korea in 1910, which was just the latest step in a military action begun years earlier; only after the conclusion of World War II would Korea be free from outside control. The Japanese military wiped out Korean newspapers, distributing in their place Japanese-language newspapers. They expected the Koreans to learn the Japanese language, so they forced the teaching and reading of Japanese. For nearly ten years, the Koreans had no press of their own, a period referred to as the "dark ages."

After significant protests, the Japanese military in 1919 agreed to allow some books and newspapers to be published in Korean. While some was better than none, the number of newspapers allowed to print in the Korean language was less than ten in the 1920s. By 1940, as war efforts intensified, Japanese military shut down the two leading Korean newspapers. The history of Korean newspapers, for much of the early twentieth century, is a history of external, severe control over messages and any form of journalism. The Korean people lacked, among many essential human necessities, legitimate sources for information about their country and culture.

USING THE CHINESE PRESS TO MOBILIZE THE PEOPLE

Protesters played a key role in establishing the Chinese modern newspaper within the society. The Chinese-run modern newspapers were started about twenty years prior to the Sino-Japanese War in 1894–1895. After China was defeated, intellectuals spread their ideas and protested through their newspapers. As reform attempts failed, the number of newspapers advocating revolution soared; "from early times the Chinese have used their press to advocate their ideas and to mobilize the people to support their cause."[19]

The intellectual awakening that occurred in Japan in the late 1800s was just as dramatic in China. Newspapers helped spark the change. According to Daniel C. Lynch, "[i]t is clear that in the decades after 1895 tens and eventually thousands of people became mobilized into politics as a direct result of media-produced changes in consciousness about China's pressing problems."[20]

Press law followed press expansion. Leaders (the Kuomintang [KMT]) in China banned many imported publications in 1906, but the Communist Party used its freedom after World War I to establish the Cultural Book Society to print revolutionary literature in its movement for power. In response, the ruling government created publication laws in the 1930s that grew tighter and tighter with each revision. By 1937, freedom was nearly eliminated for revolutionaries such as the Communist Party. And then the Japanese invaded.

Still, the 1930s offer a complex period for analyzing Chinese media—which at times, and in some locations, experienced unprecedented freedom as protesters fought the ruling party, the ruling party linked with the Communists, before the Japanese swept south from Manchuria. This brief period, before the Japanese took control, marked "a kind of golden age for the Chinese press in its content, productivity, openness, and experimentation."[21]

Obviously, the Japanese military did not give great press freedom to the Communist Party while it controlled China from 1937 until the end of World War II in 1945. But it did force a change in the political dynamics of China by displacing the KMT leadership. Mao Ze-dong and the Communist Party continued the "thought work" throughout the war years in the small villages (the Japanese controlled the larger cities) so that the Chinese citizens were converted. When war ended, the Communist Party was ready to seize power—and newspapers were essential tools to accomplish Mao's mission.

MILITARY CONTROL IN JAPAN: THE RADICAL CHANGE IN THE PRESS

The role of the Japanese military in the Chinese and Korean press history is clear, but one area remains unmentioned. The society built by the emergence of a popular press, as Huffman argues, was also devastated by the military.[22] Twelve hundred daily newspapers were publishing in 1937, about a hundred were publishing in 1940, and by 1942 only fifty-four survived.[23] Military leaders caused the elimination of about 1,150 editorial voices. The few remaining newspapers only served to deliver whatever the government wanted told.

Most of the newspapers were lost forever as institutions, but the greatest damage was to the individuals who lost their jobs and incomes. Even worse, the Peace Preservation Law of 1925—which, oddly enough, despite its name was used against dissenters, including people supporting peace and opposing the war and the military—led to thousands of arrests. More than 75,000 journalists, Communists, Christians, protesters, radicals, and intellectuals were arrested between 1925 and 1945. Beasley reasons that "[t]here is no doubt that the Japanese public was kept in ignorance of many events at home and abroad such as might show Japan in a bad light."[24]

The state rationed paper, so one significant way to control journalists was to restrict or increase the amount of paper given, depending on how favorable the newspaper was in its role of supporting the government. The other, more obvious, way was to arrest writers and editors. Journalists had little recourse in courts.

Gregory J. Kaza does argue, though, that the power of the full media was never exercised because the press never acted collectively. The large dailies were not interested in the plight of the small papers and vice versa. And papers that supported the military action were not likely to raise their voices in favor of the antimilitary press. The larger papers had influence in the military and could have helped if they had banded together, but separately, they were doomed. According to Kaza, "[t]he newspapers' battle for readers had created such bad blood that most delined to protest the liquidation of their rivals—with few exceptions, none discovered the sanctity of an autonomous press until its own coals were in the fire."[25]

FREEDOM FROM EXTERNAL CONTROL, 1945–

Korea: "Repression and Freedom"

In August 1945, at the end of the world war, Japanese military surrendered control of people and the press of three nations, China, Korea, and its own. Freedom from external control meant, for some, freedom. For others, freedom from external control meant a switch to internal control.

The Allied Powers tried to establish press freedom and a "First Amendment" in both Japan and Korea immediately after the war ended. During the occupation years, the military leaders tried to establish press freedom—without allowing much criticism of the occupation leaders, of course. The Allied Powers believed the free press, modeled on Western systems, could help establish democracies in the countries.[26] Nearly sixty daily newspapers were publishing in Korea within a year of the end of the war, despite an early requirement to register publications so that Communists could not establish themselves.[27]

The Korean press reemerged but only briefly. The conflict between North Korea and South Korea, starting in 1950, devastated newspapers again. Equipment was destroyed in the fighting, and many journalists were killed. By the late 1950s, about forty daily newspapers published in South Korea.

Adults in Korea knew only one way of life: a repressive, Japanese-controlled government and Japanese-language and -controlled newspapers. The Koreans had been forced to learn Japanese. Suddenly, without any way to prepare, they had freedom. The first years were exciting and difficult. D. Wayne Rowland concludes that "[t]he government, the press and the people were reckless, extreme and often irresponsible with their freedom, at the start, and each suspected and lacked confidence in the other."[28]

But with experience they grew stronger. The greatest danger facing the press in South Korea, according to Rowland, was economic, not governmental control. Paper was in short supply, and few of the newspapers were making a profit. Advertising was limited in a struggling economy and printing equipment needed significant upgrades. The reality, for North Korea and South Korea, was that governmental control *was* the greatest danger for those who anticipated a free press after the world war.

A 1961 military coup ended the brief experiment of free press. New standards designed to eliminate "phony" journalists only served to wipe out the existing market. About 1,200 newspapers and periodicals were closed because they did not meet the new rules.[29] Brief periods of freedom throughout the next several decades only led to further restrictions. The central guarantee was that the government could do whatever it wanted, despite the constitutions designed to keep the press free. North Korea had a constitution that guaranteed press freedom, but like in South Korea, the guarantee meant little.

Only in the late 1980s did South Korea emerge as a country with legal freedom, and the number of daily newspapers increased rapidly. Reformers led the protests against South Korea's leadership, and Roh Tae Woo, soon to be president, responded in June 1987 with a pledge to support freedom of the press, among other issues. A 1987 act implemented this pledge, and once again in their long, arduous history, the South Koreans emerged with a freer press.

Japan: A "First Amendment"

Unlike in Korea, the United States was able to implement press freedom in Japan that lasted. During the occupation years, the press was supervised through General Douglas MacArthur's headquarters for the Allied Powers, and the military did censor some journalism, especially regarding communism. The military purged all suspected Communists from newspapers—about 700 reporters at 47 newspapers and agencies.[30]

The 1952 peace treaty and Japan's ratification of a new constitution in 1947 solidified the press freedom in a model similar to that of the United States. If observers wanted a free and combative press in Japan, they got it in the 1950s. Journalists became more and more critical of the government, and when street demonstrations broke out in 1960 because of a new Japan–U.S. treaty, many newspapers—especially Japan's "big three," meaning the largest newspapers—prominently featured the protesters and wrote editorials that harshly criticized the prime minister.

While the prime minister eventually resigned, many newspapers subsequently rethought their antagonistic role in the events, which some considered the biggest postwar crisis in Japan at the time. Unlike the Chinese and the Koreans, the Japanese press has not struggled for freedom in the postwar years. Since 1960, journalists may be critical of the national leaders at times, but the biggest criticism of Japan's newspapers is about their own self-censorship within a free world.

The audience for this news is staggering. Unlike newspapers in the United States, which developed as local enterprises based mostly in relatively small towns, Japanese newspapers are mostly national with large circulations. Thus, Edwin O. Reischauer and Marius B. Jansen argue that Japanese newspapers are better examples of "mass media" than newspapers in North America or Europe,[31] as their circulations run well into the millions.

China: "Communications Is Society"

The Chinese newspaper throughout the twentieth century was linked intrinsically to society. W. Houn characterizes the four main functions of Chinese press: educate the citizens for the government, stimulate progress, form and direct public opinion, and be an instrument used by the government to control society.[32] Merrill, Carter R. Bryan, and Marvin Alisky state the Chinese press functions "not to satisfy people's needs for information or interpretation, but to make the thoughts of the masses conform to official Party policy."[33]

The Communist Party placed great importance on newspapers in distributing its messages. In the early 1920s, Communists in China started newspapers in major cities throughout the country. *Renmin Ribao (People's Daily)* developed into one of the most significant newspapers in the world—based on its influence among party leaders and, indirectly, on a billion people. "In China," according to John Howkins, "communications and society are matched to a greater degree than anywhere else. Truly, communications *is* society."[34]

When the Chinese Communist Party (CCP) took control of the nation in 1949, it established a national press system by using the *Renmin Ribao* and hundreds of papers in the provinces or cities throughout China. Just as significantly, it ordered the reregistration of all newspapers. Several hundred Chinese newspapers were not allowed to continue because they were deemed unacceptable and denied permits.

One creative way that the CCP spread its message was through the use of wall posters, one of the oldest forms of Chinese communications. The posters served a news function in early times, and the CCP relied on this traditional method to shape the thoughts of the masses, particularly those who did not read newspapers. Wall posters were especially useful in rural areas. In 1966, the party used posters to promote the cultural revolution, attack opponents, and mobilize the young people.[35]

If thought determines action, as Mao said, then control of information is essential in state-building. As such, Howkins states that "[w]ith the emergence of the communists, the [printing and publishing] workers had another code, utterly different, but just as rigid, to govern their actions."[36]

DIRECTIONS FOR THE FUTURE?

The development of newspapers in the East Asian countries of China, Japan, and Korea is a story of conflict, Confucianism, communism, and community. And while the conflict has lessened, the roots of Confucianism, the politics of communism, and the need for a sense of community—valuing harmony, belonging, cultural and national identity, and social cohesion—remain strong forces. The purpose of this chapter was to examine links between the history of newspapers and society in China, Japan, and Korea from the origins of the first newspapers to the present, but primarily over the last century. Those links show that while newspapers served an important revolutionary and evolutionary role in societies in the late 1800s, the free press was a clear victim of political battles among and within China, Japan, and Korea.

The coming of a new media age with the Internet, satellites, cellular phones, and other specialized technology cause observers to question whether the models in Asia will change once again. Can the Communist Party leaders use the twenty-first-century media, or control it, as they did in the past in China and North Korea? Will the traditions of Confucian thought cause the mainstream free press to continue a group reporting style that fails to challenge the status quo? While some say that the end of the age of mass communication is near, is it even possible to be a gatekeeper for all of the new ways that messages are distributed?

Some scholars believe that change is both inevitable and already occurring, though fundamental change takes years. Steven H. Chaffee and Miriam J. Metzger believe that the rapid growth of media outlets has caused, in some ways, the end of mass communication. East Asian media may be the prime subjects to study over coming years. "The new media bring challenges to our old models, as well as the occasion to reevaluate, extend, and perhaps even supercede them," state Chaffee and Metzger.[37]

The changes inherent in media proliferation are already being felt in China. "The Chinese propaganda state remained in place throughout the Maoist period (1949–76) and into the 1980s. In fact, it persists in name to this day." Lynch argues that "[t]he problem is that its effectiveness has crumbled dramatically; as a result, Chinese leaders can no longer rely on thought work to manage a rapidly changing society."[38]

Jamie A. FlorCruz believes that market-oriented reforms and new media diversity are changing Chinese media and audiences. "The vibrancy, diversity and enterprise of newspapers, magazines and television shows reflect growing pluralism—and Beijing's inability to control it." FlorCruz cites declining circulations for party papers and a decrease in party subsidies.[39] Media content is more diverse, and other publications are experiencing large circulation gains. The Internet offers a link to less restricted information.

Even in a free-press state, traditional values about the importance of harmony, group consensus, and the avoidance of direct confrontation influence journalists, publishers, and audiences. Asian artists and thinkers expressed themselves through theater, wood-block prints, books, and other literature well before the development of modern newspapers. So Asian leaders regulated nearly any and all forms of expression, and booksellers and artists were expected to self-regulate as well.

It is this self-regulation that causes observers to wonder about a free press in Japan and South Korea. Freedom of expression depends on both law and people's willingness to allow it. Reischauer and Jansen cite the lack of investigative reporting, or any individualized quality to daily newspapers, as the great weakness in Japanese journalism. The uniformity in journalism can lead to uniformity in the population. "Tens of millions of Japanese, intellectually armed with the same television and newspaper news and opinions, sally forth to work each day with the same facts, interests and attitudes."[40] Yet, it is this uniformity that also contributes to the strong sense of social cohesion among the Japanese.

So at the beginning of the twenty-first century, the issues of control, communism, Confucianism, and community remain to influence future media in China, Japan, and Korea just as they have over the past century. The emergence of a new media world will determine which themes survive to guide the nations' press in coming years.

NOTES

1. T. J. S. George (1998). In A. Latif, ed., "Walking the Tightrope: Press Freedom and Professional Standards in Asia." (Singapore: AMIC, 1998), p. 21.

2. John C. Merrill, ed., *Global Journalism: Survey of International Communication*, 3rd ed. (New York: Longman, 1995), p. xvii.

3. Shelton A. Gunaratne, ed., *Handbook of the Media in Asia* (New Delhi: Sage, 2000), p. 24.

4. Merrill, *Global Journalism*, xv.

5. W. G. Beasley, *The Rise of Modern Japan* (New York: St. Martin's, 1990), p. 77.

6. John C. Merrill, Carter R. Bryan, and Marvin Alisky, *The Foreign Press* (Baton Rouge: Louisiana State University Press, 1964), p. 277.

7. Anne Cooper-Chen, *Mass Communication in Japan* (Ames: Iowa State University Press, 1997).

8. Hamid Mowlana and Chul-Soo Chin, "Libel Laws of Modern Japan and South Korea Compared," *Journalism Quarterly* 48 (1971): 348.

9. John D. Mitchell, "Socialization and the Mass Media in China and Japan," *Journalism Quarterly* 46 (1969): 582.

10. Kyn Ho Youm, *Press Law in South Korea* (Ames: Iowa State University Press, 1996), p. 27.

11. Jay Rubin, Injurious to Public Morals (Seattle: University of Washington, 1984).

12. Merrill, Bryan, and Alisky, *Foreign Press*, p. 198, emphasis added.

13. Merrill, Bryan, and Alisky, *Foreign Press*, p. 168.

14. James L. Huffman, *Creating a Public: People and Press in Jeiji Japan* (Honolulu: University of Hawaii Press, 1997).

15. Beasley, *Rise of Modern Japan*.

16. Huffman, *Creating a Public*, p. 2.

17. Huffman, *Creating a Public*, p. 3.

18. Edwin O. Reischauer and Marius B. Jansen, *The Japanese Today: Change and Continuity* (Cambridge, MA: Belknap, 1995), p. 221.

19. Liqun Yan, "China: Development of Press and Broadcasting," in *Handbook of the Media in Asia*, ed. Shelton A. Gunaratne (New Delhi: Sage, 2000), p. 499.

20. Daniel C. Lynch, *After the Propaganda State: Media, Politics, and "Thought Work" in Reformed China* (Stanford, CA: Stanford University Press, 1999), p. 19.

21. Stephen R. MacKinnon, "Press Freedom and the Chinese Revolution in the 1930s," in *Media and Revolution: Comparative Perspectives*, ed. Jeremy D. Popkin (Lexington: University of Kentucky Press, 1995).

22. Huffman, *Creating a Public.*

23. Cooper-Chen, *Mass Communication in Japan,* p. 56.

24. Beasley, *Rise of Modern Japan,* p. 184.

25. Gregory J. Kaza, *The State and the Mass Media in Japan, 1918–1945* (Berkeley: University of California Press), p. 269.

26. Cooper-Chen, *Mass Communication in Japan,* p. 269.

27. Youm, *Press Law in South Korea,* p. 11.

28. D. Wayne Rowland, "The Press in the Korean Republic: Its Status and Problems," *Journalism Quarterly* 35 (1958): 450–55.

29. Youm, *Press Law in South Korea,* p. 12.

30. Cooper-Chen, *Mass Communication in Japan,* p. 56.

31. Reischauer and Jansen, *Japanese Today.*

32. W. Houn, "The Press in Communist China: Its Structure and Operation," *Journalism Quarterly* 33 (1956): 502–512.

33. Merrill, Bryan, and Alisky, *Foreign Press,* p. 180.

34. John Howkins, *Mass Communication in China* (New York: Longman, 1982), p. 4.

35. Barry M. Broman, "Tatzepao: Medium of Conflict in China's 'Cultural Revolution,'" *Journalism Quarterly* 46 (1969): 100–4, 127.

36. Howkins, *Mass Communication in China,* p. 81.

37. Steven H. Chaffee and Miriam J. Metzger, "The End of Mass Communication?" *Mass Communication and Society* 4 (2001): 81.

38. Lynch, *After the Propaganda State,* p. 3.

39. Jamie A. FlorCruz, "Chinese Media in Flux: From Party Line to Bottom Line," *Media Studies Journal* 13 (1999): 43.

40. Reischauer and Jansen, *Japanese Today,* p. 20.

Chapter 5

Pacific Rim Cultures and Newspapers

Rod Kirkpatrick

Newspapers in the Pacific Rim countries today are dominated by dailies and owned, generally, by large corporations, sometimes multinationals. The role they play and the functions they serve vary according to the nature of their societies, their political systems, and the traditions of authoritarianism or freedom in which the papers emerged and have developed. As a general rule, editors in Australia and New Zealand (NZ), with their history of stable political systems, feel freer to be outspoken politically than editors in Papua New Guinea (PNG), Fiji, and other Pacific Islands. In all the Pacific Rim countries, corporate ownership of the major newspapers is the norm. Newspapers of any form, solely inspired and produced by the indigenous population, have been rare, largely because of the oral cultures of the various indigenous peoples.

GEOGRAPHY, SIZE, AND POPULATION

The Pacific Rim countries encompassed by this chapter are Australia, NZ, PNG, and the Pacific Islands, excluding Hawaii. The most populous nation in the region—sometimes called Oceania—is Australia, a commonwealth that comprises five mainland states, an island state Tasmania, and two territories. It also holds in trust a number of external territories, such as Christmas Island. Nearly two-fifths of this island continent of three million square miles, surrounded by the Indian, Pacific, and Southern oceans, lie within the tropics. The population is about 19 million, with most of the settlement being on the coastal fringe, largely because the rest of the nation is dry pastoral and even desert country.

NZ comprises three main islands: the North, South, and Stewart Islands, with several smaller groups of nearby islands and the Chatham Islands. The total area is 26.9 million hectares. No part of NZ is more than 70 miles from the sea. Its population is about 5 million.

The Pacific Islands occupy a little more than 193,000 square miles of land scattered over the physical gap of 64 million square miles of the Pacific.[1] New Guinea accounts for about 80 percent of the land area. The serried ranges of mountains and the valleys of New Guinea have isolated people for millennia and have helped produce the variety of cultures, customs, dress, and languages that typify the nation and make it so much more varied than other Pacific Island countries. The result is a flowering of languages that have no comparison anywhere else on earth. PNG and the Solomon Islands, with 3.5 million people, share one-quarter of the world's languages, while the Pacific covers one-third of the world's surface.

HISTORY

The Pacific Rim countries share one important experience: colonization. Broadly speaking, the British colonized Australia and NZ, and various European powers, such as the French, Germans, and British, colonized the Pacific Islands. Distinctively, the Australian colonies—apart from South Australia—began life as convict settlements. By 1900, all Pacific Islands had fallen under the authority of foreign powers. Britain annexed NZ in 1840, beating France to the punch. France annexed the Marquesas in 1842 in a "calculated act of imperialism" and, almost accidentally, annexed Tahiti.[2] In 1874, Britain accepted the voluntary cession of Fiji.[3]

Australia's history of settlement began at least 540,000 years before white settlement in the late eighteenth century. It was a landmass called Sahul, extending north into PNG and south to Tasmania. More than 300,000 Aborigines are believed to have been inhabiting the Australian continent when British colonization began in 1788.[4] Captain James Cook had claimed the east coast of Australia in 1770, incorrectly assuming *terra nullius,* that is, a land that lacked human habitation, law, government, or history. The First Fleet of eleven vessels, under the command of Captain Arthur Phillip, arrived in Sydney Cove[5] with more than 700 convicts and four companies of marines to control them: a total of 1,035 people. Britain's jails were overflowing, and the country could no longer send convicts to the United States where they had been sold to local entrepreneurs. Establishing a colony with convicts, as the British decided to do in Australia, was a more ambitious undertaking. Since there was no one to buy convict labor, they were expected to become a self-sufficient community of peasant proprietors. The new colony was a product of maritime exploration, trade, and penology.[6] The plan was to send out convicts and to take back commodities such as timber and flax, available freely on Norfolk Island, 1,050 miles east of Botany Bay. Both were in keen demand by the navy for masts, sailcloth, ropes, and cordage. But the British soon discovered that the native flax could not be processed and the pine was hollow.[7] Fortunate to survive the first two years around Sydney Cove, the First Fleet contingent was followed by others. The British established a number of colonies in Australia and gradually broke up New South Wales (NSW) into what became four colonies: Victoria, Tasmania, and Queensland were separated from it. Along with South Australia and Western Australia, the electors of these colonies decided, through a process of referenda, to unite in a federal compact from January 1, 1901.

A printing press was sent out with the First Fleet, but it was fifteen years before a newspaper appeared in NSW. The first Australian newspaper, the *Sydney Gazette and New South Wales Advertiser,* was established, with the governor's approval by a printer who had been transported for life for shoplifting. When the paper first appeared on March 5, 1803, Sydney had a population of 7,000, of whom only 1,000 were free citizens.[8] In Van Diemen's Land (ultimately Tasmania), three Hobart papers appeared—in 1810, 1814, and 1816–1821. These first four Australian newspapers had many things in common: They were governmentally founded and semiofficial in character; they were not only subject to an official censorship, but they also had to be careful not to publish anything that might offend any of the official hierarchy; the proprietors of the *Sydney Gazette* and the *Hobart Town Gazette* were at first convicts and afterwards ticket-of-leave men (in effect, prisoners at large), so they had to be doubly careful not to offend; and each of the four papers had to face a number of preliminary difficulties that had been surmounted by the time their successors arrived. They also lacked the stimulus of competition, for of the Tasmanian papers there was only one in existence at a time, and none of them could be considered a rival of the far-away *Sydney Gazette.*[9] Censorship did not cease until W. C. Wentworth and Robert Wardell established the *Australian* in Sydney on October 14, 1824, without incurring Governor Thomas Brisbane's opposition.[10] The change marked the end of the period of constraint on the colony's press, and the birth of the "free press."

The third colony to possess a newspaper was Western Australia, where it is said that a manuscript issue was "appended to a stately eucalyptus tree" at Perth in October 1828, shortly after the foundation of the settlement. During the next few years, several handwritten and printed newspapers appeared, but the first to endure for any time was the *Perth Gazette and West Australian Journal* (1833–), which became the *West Australian* in 1877.[11] The first South Australian paper, the *South Australian Gazette and Colonial Register* (1836–1931), was printed in London on June 18, 1836, and brought by the editor and part-proprietor Robert Thomas, who set out for Adelaide, taking his family as well as type, press, paper, and many needed supplies. The second paper appeared in 1837 in "its own country." It settled down as a four-page weekly.[12] In the Port Phillip Bay district of NSW (to become Victoria in 1851), John Pascoe Fawkner, one of the principal founders of that colony, established the first newspaper, the *Melbourne Advertiser*, in 1838. Its early numbers were handwritten. Then Fawkner managed to get hold of a press and some type, but the first printing was suppressed for lack of the sureties required by law. Within a year he had obtained the required sureties and brought out a second newspaper, the *Port Phillip Patriot and Melbourne Advertiser*, but in the meantime George Arden and Thomas Strode had issued the *Port Phillip Gazette* (1838). Fierce rivalry ensued. In the Moreton Bay District of NSW (to become Queensland in 1859), the first newspaper, the *Moreton Bay Courier*, began on June 20, 1846, four years after the opening of the district to free settlers. It continues today as the *Courier-Mail*, the *Courier* having merged with the *Daily Mail* in 1933.

A strong country press emerged, especially during the gold-rush periods of the 1850s and 1860s in Victoria and NSW and the 1890s in Western Australia. At times, more than 400 country newspapers have been published simultaneously, with as many as four dailies competing against one another in such towns as Ballarat, Victoria, and Townsville, Queensland. In the capital cities, the number of dailies rose from twenty-one in 1903 to twenty-six in 1923 and fluctuated until 1980 when it steadied at seventeen only to fall to twelve in the early 1990s after the closure of the evening dailies. There were still twelve in 2002, including two national papers, the *Australian* (established 1964) and the *Australian Financial Review* (1951). The number of independent metropolitan owners has fallen from twenty-one in 1923 to four in 2002.

Indigenous expression in print media has not been prolific. Traditional Aboriginal culture was and still is primarily oral. Aborigines were intimately and inextricably linked to the land. Orally transmitted knowledge about Aboriginal culture and its proper relation to the land moved around the continent along well-established "dreaming tracks," or "songlines," in such quantities and so quickly that one researcher has described traditional Aboriginal culture as being "abuzz with information." The first Aboriginal newspaper in the Australian colonies was the *Aboriginal or Flinders Island Chronicle*, produced between September 1836 and December 1837. Three English-speaking Aboriginal clerks, in the employ of the commandant of the Aboriginal settlement on the island in Bass Strait, handwrote and hand copied the publication. After the last recorded date of publication of the *Flinders Island Chronicle* (December 21, 1837), a century passed before the next Aboriginal newspaper or magazine appeared. The second Aboriginal publication of which there is a clear record is the *Australian Abo Call: The Voice of the Aborigines*, a professional-quality, tabloid newspaper, six editions of which were produced by the Aborigines Progressive Association in Sydney between April and September 1938. Much of the content of the *Abo Call* dealt with the campaigns being waged by the association for justice for Aboriginal people, the granting of full citizenship rights, and the repeal of discriminatory legislation.[13]

No other significant attempt to produce Aboriginal print journalism occurred until the *Westralian Aborigine* was published by the Coolbaroo League from late 1954 until 1957. Aboriginal-controlled newspapers and magazines were published relatively frequently during the 1960s. Their size, scope, quality, and regularity varied according to the resources of their publishers and the journalistic skills of the editorial staff and contributors. Some newsletters and even newspapers were typewritten, roughly laid out and reproduced, had a very small circulation, and did not appear for long. Others were more professional in appearance and regularity of issue. Frequently, the publishers were Aboriginal legal-aid services, land councils, or self-help community groups. Many of the publications in the 1960s and 1970s had a radical tone and style that derived much from Black Power groups in the United States. The most significant recent edition to the growing list of Aboriginal periodicals is the nationally distributed *Koori Mail*, established in 1991 in Lismore, NSW, by Owen Carriage and then taken over by a cooperative of five Aboriginal communities in that region. The *Koori Mail* is significant because it is the first Aboriginal newspaper to make a sustained attempt at comprehensive coverage of Aboriginal matters on a national level, as well as seeking national distribution and commercial viability. Since late 1995, the question of its "authenticity" as an Aboriginal publication has arisen because most important editorial decisions were being made by a non-Aboriginal editor, and much of the material in the newspaper was wire copy from the mainstream Australian Association Press news service.[14]

NZ was annexed by Holland in 1642, the French in 1772, and the British in 1840, but the British were the first colonizers to settle. Initially, the British placed NZ under the administration established for the colony of NSW, and, although this lasted only fifteen months, it affected the legal framework of trading relationships for the next forty years.[15] The 1840–1880 period was one of great change in NZ society as well as in newspaper publication. The political organization of NZ changed from the status of a crown colony, through a period of provincialism, to, finally, a centralized government from Wellington. The changes in communication technology were momentous, including the connection of the NZ settlements by telegraph and the laying of sea cables between the North and South Islands and between NZ and Australia. From 1840 to 1880, the NZ settlements moved from experiencing isolation, often for months at a time, to worldwide communication on a daily basis. The European population of NZ increased greatly with corresponding changes in newspaper circulation. The demographic changes, from the point of view of newspaper controllers, were such as to allow a movement from the publication of political journals restricted by circulation to an elite, to the publication of daily newspapers oriented toward a mass readership. This was particularly so for the larger population areas and NZ newspapers came to be dominated by the dailies from the main centers.[16]

The first newspaper, the *New Zealand Gazette*, began publication on April 18, 1840, when NZ was part of NSW. After the paper, which functioned as the first government gazette in NZ, had criticized the land policy of the government, Willoughby Shortland, the colonial secretary, presented a demand that the printer of the *New Zealand Gazette* comply with the registration and bond requirements of the Newspaper Act, one of Governor Ralph Darling's notorious 1827 NSW Press Acts. The financial requirements were impossible to fulfill and the paper closed. The universal condemnation of Shortland's behavior meant that no further attempt was made to enforce the Press Acts, and all further official control of newspapers was carried out by financial manipulation or by using the law of libel. NZ was separated from NSW in July 1841, and it was 1868 before any law requiring the registration of printing presses was instituted.[17]

After the early failure of the *New Zealand Gazette*, other newspapers soon emerged and multiplied. Twenty-eight were established between 1840 and 1848 for a European population that had reached only 59,000 by 1858; 181 newspapers were established between 1860 and 1879; and 150 between 1880 and 1889. And they spread to cover a wider range of topics. Kathleen Coleridge writes: "To survive in New Zealand, newspapers had to be cautious about which of the established attitudes in Britain could be adopted and which discarded. Just as the land, soil, vegetation and climate were different, so was the community, and the most successful newspaper was the one which perceived that first and adjusted most readily."[18] Today, the longest surviving paper is the *Taranaki Herald* (established 1852), but the *Otago Times* has been a daily the longest.[19] Currently, NZ has four metropolitan dailies—one each in Wellington, Auckland, Christchurch, and Dunedin. There are two national Sunday newspapers and two major business weeklies that also circulate nationally. In the provinces, there are 20 dailies—most of them evening publications—and more than 100 community newspapers, principally weeklies but also a significant number of biweekly and triweekly papers. The national news agency—the New Zealand Press Association—is a cooperative owned by the newspapers that subscribe to (and provide copy for) its services.[20]

European and American missionaries introduced the print media to the Pacific Islands. Individual missionaries or missionary groups published each of the first three Pacific Island newsletters: *O Le Sulu Samoa* (1839), *Fiji Weekly News and Planters' Journal* (1868), and *Ko E Bo'obo'oi* (1874). The printers of the London Missionary Society established the first printing press in what is now French Polynesia on June 9, 1817. Under missionary guidance, King Pomare set and printed the first page of the first publication, a speller. Demand for the book was huge and led missionaries William Ellis and William Pascoe Crook to charge quantities of coconut oil and arrowroot for their printed material. Other presses followed in Tonga (1831), Samoa (1839), and Fiji (1839). A similarly high demand for reading matter was shown in other Polynesian islands. In 1854, the circulations of the Samoan-language *O Le Sulu Samoa* (19,500) and English- language *Reporter* (1,200) far outstripped the European population in western Samoa. In Tonga in the 1830s, mission printer William Woon wrote "so many Tongans clamored for reading matter that they became quite troublesome." Controversial Wesleyan missionary Shirley Baker founded the first substantive Tongan-language newspaper, *Ko E Bo'obo'oi*, in 1874 to further his political agenda and raise money for the church. It contained "Baker's views on religious and political matters mixed with selected items of local and foreign news." In the Solomon Islands, the first newspaper published was *O Le Sala Ususur (The Messenger)*, by the Anglican missionary E. E. Fox in 1903. Tonga's first newspaper, *Fetu'u 'o Tonga (Star of Tonga)*, was published by the government in September 1869 to explain the country's new constitutional monarchy.[21]

In New Guinea, colonial newsletters produced in German New Guinea were the first form of print media in the late nineteenth century, followed in the early twentieth century by mission-produced pamphlets. The German government papers, both in Samoa and New Guinea, used German whereas the mission papers used indigenous vernacular languages. A number of Papua New Guineans were trained as printers and compositors to assist missionaries in their work. While most missions published pamphlets and newsletters, these periodicals lacked the penetration of the print media produced under indigenous patronage in Pacific Islands with monolingual cultures, such as Fiji, Tonga, and Samoa. The German New Guinea Company, which administered the German colony in the northern part of New Guinea and adjacent islands, founded in 1885 the first New Guinea newspaper, a general-interest monthly that appeared until 1898. Aside from government gazettes, the earliest forms of printed news in British New Guinea, which became known as Papua when the Australians replaced the British as colonial administrators in 1906, were a few commercial papers—beginning with the *Papuan Times and Commercial (Tropical) Advertiser* in 1911—published by and for the expatriates, reflecting their views before and between the two world wars. In 1929, Sir Hubert Murray, the lieutenant governor, introduced a monthly English-language newspaper, the *Papuan Villager*, the first government or commercial publication to address an indigenous audience. It set out to turn Papuans into model territorial subjects loyal to the British Crown. There was an authoritarian element about the newspapers in American Samoa from 1903 to 1955, with officers of the U.S. Navy administration editing the publications.[22] While missionary presses operated on various islands of Micronesia, no newspaper press developed, possibly because of a lack of population and a diversity of languages. The German and later Japanese administrations did not produce local media. An exception was the *Guam News Letter* published by the American administration on Guam since 1909.[23]

After World War II, political change was initiated in most Pacific Island territories, with the result that most of them have become independent nations since 1962. This transition has occurred sometimes earlier and faster than the inhabitants wished, particularly when Western ideology has proven a more important factor than island nationalism. The new nations of the Pacific Islands, however, have found that political independence has not enabled them to meet all the social and economic goals that they optimistically envisaged. The desire for progress beyond the means of their own resources has induced a dependency and an accelerated change far greater than during the colonial era before 1950.[24]

The number of Pacific Island newspapers doubled between 1973 and 1989, with the largest increases occurring in PNG (from five to fifty-six titles), Guam (from two to fifteen), the Solomon Islands (from two to eight), Tonga (from two to seven), and Fiji (from fifteen to twenty-two). Circulation more than doubled in the same period, while regional population rose by 42 percent.[25] In 1999, twenty-four Pacific nations and territories had at least one locally published newspaper, and eleven had two or more competing newspapers, along with a variety of specialist periodicals. In addition, six major news magazines were available. The biggest newspapers were dailies located in the major English-speaking markets, such as the *Post-Courier* in Port Moresby, PNG (circulation 41,000), and the *Fiji Times* in Suva (31,000). Dailies in the French territories also are significant in regional terms: *Les Nouvelles Calédonnienes* (13,000) and *La Depeche de Tahiti* (12,000). All the dailies are owned by foreign-based media corporations. Some of the best newspapers in the region are quite small; in 1996, the *Cook Islands Press* (1,500) won the Pacific Islands Newspaper Association Media Freedom Award. Weekly newspapers are such a significant force that they claim a circulation nearly double that of the dailies. Church and nongovernment organizations publish most of the smaller weeklies. Though the newspapers primarily serve an urban audience, the Tok Pisin–language weekly *Wantok* has a significant near-urban and rural circulation in PNG.[26] For the publisher, the cost of transporting goods, books, or newspapers throughout the Pacific Islands is horrendous (postage takes up 60 to 80 percent of the subscription for most overseas subscribers to the *Times of PNG*).[27]

SOCIAL FUNCTIONS

The social functions of newspapers vary according to the societies in which they operate—not only the political nature of those societies, but also their size, as well as their hierarchical and religious nature. In Australia, just as news values differ between Sydney dailies and the provincial triweeklies and dailies, they also differ between larger country papers and smaller ones. In the first half of the twentieth century, the *Wingham Chronicle*, the *Molong Express*, and the *Lockhart Leader* were the type of "local rag" or small country paper that, in the words of T. J. Hebblewhite, editor of the *Goulburn Evening Penny Post* (1885–1900), "acted as a bond to the countryside, chronicling things which, although of no interest to the great outside world, were, within its little circle, quite family affairs—so and so's death, with brief biographical sketch; who of where were married; social functions with perhaps the names and dresses of the ladies participating; echoes from without, with probably a serial love story which opened magic casements giving entrancing glimpses of fairyland."[28] In this way, the local newspaper served as a genial gossip who, passing from house to house as the gaberlunzies (beggars) of Scotland used to do in the days when "Waverley" was in every literary man's mouth, distributed the assorted news of a dozen parishes in return for a few pence.

News in the twentieth-century Australian provincial newspaper changed in definition and in the styles of writing, presentation, and production. The most obvious changes were that news, from about the late 1930s, took precedence over advertising on the front page of most provincial newspapers; the tombstone style of layout was increasingly shunned as headlines were enlarged and the introductions of some stories were set over two or three columns; the news writing style adopted the inverted-pyramid style of writing, with the most important information at the top and the rest of the story in a generally descending order of importance; stories and sentences became shorter for reasons of cost, presentation, and readership; pictures were used increasingly from the 1930s, and they gradually became up-to-date pictures rather than almost dateless pictures of, for instance, agricultural activity or coastal scenery; and the newspapers changed from a broadsheet format to tabloid—generally in the 1970s when they converted from letterpress to web offset printing. In the 1980s, most papers adopted modular layout—that is, the presentation of stories in rectangular modules with an emphasis on the horizontal. In the 1990s, the big swing was to the use of full-color, mainly on the front page but also in features and supplements.

A major influence on the functions performed by the press in colonial Australia was the perception, held strongly by many proprietors and editors, that the press had a fourth-estate role. This belief in the independence of the press from government—of a watchdog function—arose directly from the British notion of press freedom based on the doctrine of publication without prior restraint, such as censorship or regulation.[29] This was seen to give editors great power. Through their constant editorializing and sheer weight of words, editors exerted greater influence than the politician who might make only three or four speeches in a year. One editor suggested in 1864: "The 'line upon line and precept upon precept,' the constant dropping of the fountain, wears itself a channel in the firmest mind. Good political judges and those not newspaper men, have predicted that, if the force and influence of the 'fourth estate of the realm' shall ever be brought to bear unanimously on any one point, it will have a fair chance of victory against the other three."[30]

Another editor suggested that the press was the greatest institution of modern days. Armies, navies, arts, science, and commerce would be nothing without it. It was the "shield of the people" that protected them from tyranny and wrong. It was the great bond that held civilization together. In South Australia, however, the *Border Watch* (Mount Gambier) regarded it as its duty to "protest against the commonly received doctrine that a free press is the chief leader and guide of public opinion." The truth was that the press and public opinion acted and reacted on one another in a manner that could never be clearly traced. The press sometimes guided public opinion, but more frequently followed it.[31] Grant Harman finds in his study of the NSW New England press and politics over three-quarters of a century to 1930 that the local press saw itself as a watchdog over the actions of ministers and public servants alike. It carefully scrutinized public expenditure and at times not only attempted to secure modification of administrative practices, but also put forward definite proposals for new legislation and for legislative amendments.[32]

At Melbourne's *Age*, for nearly fifty years from 1860, proprietor-editor David Syme was a campaigning newspaperman whose strong advocacy earned him such titles as "kingmaker" and "the father of Protection." In one strenuous campaign he called on Victoria to impose import duties on goods from England, the United States, NSW, and everywhere else in the world. Victoria should make its own furniture, locomotives, and wines rather than import them, he argued. This man—who did not speak in public, was unrecognized in the street, and was outwardly shy when approached—seemed to possess more power than any single Victorian politician. His long, thin editorials, usually running to about 400 lines of type, appeared six days a week, and daily reached a wider audience than could be fitted into the ten largest town halls in Victoria. Syme believed he was the teacher of people who had not previously enjoyed the right to vote, who could not always shape their arguments with fluency, but who had a wonderful opportunity to create a prosperous society in a new land.[33]

In NZ, too, British fourth-estate rhetoric was "lifted bodily over the seas to be transplanted in the antipodean colony," but the practice was distinctly different from the rhetoric. The rhetoric bore no relationship to the reality of newspapers as businesses governed only by the usual commercial imperatives. Commercial, local, and regional interests, not class struggle or opposition to censorship, seem to be the best way of interpreting the nineteenth-century NZ press.[34] The only powers of the press that interested most New Zealanders were the powers to earn money (for the newspaper proprietor), to sell goods and services (for the advertiser), and to provide local information (for the purchaser). Any other power ranked way below these in importance. In NSW, the editor in 1894 of the leading provincial journal, the *Maitland Daily Mercury*, would have agreed. "A newspaper is primarily in most cases a commercial speculation. And the more successful the speculation as a rule, the better the newspaper."[35]

In the NZ press, partisan political advocacy was normal in the 1840s and 1850s. The practice had developed before self-government was granted in 1852 and had intensified in the final years before the first elections were held. Intense political agitation was coordinated through the colony's newspapers as self-government was sought. This agitation, says Patrick Day, became "partisan political advocacy on behalf of particular politicians" and was seldom conducted according to standards of decorum or fair play. Most of the major elected officials had connections with NZ newspapers; these connections varied from actual ownership to a period of intermittent contributions to a newspaper. Day states that "[p]ress political advocacy was not usually advocacy for a political party—these were as yet generally undeveloped—but personal advocacy for a particular politician." Mostly, the politician also happened to own the newspaper.[36]

In the Pacific Islands, the big question facing newspaper owners has always been: How do you provide for the cultural, social, and educational information needs of small, often scattered, populations? For many years, a very serious problem in the Pacific Islands was the lack of appropriate and credible reading materials with a Pacific Island background. Because of the small number of people speaking or reading any one of the vernacular languages, it has generally been unprofitable for commercial publishers to venture into publishing materials in the vernacular. The exception has been in Fiji, where there is a relatively sizable number of Fijian, Urdu, Tamil, and Hindustani people. But even in Fiji's case, the population is only about 750,000. In PNG, where 700 languages are spoken, and other parts of Melanesia, by 1984 Pidgin was increasingly appearing in published form, especially in newspapers, magazines, and official government notices for the public.[37] Newspapers have been published in the Pacific Islands for more than 160 years. Introduced as a social artifact by adventurous Europeans, they reflected differing social, moral, and political forces during the missionary, colonial, and postcolonial periods. They have served as voices for religious orthodoxy, for the interests of planters, administration officers, and military commanders, and for nascent independence movements. Most of the islands have assumed control of their own affairs in recent decades, within the context of accelerating global integration fueled by new communication technologies. Multinational media corporations have bought the major newspapers in the islands.[38]

SOCIAL ADVANCEMENT

In his study of the nineteenth-century NZ press, Ross Harvey downplays suggestions that it functioned as a powerful political instrument. Instead, he suggests a list of "perceived" powers: the power to evoke nostalgia; the power inherent in a tool for effective colonization, settlement, and government; commercial power (to make money); the power to promote a new settlement or district; the power to assist a person into, and out of, politics; the power to educate, to influence, and perhaps even to change public opinion; the power to proselytize; and the power to civilize. In a NSW setting, boosterism was one of the main powers of the press in the provinces. R. B. Walker notes that one principle to which all country newspapers firmly adhered was the vigorous promotion of their town and district. "In the absence of local government, the conferment of such benefits as roads, bridges, schools, public buildings, railways and other amenities depended much on the local member supported by a public marshalled by the press. A newspaper proprietor also had a personal pecuniary interest in development; prosperity, closer settlement by free selectors, meant more subscribers."[39]

This was put into a nutshell by one provincial editor in 1863. He summarized his political belief thus: "PROGRESS: social, moral, and material."[40] In Victoria, Elizabeth Morrison finds that although newspapers were not present at the initial occupation of the colony, they were active in its legitimization—and the country press particularly so—reinforcing the process of claiming, naming, profiting from, and praising.[41] In NSW, in many instances, the establishment of a town's first newspaper predated the advent of local government. This placed a heavier onus on the newspaper to "represent" or to advocate the interests of the town. At least two other factors contributed to the need in NSW for a newspaper to advocate the material and social interests of town and district. One was the general slowness of communications. Another was that elected members of Parliament often did not live in their electorates. Certainly, the NSW provincial newspapers that boosted their communities in many cases had political affiliations or patronage. Mining newspapers were outspoken in advocating the cause of their primary clientele.

The pioneering Australian provincial papers did not ignore social goals. Some of these proclaimed goals were to civilize, to assert the rights of the local people, to promote equity, to educate, and to entertain. The *Maitland Mail* [11 November 1882] said it planned to become "not merely a vehicle for local items and information, but also an instrument for the elevation and instruction of our readers in all those departments of knowledge best calculated to promote the progress of humanity." At Albury in 1869, when George Henry Mott left the *Border Post,* he was "proud to be able to say that the press as a general rule has done its work vigorously in this part of the world." Because of the isolated nature of the town and surrounding districts, it had "devolved upon local journalists not merely to lead public opinion, but to create it—not merely to write and publish, but to look after and take part in the more practical business of agitation." Mott concluded: "The reforms inaugurated, the local requirements satisfied, the general progress of the various towns, all bear witness that these exertions have not been altogether unproductive."[42]

In a fascinating study of Sydney's *Bulletin,* Sylvia Lawson suggests that from 1880, when it began publication, to the years after federation (1901), this journal penetrated its society and gripped attention in ways for which it is hard to find any parallel, even in the highest times of national radio and television. The reasons were much more than "mass appeal," Lawson argues. She says that historians generally have looked strictly for the "literary" or the explicitly political, ignoring journalism and its special strategies. Hence, they failed to see the workings of a vast and extraordinary text—of an unusual social function, we might add. Lawson focuses on the "Archibald paradox," which is simply the paradox of being colonial, of being so removed from the center of language and of the dominant culture and its judgments, and yet of having to love and communicate and teach not Elsewhere but Here. "To know enough of the metropolitan world, colonials must, in limited ways at least, move and think internationally; to resist it strongly enough for the colony to cease to be colonial and become its own place, they must become nationalists."[43]

Lawson tracks this paradoxical process in founding editor J. F. Archibald, whose first allegiances were to "his jumbled images of European cosmopolitanism and insurgency." He hated, and was irresistibly drawn to, a London written by Charles Dickens and the pamphleteers of poverty, a London of cruel hierarchies that was also the great urban parade and performance, not least the parade of journalism. He loved the Paris of Gustave Flaubert and Émile Zola, the mythology of boulevards and barricades, still vital memories of the commune, and a cunning, insurrectionary press. It was the mythic metropolis. Archibald looked also, as British radicals did, to the United States. From these quarters of his known world, the messages that counted were about resistance to imperial dominance. Back in Australia, dreaming of flamboyance, he could link those messages only to the broken echoes of the Eureka Stockade, a rebellion by gold miners in 1854 against government authority. That was one available way of bringing the world home to the province.

The *Bulletin*'s republicanism and nationalism flowered out of the paradox. The republicanism worked as an inspiriting argument for a time, but nationalism supervened. It was expressed strongly, through the late 1880s in particular, as viciously chauvinistic racism—directed especially, but not only, against the Chinese. In this the editor, with all his compassionate, world-ranging perspectives, was not alone; but he was responsible. The paradox worked because the dominant culture, which in one breath the *Bulletin* lampooned and disavowed, was upheld vigorously in the next. The prospective Utopia, the dream of "Australia"—federated, republican, and democratic—was landscaped for white men only. The internationalist humanism, enacted so brilliantly in the journal's range of reference and its open-pages policy, was denied in the racist argument; it was also undermined and disfigured perennially in much of the *Bulletin*'s discourse on women.[44] Another perspective of the functions performed by the *Bulletin* came from Graeme Davison: "Towards the end of the nineteenth century, through the powerful influence of the Sydney *Bulletin* and the new unionism the rural traditions of egalitarianism and collectivism, of 'mateship,' were imported from the pastoral frontier to the coastal cities where they formed the basis of a national, rather than merely sectional, culture. As the 'bush' became the 'Bush,' folk tradition was transmitted into literature."[45]

Generally, in the Pacific Islands oral societies have prevailed. Reading has not been appreciated widely as a useful accomplishment; it has been regarded as antisocial and useless. A change in this attitude is taking place, but the evolution is all the slower because the boy who is literate and can read and write cannot necessarily get a job.[46] For newspaper publishers, the problems have been immense: small markets, multiplicity of languages, low economic bases, vast distances, inadequate transportation, high costs, lack of trained personnel, and lack of attention by the bigger world of publishing. Clearly, the financial rewards are uncertain at best.[47] Kevin Walcot, as the manager of Word Publishing in PNG, said in 1984 that the Pacific Islanders "know so little of each other."[48]

LITERATURE IN NEWSPAPERS

In Australia and NZ, one of the major social functions of newspapers in the nineteenth century was to provide a vehicle for literary expression. For example, in the Port Phillip District of NSW, many issues of the Geelong and Portland publications of the 1840s contained one or more poems. Often, these were reprinted from elsewhere, but many appear to be original contributions. Elizabeth Webby, an indexer, shows that hundreds appeared in these country papers and that the titles presented a wonderful spread, giving promise of whimsy, social commentary, and political satire, but for the most part doing so anonymously. Webby, who considers that to "study the literature written in Australia before 1850 is mainly to study poetry," comments that in the 1840s there was "a marked increase ... in the number of poems on local topics, a significant proportion of which were humorous or satirical, the equivalent of the modern paper's daily cartoon." In the Port Phillip papers, with the striking exception of the *Corio Chronicle*, very little fiction, long or short, is to be found.[49]

In colonial NZ, Coleridge, Day, and others note problems arising from the irregular supply of news. One of the expedients adopted was to reprint literary extracts to fill the gaps between the advertisements. In 1866, J. G. S. Grant commented that of the seventeen dailies then being published in NZ, "eleven are purely advertising sheets, plus the insertion of a piece of a novel or rattle successively published for the amusement of the gaping settlers who have no other sources of literature." Thomas Morland Hocken noted the very broad spread of subject matter in NZ colonial newspapers. Commenting specifically on Wellington's *New Zealand Gazette* between 1840 and 1844, he said: "From time to time the journals of exploration into the unknown country around are given at length, and occasionally there are articles on the natural history and production of NZ."[50] From the late 1850s, various NZ papers serialized fiction. In January 1858, the *Hawkes Bay Herald* began to serialize Bulwer Lytton's novel *What Will He Do with It?*; in 1862, the *Otago Daily Times* serialized Mary Elizabeth Braddon's *Lady Audley's Secret*; and in 1862–1863, the *Otago Witness* serialized *The Life and Adventures of Christopher Congleton* by the local author B. L. Farjeon.[51]

British press historian Alan J. Lee says the British newspaper press began the serialization of novels in 1871. At about the same time, U.S. newspapers began to serialize popular fiction. If Lee's date for Britain is correct, the antipodean newspapers were in fact the true pioneers of serialized fiction in newspapers; Australian dailies had begun serializing fiction well before 1871. Morrison notes that the *Sydney Mail*, the weekly edition of the *SMH*, began serializing fiction in 1860, the Melbourne *Australasian* in 1867, and the Melbourne *Age* in 1872. She also comments that most new novels by Australian authors were published in newspapers and periodicals until the 1890s.[52] Dirk H. R. Spennemann notes that the third Albury paper, the *Banner,* published fiction. After a faltering start in 1864, when the serialization of Charles Dickens's *Our Mutual Friend* was terminated without conclusion, the *Banner* embraced the serialization of novels in March 1869. By the end of the century, a total of thirty-eight novels and been reproduced, usually in weekly installments. Fourteen of these novels were written by Braddon, the single most represented author.[53] In NZ, in the late 1890s and in the years of intense competition in the 1920s and 1930s, the newspapers followed the British pattern by resorting to widespread serialization of popular fiction to boost readership, but the reasons were different for the earlier period.[54] In Australia, at the beginning of the 1890s, journalism was seen as "the only field in which literary talent can find profitable occupation."[55]

NOTES

1. Kevin Walcot, "Perspectives on Publishing, Literacy, and Development," *Proceedings of Pacific Islands Symposium,* 1984, p. 12.

2. I. C. Campbell, *A History of the Pacific Islands* (Brisbane: University of Queensland Press, 1990), pp. 136, 138–39.

3. Campbell, *History of the Pacific Islands,* p. 143.

4. Stuart Macintyre, *A Concise History of Australia* (London: Cambridge University Press, 1999), pp. 3–4.

5. They first visited Botany Bay, Captain Cook's choice in 1770, but found it uninviting in midsummer, so they moved on to the harbor of Port Jackson or Sydney Cove.

6. Macintyre, *Concise History of Australia,* p. 31.

7. Macintyre, *Concise History of Australia,* p. 32.

8. R. B. Walker, *The Newspaper Press in New South Wales, 1803–1920* (Sydney: Sydney University Press, 1976), p. 3.

9. H. M. Green, *A History of Australian Literature: Pure and Applied,* vol. 1, *1789–1923* (Sydney: Angus and Robertson, 1961), p. 67.

10. Walker, *Newspaper Press in New South Wales,* p. 6; F. J. Meaney, "Governor Brisbane and the Freedom of the Press in New South Wales 1824–25," *Armidale and District Historical Society Journal and Proceedings* 12 (1970): 73; Clem Lloyd, "British Press Traditions, Colonial Governors and the Struggle for a 'Free' Press," in *Journalism: Print, Politics and Popular Culture,* ed. Ann Curthoys and Julianne Schultz (Brisbane: University of Queensland Press, 1999), p. 11.

11. Green, *History of Australian Literature,* pp. 72–73.

12. Green, *History of Australian Literature,* p. 73.

13. Michael Rose, ed., *For the Record: 160 Years of Aboriginal Print Journalism* (Sydney: Allen and Unwin, 1996), pp. xviii–xix, xxix–xxx, 22.

14. Rose, *For the Record,* pp. xxx–xxxi.

15. *Concise Encyclopaedia of Australia and New Zealand* (Sydney: Collier's, 1995), pp. 1:17–18; K. A. Coleridge, "Printing and Publishing in Wellington, New Zealand, in the 1840s and 1850s," *Bibliographic Society of Australia and New Zealand Bulletin* 10, nos. 2–3 (1986): 63.

16. Patrick Day, *The Making of the New Zealand Press: A Study of the Organizational and Political Concerns of New Zealand Newspaper Controllers* (Wellington: Victoria University Press, 1990), pp. 1–2.

17. Coleridge, "Printing and Publishing," pp. 64–66.

18. J. E. Traue, "But Why Mulgan, Marris and Schroder?: The Mutation of the Local Newspaper in New Zealand's Colonial Print Culture," *BSANZ Bulletin* 21, no. 2 (1997): 109.

19. *Concise Encyclopaedia of Australia and New Zealand* (Sydney: Collier's, 1995), p. 2:1006.

20. John Tidey, e-mail to author, 26 October 2001.

21. Suzanna Layton, "Media Freedom in the Pacific Islands: A Comparative Analysis of Eight Nations and Territories" (Ph.D. diss., University of Queensland, 1993), pp. 68–70, 75.

22. Layton, "Media Freedom in the Pacific Islands," pp. 90–94, 99.

23. Dirk H. R. Spennemann, e-mail to author, 8 October 2001.

24. Campbell, *History of the Pacific Islands*, p. 12.

25. Layton, "Media Freedom in the Pacific Islands," p. 9.

26. Michael R. Ogden and Suzanna Layton, "Communications," in *The Pacific Islands: Environment and Society*, ed. Moshe Rapaport (Honolulu: Bess, 1999), p. 410.

27. Walcot, "Perspectives on Publishing," p. 12.

28. Thomas J. Hebblewhite, "Recollections of a journalist: XXX," *Goulburn Evening Penny Post*, May 13, 1922.

29. Yet, as C. J. Lloyd states, freedom of the press was not written into any Australian constitution; newspapers depended on convention for access to Parliament and its sanction to publish debates. See C. J. Lloyd, *Parliament and the Press: The Federal Parliamentary Press Gallery 1901–88* (Melbourne: Melbourne University Press, 1988), p. 20.

30. *Clarence and Richmond Examiner*, 5 April 1864.

31. *Bega Gazette*, 25 March 1865, editorial; *Border Watch* (Mount Gambier), 26 April 1861.

32. *Bathurst Free Press*, 9 January 1886, editorial; cited in *Sydney Morning Herald*, 1 October 1868, p. 5; Grant Harman, "The Provincial Press and Politics in the New England Region of New South Wales, 1856–1930," *Journal of the Royal Australian Historical Society* 61, no. 4 (1975): 231.

33. Geoffrey Blainey, introduction to *125 Years of Age* by Geoffrey Hutton and Les Tanner (Melbourne: Thomas Nelson Australia, 1979), p. ix.

34. Ross Harvey, "The Power of the Press in Colonial New Zealand: More Imagined Than Real?" *BSANZ Bulletin* 20, no. 2 (1996): 130.

35. *Maitland Daily Mercury*, 1 January 1894.

36. Day, *Making of the New Zealand Press*, pp. 107–8.

37. Miles M. Jackson, "Pacific Islands Publishing: A Symposium," *Proceedings of Pacific Islands Symposium*, 1984, p. 1.

38. Suzanna Layton, *The Contemporary Pacific Islands Press* (St Lucia: Department of Journalism, University of Queensland, 1992), p. 3. (Correct.)

39. Walker, *Newspaper Press in New South Wales*, p. 176.

40. "Our Introduction," *Manaro Mercury* (Cooma), 3 April 1863.

41. Elizabeth Morrison, "The contribution of the country press to the making of Victoria, 1840–1890," PhD thesis, Monash University, Melbourne, 1991, p. 2.

42. *Border Post*, 20 January 1869, p. 2.

43. Sylvia Lawson, *The Archibald Paradox: A Strange Case of Authorship* (Melbourne: Penguin, 1987), p. ix.

44. Lawson, *Archibald Paradox*, pp. ix–xii.

45. Graeme Davison, "Sydney and the Bush: An Urban Context for the Australian Legend," in *Intruders in the Bush: The Australian Quest for Identity* (Melbourne: Oxford University Press, 1989), p. 110.

46. Walcot, "Perspectives on Publishing," p. 20.

47. Jim Richstad, "Publishing in Hawaii and the Pacific Islands: An Overview", Proceedings of Pacific Islands Symposium, 1984, p. 7.

48. Cited in Richstad, p. 7.

49. Morrison, "The contribution of the country press to the making of Victoria, 1840–1890," p. 41.

50. Traue, "But Why Mulgan, Marris and Schroder?" p. 110.

51. Traue, "But Why Mulgan, Marris and Schroder?" p. 111.

52. Elizabeth Morrison, "Serial Fiction in Australian Colonial Newspapers," in *Literature in the Marketplace*, ed. John O. Jordan and Robert L. Patten (London: Cambridge University Press, 1995), p. 309.

53. Dirk H. R. Spennemann, *Albury and District Historical Society Bulletin* (April 2001).

54. Traue, "But Why Mulgan, Marris and Schroder?" pp. 111–12.

55. Davison, "Sydney and the Bush," p. 111.

Chapter 6

Newspapers in Europe before 1500

Ralph Frasca

William Caxton faced a dilemma.[1] He finished translating to English Raoul Le
Fevre's manuscript *Le recueil des histories de Troyes*[2] in 1471, and soon found
public demand for the book exceeded his ability to copy it by hand. At the advanced age, for the era, of 49, he concluded it was time to learn the new art of
printing.

"Therefore I have practysed and lerned at my grete charge and dispense to
ordeyne this said book in prynte after the maner and forme as ye may here se,"
Caxton informed readers in the book's prologue. "And it is not wreton with
penne and ynke as other bokes ben." Marveling at the alacrity that the printing
press afforded him in reproducing the seven-hundred-page book, which is generally accepted as the first book printed in the English language, Caxton noted
that the saga "thus empryntid as ye see here, were begonne in oon day, and also
fynyshid in oon day."[3]

Other early printers felt compelled to explain this new art to their readers.
"This volume of the Psalms, adorned with a magnificence of capital letters and
clearly divided by rubrics, has been fashioned by a mechanical process of printing and producing characters, without use of a pen," German printers Johann
Fust and Peter Schoeffer informed readers of the *Mainz Psalter* in 1457. Three
years later, an unknown German printer identified God's providence in the invention of the printing press. "By the aid of the most High, at whose nod the
tongues of the dumb are made eloquent, and who ofttimes revealeth to children
what He hides from the wise...this book, *The Catholicon*, was printed and
completed not by the use of reed, stylus, or quill, but by a wonderful agreement, conformity, and precision of patrices and forms."[4]

NEWS BEFORE PRINTING

Printing had changed the manner and function of the dissemination of information to the literate European public, but it was not the first form of news.

Before the invention of printing, people conveyed news through spoken language, written letters, or public notices. Churches served not only as places for people to worship God, but also to learn of events outside the confines of the villages. People craved not only information of God and His instructions for the salvation of their souls, but also of more temporal matters. They desired news of their government, their society, and their hemisphere, and Roman Catholic priests provided it to them as best as they could. Overseas traders and traveling merchants transported news from one village to the next, and often parlayed their access to knowledge into customer trade. This oral tradition was saddled with many flaws, though, including alteration of the news and the introduction of errors as it passed from one mouth to another and the profound limitations of the distances of time and space. The unreliability of communication did little to foster a sense of unity among highly provincial people. A powerful government that wished to be powerful required an effective means of news dissemination. Julius Caesar understood this. Seeking to develop his neoteric Roman Empire, he devised a method to unite distant peoples through standardized and regulated news.

The earliest recorded means for mass news distribution was the *Actis Diurna* (*Daily Events*). Beginning in 59 B.C., Caesar ordered copies of it to be posted every day in public places throughout Rome, such as church doors and marketplaces. According to Roman historian Suetonius, "Caesar's very first enactment after becoming consul was, that the proceedings [*acta*] both of the Senate and of the people should day by day be compiled."[5]

As government publications, the *Acta Diurna* were subject to censorship, but they did contain a variety of news, such as marriages, births, accidents, deaths, crimes, trials, executions, political intrigue, legal decisions, and military battles. Even human interest stories received coverage. In the first century A.D., Roman historian Pliny the Elder included in his writings a story he had read in the *Acta Diurna* about the faithfulness of an executed man's dog. Even after the man's death, the dog would not leave his side. When the corpse was thrown into the Tiber River, the dog jumped in as well, in an effort to keep the body afloat.[6]

The diverse types of news were gathered by *actuarii*, government-employed reporters who handwrote the news onto parchment, which was then affixed to whitened boards for more prominent display. Caesar also ordered public distribution of the *Acta Senatus et Populi*, chronicling the topics and outcomes of debates of the Roman Senate, but this publication was soon terminated.[7]

Although every copy had to be handwritten, the *Acta Diurna* circulated widely throughout the Roman Empire. The empire remained intact from the first century B.C. to the fifth century A.D., stretching from what is now Scotland to Egypt. Besides military might and multitiered government, communication was the glue that held the empire together. The *Acta Diurna* created a sense of "community" as it united the far-flung empire and standardized governance.

LATER HANDWRITTEN NEWS

After the fall of the Roman Empire, there were no other examples of written news for nearly a millennium. The small percentage of literate Europeans continued to write, but the spread of news chiefly depended on word-of-mouth transmission. Organized services for the distribution of news and messages appeared in the twelfth century, though, and by the close of the fourteenth century, town clerks in the German empire were securing news from other towns. This information was important because commercial and political interests of medieval Europe required accurate reports. As news became an increasingly valued commodity, the intellectual life of Europe developed throughout the fifteenth century.

These were typically generated by trading companies, the most prominent of which was the Fugger family of Augsburg. The cornerstone of this family financial dynasty was Jacob Fugger, whose desire for commercial and political news that might affect his investments prompted him to establish a network of correspondents. These writers handwrote business news for Fugger, during whose lifetime Ferdinand Magellan circumnavigated the globe, Christopher Columbus discovered America, and Martin Luther nailed his ninety-five theses to the door of the Wittenberg Cathedral. Fugger built his commercial empire of mining, banking, trade, and real estate by using information of these important occurrences to make business decisions. Information that was not reserved for the family's private use was recopied into specialized newsletters and sent to select subscribers and business clients.[8]

In the preprinting era and the early years of printing, most writers and printers were either clerics serving the Roman Catholic Church or employees of aristocratic families. In either case, these men wrote and published to order, handcopying religious tracts and Bibles, or promoting the accomplishments of their employers. A smaller group of book producers worked independently in western Europe, copying schoolbooks for children and textbooks for students at the emerging universities. At these shops, a "stationer" accepted orders for copies to be made by a scribe, illustrated by an artist or limner, and assembled by a binder. The scribe's work of handcopying was extremely time consuming and created the possibility of errors being introduced into various copies of the manuscript.[9]

PRINTING GIVES NEWS PERMANENCE

The invention of the printing press virtually eliminated the inconsistency of scribal work, reduced factual errors, and began to freeze the spelling and syntax of the various nations' language in place. The art of printing spread rapidly throughout Europe, and by 1500 every major European city had at least one printer. In addition to stabilizing European languages, printing began to invest some truth-claims with the authority of "fact" in the collective consciousness of the literate Western world. In essence, if something was in print, people believed it. Columbus's "discovery" of the New World exemplifies this.

Vikings became the first Europeans to discover North America, landing on the desolate northern tip of what is now the Canadian province of Newfoundland in 986 and establishing a settlement there. Approximately forty Vikings lived there for about three years, fishing and operating an iron forge on the barren tundra near what is now the village of L'Anse aux Meadows. News of this settlement traveled by word of mouth back to Scandinavia via Greenland across the North Atlantic. This discovery was recorded in a ledger nearly a century later by the German cleric Adam of Bremen, who called the island "Vinland."[10]

However, this discovery and subsequent chronicling lacked the mass communication necessary to plant it firmly in the European mind, so when Columbus rediscovered the North American continent five centuries later, his find was heralded as the first, courtesy of an active Spanish press. Printers in Barcelona distributed a pamphlet throughout Spain containing Columbus's 1493 report to King Ferdinand of his discovery of a trade route to what he thought was India. "I found a great many islands peopled with inhabitants beyond number," Columbus recounted. "The people...all go naked, men and women, just as their mothers bring them forth; although some women cover a single place with the leaf of a plant, or a cotton something which they make for that purpose. They have no iron or steel, nor any weapons; nor are they fit thereunto; not because they be not a well-formed people and of fair stature, but that they are wonderously timorous."[11]

This tale was later reprinted and circulated throughout Rome, Paris, Florence, and other fifteenth-century European cities. As a result, the new art and technology of printing cemented the Columbus discovery myth as historical fact in the European—and subsequently American—culture.

THE INVENTION OF PRINTING

Who invented this powerful technology? The common understanding is that Johann Gutenberg created movable type in 1450, made some alterations to a wine press, and began work on the Bible at his shop in Mainz, Germany, completing it about 1455. However, printing literature throughout the centuries has posited several other printers for the claim of inventor.

In the earliest-known printed testimony in which the art's invention is attributed to an identified individual, Omnibonus Leonicenus wrote in the *Quintilian* in 1471 that his own publisher, Nicolas Jenson of Venice, was the first printer. "He, the inventor of the admirable art of printing, first of all men, ingeniously showed how books should not be written with a pen, but printed as though with a gem or seal."[12]

Other scholars have placed its discovery in the Netherlands, crediting Lourens Janszoon Coster of Haarlem. Those scholars rely on a passage in the book *Batavia*, written in 1568 by Dutch scholar Adriaen de Jonghe under the pseudonym Hadrianus Junius. Junius wrote that to Coster "should be restored the fame, at present usurped by another, of the invention of the whole art of printing." As Junius explained it, Coster cut some letters from the bark of a beech tree while he was strolling the woods one day. Using ordinary ink, he impressed these letters on paper, and thus "composed one or two lines to serve as an example for the children of his son-in-law. When this succeeded, he began to contemplate greater things," Junius wrote. Developing more substantial ink, Coster printed entire pages using his beech wood letters. He eventually produced his first book, the Dutch-language *Spieghel onzer behoudenisse* (*Mirror of Our Salvation*), circa 1441. Soon after, Coster replaced the beech wood letters with lead and tin type and printed more books. "And so the new art was greeted with enthusiasm, and its ware, of a kind never seen before, drew purchasers from all sides and brought in rich profits," Junius recounted.[13]

However, treachery soon followed Coster's invention, according to Junius's tale. The profitable nature of the business prompted Coster to take on apprentices, including one named Johann. "This Johann, who was bound to the work of printing by oath, as soon as he thought he knew enough about the art of joining the letters and of casting the types—in fact, the whole trade—sought the first favorable opportunity to make off," Junius wrote. Johann fled to Amsterdam, then Cologne, and finally to the German city of Mainz, where he "could live in security and harvest the rich fruits of his theft by opening a printing workshop." Junius then claimed that Johann (he avoids using the surname Gutenberg because "I do not wish to trouble the shades of the dead, who during their lifetime were tormented enough by conscience") printed the *Doctrinale* by Alexander Gallus, the *Tractatus syncategorematum* of Petrus Hispanus, and a grammar book beginning in late 1442.[14]

Most scholars, though, credit Gutenberg as the inventor of the printing press and type. The earliest printing presses were adaptations of the screw press used in wine making. The press consisted of a bed of stone with a smooth and level face on which the printing surface rested and a flat piece of wood or metal called a "platen" that could be pressed down by a screw onto a piece of paper resting on the inked type. The type was held together in a frame for uniformity. This is the type of printing press Gutenberg and his pre-1500 contemporaries used, and the printing press remained largely unchanged for the next 350 years.

Although Gutenberg is usually hailed as the inventor of the art, there is some doubt as to when he actually invented the press and what his first printed work was. Tradition holds that it was the famous forty-two-line Bible. There are other publications of the era that are of uncertain dates and origin, but that have been ascribed to Gutenberg's press. These publications include Aelius Donatus's Latin grammar book; an astronomical wall calendar believed to be from 1448; and the "Fragment of the World Judgment," a German poem about the biblical End Times and God's judgment of humanity, which some scholars believe to have been published in the 1440s.[15]

Once printing was invented, it spread rapidly, and European officials and merchants soon began using it to publish news. By the early sixteenth century, news books and pamphlets reported newsworthy events in prose and were joined by news ballads, which delivered reports in verse. These were succeeded in the early seventeenth century by newspapers.

FINANCING AND LIBERTY

Like most of the fifteenth-century printers, Caxton learned printing in Germany, the early center of the new trade. He took his new skills to Bruges, Flanders (now Belgium), and published Le Fevre's *The recuyell of the histories of Troye* under the patronage of Margaret, the duchess of Burgundy. Indeed, she had commissioned the translation and book and overruled Caxton on some points of translation from French to English. "Y durste in no wyse disobey because y am a servant unto her sayde grace and resseive of her yerly ffee and other many goode and great benefets, and also hope meny moo to resseyve of her hyenes," Caxton admitted.[16]

In doing so, Caxton was following the customary course of events: The patron commanded and the scribe obeyed. Early scribes and printers often worked under the patronage of nobles, who provided financial support and a stamp of aristocratic approval for the work. When Caxton returned to his native England and set up a printing house at Westminster, he published *The Dictes or Sayengs of the Philosophres* at the behest of Earl Rivers. "I am bounden so to do for the good reward that I have resseyved of his sayd lordship," Caxton informed readers.[17]

The liberty of early presses was largely regulated by the extent to which printed products might meet with royal approval and subsidy. Accordingly, Caxton and other early printers produced what was safe—poetry, histories, religious works, and morality tales—and dedicated them to prominent people. Gutenberg also accepted job-printing orders that met with official approval. In 1454, Gutenberg produced the first *dated* piece of printing, a papal indulgence for the remission of sins. Constantinople had been conquered by the pagan Turks the previous year, and the king of Cyprus asked that Pope Nicholas V grant indulgences to Roman Catholics who would contribute funds to mount a military campaign to take back the city. Ordinarily, these indulgences were written by hand, but since so many were needed, the new art of printing was enlisted for the cause. Cyprian delegate Paulinus Chappe traveled to Mainz to order a mass quantity of these forms from Gutenberg, with blank spaces left to fill in dates and names of donors.[18]

THE REVOLUTION OF PRINTING

The invention of the printing press represents a major "dividing line" in world history, between print culture and scribal culture, and catalyzed the Italian Renaissance, the Protestant Reformation, and the Scientific Revolution.[19]

This has been the widely accepted view, but it is certainly not the only one. There is also a school of thought that asserts many of the supposed innovations brought about by print culture were already present in scribal culture. For instance, the fifteenth-century printed book, which supposedly revolutionized Western thinking and drew the Dark Ages to a close, owes much of its form and substance to manuscript books, which continued to be made and read alongside their printed counterparts for generations.[20]

Thus, the "dawn" of printing did not really end one era and commence another; rather, it represents a gradual transition from one mass medium to another. As such, printing does not really represent the inception of mass communication, but instead a more efficient and expeditious means of delivering the same product to a growing audience. Printing made the written products more affordable to the masses by reducing the per-unit cost and also by increasing the availability of books. With more books, printers could begin trying to attract certain market niches, while still trying to appeal to a broad audience. Caxton's *Reynard the Fox* is a story suitable "for all good folk," he wrote, while *The Order of Chyvalry* "is not requysyte to every comyn man to have, but to noble gentylmen that by their vertu entende to come and entre into the noble ordre of chivalry." Other books were intended principally for "ladies and gentilwomen" or "every gentilman born to arms." Caxton even noted that certain books are inappropriate for every "rude and unconnynge men to see," but are intended for "clerkys and gentylmen that understande gentilnes and scyence."[21]

Printing also enabled news to flow with greater clarity and rapidity. With the new ability to produce hundreds or thousands of exact duplicates of the same news report, printing ensured that the original news was not distorted or misunderstood in its transmission from the press to the readers. Once the story was in print, there was not as much room for interpretation and alteration as existed in the oral or scribal cultures.

Printing also gradually increased the rate at which ideas were transmitted, but it took several generations before European society adapted to the speed and distance at which written thoughts could be transmitted. Manuscript and print books coexisted for generations before the former eventually yielded to the latter.[22]

Other factors that limited the immediate impact of printed information were illiteracy and transportation difficulties. However, this new technological device, the printing press, was a world of potential waiting to be tapped. Governments, the Roman Catholic Church, and financiers all saw the opportunity and sought to employ it to serve their aims of regulation, evangelization, and influence. At the same time, printing's ability to enhance the public's access to news was just beginning to be recognized.

NOTES

1. Probably pronounced "Causston." See Colin Clair, *A History of Printing in Britain* (New York: Oxford University Press, 1966), p. 8.

2. Published by Caxton as *The recuyell of the histories of Troye* in Bruges in 1475.

3. W. J. B. Crotch, ed., *The Prologues and Epilogues of William Caxton*, Early English Text Society, Ordinary Series, no. 176 (1928), p. 5, cited in H. S. Bennett, *English Books and Readers, 1475 to 1557* (Cambridge: University of Cambridge Press, 1952), p. 11.

4. Cited in Pierce Butler, *The Origin of Printing in Europe* (Chicago: University of Chicago Press, 1940), pp. 91–92.

5. Cited in Mitchell Stephens, *A History of News: From the Drum to the Satellite* (New York: Viking, 1988), p. 64.

6. Stephens, *History of News*, p. 65.

7. Stephens, *History of News*, p. 64.

8. For background on the Fugger dynasty, see Jacob Streider, *Jacob Fugger the Rich: Merchant and Banker of Augsburg, 1459–1525*, trans. Mildred L. Hartsough (Westport, CT: Greenwood, 1984); Lisa Jardine, *Worldly Goods* (New York: Talese, 1996); George T. Matthews, *News and Rumor in Renaissance Europe: The Fugger Newsletters* (New York: Capricorn, 1959).

9. P. M. Handover, *Printing in London from 1476 to Modern Times* (Cambridge, MA: Harvard University Press, 1960), pp. 20–21.

10. Gwyn Jones, *A History of the Vikings* (London: Oxford University Press, 1968), pp. 295–303.

11. Cited in Stephens, *History of News*, p. 83.

12. Butler, *Origin of Printing in Europe*, p. 98.

13. Cited in Albert Kapr, *Johann Gutenberg* (Brookfield, VT: Scolar, 1996), pp. 100–2; see also André Blum, *The Origins of Printing and Engraving* (New York: Scribner's, 1940), pp. 3–5.

14. Kapr, *Johann Gutenberg*, p. 102.

15. Douglas C. McMurtrie, *The Book: The Story of Printing and Bookmaking*, 3rd ed. (New York: Oxford University Press, 1943), pp. 143–47; George Parker Winship, *Books Printed in the Fifteenth Century* (Philadelphia: Rosenwald, 1940), pp. 1–19.

16. Crotch, *Prologues and Epilogues*, p. 10.

17. Crotch, *Prologues and Epilogues*, p. 12.

18. McMurtrie, *Book*, pp. 148–49.

19. For this argument, see Elizabeth L. Eisenstein, *The Printing Press As an Agent of Change: Communications and Cultural Transformations in Early Modern Europe*, 2 vols. (Cambridge: Cambridge University Press, 1979); Elizabeth L. Eisenstein, *The Printing Revolution in Early Modern Europe* (Cambridge: Cambridge University Press, 1983); Marshall MacLuhan, *The Gutenberg Galaxy: The Making of Typographic Man* (London: Routledge and Kegan Paul, 1962).

20. Curt Bühler, *The Fifteenth-Century Book: The Scribes, the Printers, the Decorators* (Philadelphia: University of Pennsylvania Press, 1960); Anthony Grafton, "The Importance of Being Printed," *Journal of Interdisciplinary History* 2, no. 11 (1980): 265–86; Sandra Hindman, ed., *Printing the Written Word: The Social History of Books, circa 1450–1520* (Ithaca, NY: Cornell University Press, 1991).

21. Crotch, *Prologues and Epilogues*, p. 11.

22. William Wallace, "Galileo's Sources: Manuscripts or Printed Works?" in *Print and Culture in the Renaissance: Essays on the Advent of Printing in Europe,* ed. Gerald P. Tyson and Sylvia S. Wagonheim (Newark: University of Delaware Press, 1986); Steven Rowan, "Jurists and the Printing Press in Germany: The First Century," in *The Prologues and Epilogues of William Caxton,* ed. W. J. B. Crotch, Early English Text Society, Ordinary Series, no. 176 (1928).

Chapter 7

Newspapers in Europe after 1500

Tamara Kay Baldwin

The printing revolution that began with Johann Gutenberg and his counterparts in the fifteenth century laid the groundwork for the expanded role of methods of the dissemination of news by its introduction of the means to provide mass circulation print media, or in modern terms, the newspaper, for the first time. Thus, throughout Europe after 1500 were developed in the various nations of the continent broadsides, pamphlets, and chap books that led to great national newspapers of succeeding centuries, particularly in Europe's great metropolitan centers, which ultimately provided a medium for the dissemination of news of "historical" events such as wars, revolutions, and governmental affairs, as well as the means for social and cultural communication both within national and linguistic groups and across national language boundaries as a distinctively European culture was developing and being promoted via the great national newspapers.

Chapter 6 reviewed developments in communication that culminated in detailing the spread of the movable type printing press technology across Europe in the mid and late 1400s. In hindsight, the development of the movable type printing press and its rapid spread to numerous European cities made many things possible, affected nearly all aspects of life, and changed literate societies forever in ways that deserve scrutiny even today. That is, in fact, part of the problem in examining the impact the printing press and its output had on European society. Its impact was so vast as to make it largely immeasurable, according to many historians. This has led many interested in European civilization to dismiss the printing press and its impact rather quickly, or, at best, to give it a quick nod of acknowledgment and move on to developments and characteristics easier to gauge.[1] Others, however, acknowledge the tremendous impact the printing press had on every aspect of European life and culture. In fact, if not largely for the printed artifacts from earlier times, we would know far less about the earlier societies and people and what their lives and worlds were like. Elizabeth L. Eisenstadt notes that "the condition of scribal culture can only be observed through a veil of print."[2]

By the end of 1470, printing presses had been set up in at least seven towns in Germany, thereby creating the cradle of printing technology for the Western world, and by the end of the 1400s, printing was being done in at least fifty places in Germany.[3] Clearly, the stage was set for the rapid spread of this technology beyond Germany. Printers from Germany traveled to other countries to set up printing shops, no doubt in an effort to earn their living with this new technology. Some of the earliest printers in Italy bore German surnames, and William Caxton, who had learned printing in Germany, brought the technology back to England and set up the first printing press there. While Bibles and other religious books were among the first and foremost products of these early presses, printers also produced single sheets of printed information that provided the public with opinions, news, gossip, and entertainment—all of the things modern newspapers provide for their readers today.

FROM BALLADS TO BROADSIDES IN THE 1500s

In earlier centuries, news and information of all kinds were conveyed in the oral tradition or through handwritten accounts. With the spread of printing across Europe, news and information that was formerly spoken, sung, or handwritten was now printed and mass produced. The ballad—the spoken, recited, or sung account of information, gossip, or commemoration of a memorable event—had long been a part of European popular culture, and the printing press brought a change in the delivery of this traditional mode of communication. The early single printed sheets of information that formerly were delivered orally were known by several names—news ballads, broadsides, broadsheets, and street ballads. Whereas before these ballads were sung or recited in the street or handwritten, now they were available in printed form to enjoy later or share with others. Sometimes, these were printed on both sides, they often carried advertising on the back, and they may have even been folded to make a small pamphlet or booklet.[4] These broadsheets or broadsides were the popular literature of the day and served much the same function for the sixteenth-century European as modern newspapers do today for the twenty-first-century European. They dealt with all manners of topics, ranging from the everyday and trivial to the heroic and the mystical and magical.[5] One ballad surviving from 1628 managed to combine several such topics for the public's information and no doubt entertainment when it detailed the murder of a magician named Dr. Lambe, who was killed by a mob: "The TRAGEDY of DR. LAMBE, The great supposed Conjuror, who was wounded to death by saylers and other Lads, on Friday the 14 of June 1628. And dyed in the Poultry Counter, neere Cheap-side, on the Saturday morning following. To the tune of Gallents come away."[6]

Religion and politics also were popular topics treated in the broadsides.[7] Besides the everyday topics and opinions they often carried, broadsides also aided people in understanding the human condition[8] and without a doubt helped them to feel more connected to their world and others in it. By the time of Henry VIII's reign in England, broadsides were exerting great influence on public opinion and often reflected the period of social upheaval Europe was undergoing.[9]

Few of the many broadsides that remain today bear a printing date, which may indicate that their usefulness or "shelf life" was not expected to be long. They were, like newspapers today, not meant to be kept in the same way as books were. They made excellent waste paper, and fortunately for historians, many of them wound up being used in the binding of books printed during this time. This use of them has enabled historians to recover many of the ones in existence today. One of the earliest known ones was discovered in the cover of a book printed in Paris in 1513. The book had been bound in England, and its cover held a ballad written by John Shelton, poet laureate to Henry VIII. It was titled "The Ballade of the Scottysshe Kinge" and detailed the Battle of Flodden Field that took place in 1513.[10]

What effect did this new and more efficient method of delivering news and information have on the professional minstrel, the person who previously delivered such news and information in the oral tradition? The printed broadside replaced the minstrel; in fact, by the 1600s minstrels were viewed in the same way as rogues.[11] European society quickly adjusted to and accommodated this new and more efficient way of delivering news and information. The news or information itself did not change, however; printing was, according to Leslie Shepard, "merely superimposed...on an oral tradition."[12]

Like printed news that came after the 1500s, these broadsheets and ballads often came under attack by authorities. As early as 1533 in England, a proclamation was issued suppressing ballads and other lewd works. Ten years later England passed an act to purge the country of ballads that got in the way of the "true" religion. In part, the act read: "'For reformation whereof, his majesty considereth it most requisite to purge his realm of all books, ballads, rhymes and songs, as be pestiferous and noisome.'"[13] Later in the 1550s, the Stationers Company in England required ballads to be registered at a fee of fourpence per ballad, which was another way of exerting governmental control over them. Some of the titles recorded give an indication of the vast array of subject matter ballads encompassed. The titles of ballads issued from the printing press of the widow of a printer named Robert Toye suggest that nearly anyone or any topic was possible fodder for a ballad: "The Day of the Lorde Ys At Hande," "Women Beste When They Be At Reste," "The Murnynge of Edwarde Duke of Buckyngham," "A Mayde That Wolde Mary with a Serving Man," and "An Epytaph upon the Death of Kynge Edward Ye Sixte."[14]

NEWS BECOMES MORE REGULAR IN THE 1600s

By the dawn of the seventeenth century, printing was widespread through-out Europe, and broadsides, pamphlets, religious tracts, and books continued to inform people of events in their world. Europe was experiencing tremendous growth and change in this century. The Renaissance, the Scientific Revolution, and the Reformation led to changes in the European world. It was the time of Galileo Galilei, René Descartes, Francis Bacon, Blaise Pascal, and of the settling of colonial America by the Dutch and English. It saw the foundation of the Dutch East India Company in 1602 and the beginning of the world's first known stock exchange in Amsterdam that same year. It was a time of the Thirty Years War, which left its mark on Europe as well.[15]

The seventeenth century saw the introduction of the news book, which some historians cite as the forerunner of the modern newspaper.[16] The first of these in Europe appeared in Germany around 1609. Two of these, *Advise, Relation oder Zeitung* and *Furnemen und gedenkwurdigen Historien*, appeared in January of that year, and a third appeared the following year.[17] Similar news books, or corantos, as they also were called, appeared early in this century in the Netherlands and in cities all over Europe. In September 1621, the first such news book printed in England appeared. It was called *Corante, or Newes from Italy, Germany, Hungary, Spaine and France*. As the title suggests, the content focused on news from abroad. This was a common characteristic of the news books and corantos of the day. Their focus was a broad one. News of events in neighboring countries, particularly if battles and wars were involved, made up much of their content. They attempted to provide readers with an accounting of the "whole world,"[18] an ambitious undertaking.

Another feature in the printed news of this period, and the most significant, was the regularity of its printing. No longer would sheets of news be printed only when events considered newsworthy occurred. Now, the reading public could expect these on a regular basis. It was the genesis of what Anthony Smith identifies in his *Newspaper: An International History* as the phenomenon of a "continuing relationship between reader, printer, and originator of the news."[19] Smith quotes a publisher of an early coranto who recognized the expectations the public had for a regularly appearing news product: "Custom is so predominant in everything that both the Reader and the Printer of these pamphlets agree in their expectation of Weekly News, so that if the Printer have not the wherewithal to afford satisfaction, yet will the Reader come and ask every day for new Newes."[20] Thus, this began the progression toward more modern characteristics of news—that of regularly appearing, periodic publications. The seventeenth century set the stage for the birth of a full-fledged "newspaper."[21]

Inevitably, with the increase in printed news available in a more regular, standardized form, an increase in censorship occurred as well. In England, for example, news sheets were printed until 1632 when the Star Chamber ordered that they cease to be printed. For six years, none were printed in England, until

Nathanial Butter and Nicholas Bourne were given the exclusive right by Charles I to resume printing some.[22] Because theirs were in essence sanctioned and approved by the government, it raises the question as to how well these news sheets served the public's information needs.

While the former news sheets and corantos provided or, at least, attempted to take an international or broad view of happenings in their readers' world, they did not satisfy the readers' needs for domestic news. In the 1640s, the diurnal appeared, which focused on domestic news. The first one of these in England appeared in 1641 and was titled *The Head of Severall Proceedings in the Present Parliament*. It became known as *Diurnall Occurrences* and was printed weekly by Samuel Pecke.[23] In 1649, the diurnal *A Perfect Diurnall of Some Passages in Parliament and the Daily Proceedings of the Army under His Excellency the Lord Fairfax* was printed. It described in detail the execution of Charles I:

The Scaffold was hung round with black, and the floor covered with black, and the Ax and Block laid in the middle of the Scaffold. There were divers companies of Foot and Horse, on every side of the Scaffold, and the multitudes of people that came to be Spectators, very great. The King, making a Passe upon the Scaffold, look'd very earnestly on the Block, and asked Col. *Hacker* if there were no higher; and then spake, Directing his speech to the Gentlemen upon the Scaffold.[24]

In England, credit for that country's first newspaper goes to Henry Muddiman, who started the *Oxford Gazette* in 1665. The paper was originally printed twice a week in Oxford, but after twenty-four issues, Muddiman moved the operation to London and changed the paper's name to the *London Gazette*. The paper was an official government mouthpiece whose creation was suggested by Joseph Williamson, the undersecretary of state at the time. The paper is significant because it carried features that are common to newspapers today. Its pages were printed in two columns rather than in the familiar pamphlet form, and it included datelines and the place of origin at the beginning of each piece of news, a practice that modern newspaper readers are familiar with. The paper also began to be called "newspaper," a name that is still used today.[25]

NEWSPAPERS TAKE ON A MORE MODERN LOOK IN THE 1700s

Europeans began to see a "daily" accounting of news, foreign and domestic, in the middle part of the 1600s. Germany had its first daily newspaper in 1660 called *Neueielaufende Nachtrict von Kriegs-und Welthandeln*, which was published in Leipzig by Timotheus Ritzsch, and this was followed closely by the appearance of daily papers in Konigsberg, Vienna, and Frankfurt am Main.[26] France's first daily paper, the *Journal de Paris*, began in 1677.[27] The first daily paper in England appeared in March 1702. Called the *Daily Courant*, the paper began as a half sheet of information printed on one side of the paper. The first nine issues were printed by Elizabeth Mallet, but after that, Samuel Buckley printed and sold the paper. Historians note that these first issues of the *Daily Courant*, other than being published daily, were really no different from the news sheets that had come before it.[28] Content-wise, nothing had changed.

While newspapers, many of them by now daily newspapers, flourished in the early years of the eighteenth century, a new type of news and information product also developed. The first literary journal, the forerunner of today's periodical literature, or magazines, appeared in 1704 and became the prototype for a number of similar journals that followed. Printed and written entirely by Daniel Defoe, it was titled *A Weekly Review of the Affairs of France: Purg'd from the Errors and Partiality of News-Writers and Petty Statesmen, of all Sides*, and was shortened to the *Review* a while later. At first, the *Review* was printed twice a week, but after the first year of publication it appeared three times a week. It continued to be printed for nine years and contained articles and essays on political, social, and commercial topics of interest to its readers.[29] In the December 26, 1704, issue of the *Review*, Defoe shared with his readers his strong feelings about the often unfair way justice in Britain was handled. He took the magistrates and justices to task for this: "Every Man who is subject to the Law and punishable by it, has a Right in the Execution of the Law upon all Offenders equally with himself; and if one is punish'd for a Crime, and another goes free, the first Man is Injur'd, because he has not Equal Justice with his Neighbors. Again, I have a Right of Complaint, when any Offender is not brought to Justice because it is an Encouragement to the Offense; and I may one time or other find the Effect of it.'"[30]

It did not take long for others to imitate and improve on the type of publication Defoe introduced. From modest beginnings, the periodical essay found its earliest and arguably most permanently influential examples in the *Tatler* and *Spectator* of the early eighteenth century. Extremely popular in their day and in numerous collected editions published over the years, these two set a pattern for "magazine" publications that may still be noted today.

The collaboration of Sir Richard Steele and Joseph Addison in the publications—Steele being primarily responsible for the *Tatler* and Addison for the *Spectator*—played a major role in refining the manners and morals of the eighteenth century and contributed significantly to the "Age of Reason" designation for the era. The *Tatler*, with 271 issues in 1709–1711, and its successor the *Spectator*, with 555 issues in 1711–1712 and 80 in a 1714 revival, addressed in their essays issues of taste, particularly in literature, but also in music, art, and other aesthetic areas. They wrote about a variety of social and cultural issues such as modes of dress, dueling, drunkenness and other social ills, and political concerns. Regarding political issues, both Addison and Steele and their periodicals took a mildly but firm Whig position in the controversy with the Tories of the time.[31]

Their type of journalism appealed to the coffeehouse "set," who no doubt enjoyed and perhaps even benefited from Addison's and Steele's commentaries on society. In the tenth issue of the *Spectator*, Addison explains the purpose of the paper and reveals his target audience:

It was said of Socrates, that he brought philosophy down from heaven, to inhabit among men; and I shall be ambitious to have it said of me, that I have brought philosophy out of closets and libraries, schools and colleges, to dwell in clubs and assemblies, at tea-tables and in coffee-houses.

I would therefore in a very particular manner recommend these my Speculations to all well-regulated families, that set apart an hour in every Morning for tea and bread and butter; and would earnestly advise them for Their good to order this paper to be punctually served up, and to be looked Upon as a part of the tea equipage.[32]

Much imitated in their own time and subsequently, in primarily British and U.S. journals, but also in other European nations, the *Tatler* and *Spectator* presented in their essays models of middle-class behavior that were influential in "softening" the manners, customs, and social outlooks of the eighteenth-century Englishman—and woman, as Addison and Steele specifically addressed both sexes in a significant departure from the almost exclusively masculine approach of prior literature. Sometimes referred to as the "first Victorians," Addison and Steele cultivated the image of the English "gentleman" (and "lady") and the notion of common sense and good taste as underlying values of civilized society. Prominent imitations of these two publications in the century were the *Guardian*, the *Examiner*, the *Englishman*, and particularly Samuel Johnson's the *Rambler* with 208 issues in 1750–1752.[33]

Periodicals aimed specifically at the female audience emerged during this time as well. Eliza Haywood produced some of the first periodicals for women, with her first taking the name the *Female Spectator*, which she produced in 1744–1746, and later with the *Parrot* in 1746. She published the *Female Spectator* monthly in essay form, no doubt because of the influence and success that Defoe, Addison, Steele, and others had found using this format. Haywood aimed to provide her audience with timely information, and to this end, she reveals to her readers her use of a network of "spies," whose job it was to seek out all the information and news of interest to her female audience. She wrote,

To secure an eternal Fund of Intelligence, Spies are placed not only in all the Places of Resort in and about this great Metropolis, but at Bath, Tunbridge, and the Spas, and Means found out to extend my Speculation even as far as France, Rome, Germany, and other foreign Parts so that nothing curious or worthy of Remark can escape me.... simply by tumbling over a few Papers from my Emissaries, I have all the secrets of Europe, at least such of them as are proper For my purpose, and laid open at one View.[34]

Soon after it began publication, the *Female Spectator* began including a correspondence column from readers about their concerns and problems with manners and decorum of the day. Haywood would respond to these and offer advice, and this is a feature that many modern newspapers include today.

While there was a relative loosening of some restrictions on the press in England by the end of the eighteenth century, this was not true of other parts of Europe. The 1700s saw many censorship means used throughout the rest of Europe. Early in the century various governmental or religious bodies imposed restrictions of various kinds on the press. As early as 1715, the Holy Roman Empire under Charles VI instituted an edict regarding slander that had been largely unenforced in previous times. Near the end of the century, France strengthened its laws against importing printed materials that disturbed the peace or that advocated the overthrow of the government. The king of Prussia set up an official censor in the Department of Foreign Affairs, and in Austria a Censorship Committee was set up in midcentury that exercised tight control over printed material there.[35]

Despite a veil of restrictions, a type of commercial newspaper known as *Intelligenzblattler* flourished in the German-speaking parts of Europe. These were government-sanctioned papers allowed to carry advertising (which was controlled by a state monopoly). After this type of commercial paper became established in this region, it was copied in other parts of Europe.[36]

THE 1800s BRING TECHNOLOGICAL INNOVATIONS

The Industrial Revolution in the 1800s brought sweeping economic and social changes to Europe and, with it, a profound effect on newspapers. All across Europe, cities experienced significant and rapid growth in population as society moved from a largely agrarian one to a more industrialized and urban one. The invention of the steam engine by James Watts in 1769 revolutionized industry and made mass production of goods a reality. Many Europeans who had once made their living by farming or raising livestock found themselves moving to metropolitan areas in order to work in factories.[37]

Technological advances also made possible innovations and developments in newspapers of this age as well. The steam engine made it possible to print papers more rapidly, thus enabling editors to keep up with the growing body of readers. Coupled with a more efficient method of making paper possible by the 1820s and the development of the telegraph in the transmission of news, newspapers were for the first time able to truly serve the "mass" audience. Improved technology involved with printing and an increasing audience of potential readers led to the development of Sunday newspapers, regional and local papers, and most importantly, highly affordable newspapers. In England, the *Daily Telegraph and Morning Post*, later shortened to the *Daily Telegram*, began in 1855 at a cost of two pennies per copy. A few months after it began, its price was lowered to one penny, making it one of the early papers in England to sell for a penny.[38] On the first day that the paper sold for one penny, it carried a statement that typified the thinking behind the idea of a cheap newspaper or a paper "for the masses": "'There is no reason why a daily newspaper, conducted with a high tone, should not be produced at a price which would place it within the means of every class of the community.... The future stability of the revered institutions of this country must depend more upon the enlightenment of the million than all the bayonets and legions the enormous wealth of the nation would enable it to collect upon its shores.'"[39]

During the 1800s, the *Times,* established in London in 1785 by John Walter under the name the *Daily Universal Register,* experienced tremendous growth as a powerhouse of a newspaper under a series of influential editors. The paper earned itself the nickname "Thunderer" for its influence on behalf of the English middle class. The paper boasted the hiring of the first true war correspondent, William Howard Russell, who actually traveled to the battlefields to bring the public eyewitness accounts. He covered the Crimean War (1853–1856) for the *Times,* and later he reported for it on the U.S. Civil War (1861–1865) from abroad.[40]

Despite great strides in the technological side of the newspaper industry that were taking place in the 1800s, for much of the century many of Europe's newspapers operated under heavy governmental control. Newspapers in France, for example, suffered greatly under layers of regulation. An example of the stifling extent of governmental regulation and control exerted on the French press was the Organic Decree of 1852, which among other things, outlawed foreign papers, increased taxes and postal rates for newspapers, imposed huge "caution" money charges, or money put forth as a security or a guarantee, on political papers, and imposed stiff penalties for those who broke any of the regulations.[41]

It was not until 1876 when France introduced new legislation regarding newspapers that their freedom increased dramatically. When the restrictions were finally lifted, a number of large circulation newspapers were allowed either to begin or flourish. Papers such as the *Petit Journal* (1863), the *Petit Parisian* (1876), *Le Matin* (1882), and *Le Journal* (1889) were better able to serve the public's needs.[42]

Heartened and inspired by events in France and the press freedom it won, other European countries underwent their own moves toward gaining more press freedom.

TECHNOLOGY DOMINATES IN THE 1900s

Building on the technological advances of the nineteenth century, the European newspaper of the twentieth century became increasingly dominated by press concentration through the development of huge metropolitan dailies with circulations in the hundreds of thousands and even millions, and the establishment of newspaper chains with capitalistic concerns, that is, advertising, became increasingly significant. As the century progressed, totalitarian political systems led to the controlled press with newspapers such as *Volkischer*

Beobachter (1920), Adolf Hitler's personal newspaper, *Il Popolo d'Italia*, founded in 1914 by Benito Mussolini and edited by him until 1922, and in Russia *Pravda*, representing the Communist Party and *Izvestia* representing the government.[43]

In England, the London press became increasingly the national news source (augmented, of course, by the British Broadcasting Corporation) along with some provincial additions, most notably the Manchester *Guardian*. The *Times* continued as the premier British newspaper as it had been since shortly after its founding in 1785. Under Lord Northcliffe's direction, it became a national institution, and though its circulation did not match those of the popular organs, its influence continued to be great. By midcentury, the popular London newspapers, the *Daily Express*, the *Daily Mirror*, the *Daily Herald*, and the *Daily Mail*, had achieved circulations in the millions.[44] Also important as a "quality" paper rivaling the *Times* in influence but with a larger circulation (around 900,000 to the 240,000 of the *Times*) was the *Daily Telegraph*.[45]

Significant developments in twentieth-century British newspapers were the evening newspapers, most notably the *Evening Standard*, the *Evening News*, and the *Star*. Added to the newspaper mix were several illustrated newspapers and Sunday newspapers, which had first appeared in the 1800s,[46] with the sensational *News of the World* attracting the world's largest circulation by midcentury of nearly 8 million.[47] By the end of the century, competition from the electronic media, increased operating costs, and competitive pressures within the newspaper industry itself had reduced the number of British papers significantly with the *Times* retaining its preeminent position and the popular dailies having the largest circulations.[48]

The early twentieth century in France saw the number of daily newspapers produced per capita to be first in Europe (244 for every 1,000 inhabitants—in Britain, the figure was 160 per 1,000). Four dailies, *Le Petit Parisien, Le Petit Journal, Le Matin*, and *Le Journal*, each had circulations of around a million. There were as many as 80 Paris dailies and 242 provincial dailies.[49] These numbers declined between the two world wars as did daily readership in comparison with Britain. Near the end of the century, there were eleven Paris dailies with *Le Figaro* having the largest circulation (423,000 in 1991) and the greatest influence, while the regional paper *Ouest France*, published in Rennes, was the biggest selling daily (794,000 in 1991).[50] Press concentration as just described has been significant in France, most notably under Robert Hersant, the proprietor of *Le Figaro, Le France-Soir*, and *L'Aurore*, which merged with *Le Figaro* in 1980, but government policies have increased the role of the state in the press, even taking the form of financial assistance.[51]

In Germany, the press operated under strong governmental controls through the period of World War I. The greatest German newspaper, the *Allgemeine Zeitung*, however, survived the Bismarck period only to cease publication during the Hitler regime. During the German republic years (1919–1932), newspapers had their greatest degree of freedom as large circulation dailies increased their circulation in Berlin and other cities, with the largest paper being the *Berliner Morgenpost*, which had a circulation of 600,000 by 1932. Following the controlled press of the Nazi period was the occupation press with the Soviet-controlled *Tagliche Rundschau* in Berlin, the U.S. *Die Neue Zeitung* in Munich, the British *Die Welt* in Hamburg, and the French *Der Kurier*, an afternoon Berlin paper. Following reunification, the press in Germany became increasingly concentrated with the Springer group (the *Bild, Bild am Sonntag, Welt am Sonntag, Die Welt,* and Hamburg's *Abendblatt*) and the *Westdeutsche Allgemeine Zeitung* group being prominent.[52]

The number of daily newspapers in Italy was greatly reduced by the rise of Mussolini and totalitarianism in the 1920s; the remaining papers had their editorial policies entirely determined by the government. Many of these papers were shut down by World War II, and those remaining were largely bought up by the country's prominent businessmen seeking not profits so much as political influence with the Mondadori group's *La Repubblica* and the Rizzoli/Fiat group's *Corriere della Sera* heading the list.[53]

In Spain and Portugal, heavy government censorship inhibited the development of major independent newspapers during the first half of the twentieth century, with Madrid's *ABC* a notable exception. More recently, state aid to the press in each country has aided in establishing a more effective newspaper industry.[54]

Like other small European countries, Belgium and the Netherlands saw national newspapers in competition with and frequently overshadowed by their larger neighbors. Among Scandinavian countries, Denmark's *Berlingske Tidende*, Norway's *Aftenposten*, and Sweden's *Dagens Nyheter* and *Svenska Dagbladet* are "quality" papers with significant circulations.[55] *Pravda*, with a peak circulation of 3 million, and *Izvestia* with about 1.5 million, were among the world's largest circulation newspapers, but as Soviet propaganda organs, they could not be compared to the nontotalitarian press.[56] Since the breakup of the Communist state, Russian newspapers, like other aspects of the nation, have become subject to market forces and competitive concerns.

Although it is obviously impossible to briefly summarize the effects of 600 years of development of the popular print media on the social and cultural climate of a diverse geographical region such as Europe, it is certainly tremendous. Clearly, the atmosphere of the twentieth and twenty-first centuries in Europe as well as the rest of the world is very much a product of the media, with the electronic media having a huge influence in contemporary times. In spite of the use of radio, television, and now the Internet, however, much of the European continent remains dependent on the great circulation daily newspapers and its host of local and regional newspapers, perhaps not so much for news per se, but for the more reasoned and in-depth factors underlying daily news events and life. The deliberate evaluation of cultural phenomena such as popular entertainment, modes of dress, science and health information, and all of the many manifestations of society and popular culture are promulgated by the daily newspapers. Evidence of this pervasive influence is readily noted if one simply takes a morning ride on the London underground, the Paris Metro, or the popular transportation modes of any of the great European cities. Almost without exception, each person on his or her way to daily activities can be seen reading the *Times, Le Figaro,* the *Daily News,* or whatever the local newspaper of choice might be. Truly, the newspaper counts as a major social force today just as its earlier counterparts did.

NOTES

1. Elizabeth L. Eisenstein, *The Printing Press As an Agent of Change: Communications and Cultural Transformations in Early Modern Europe* (Cambridge: Cambridge University Press, 1979), p. 8.

2. Eisenstein, *Printing Press,* p. 8.

3. Colin Clair, *A History of European Printing* (London: Academic, 1976), p. 23.

4. Leslie Shepard, *The Broadside Ballad: A Study in Origins and Meaning* (London: Herbert Jenkins, 1962), p. 26.

5. Shepard, *Broadside Ballad,* p. 55.

6. As cited in Shepard, *Broadside Ballad,* pp. 24–25.

7. Shepard, *Broadside Ballad,* p. 55.

8. Shepard, *Broadside Ballad,* p. 51.

9. Shepard, *Broadside Ballad,* p. 51.

10. Shepard, *Broadside Ballad,* pp. 49–50.

11. Shepard, *Broadside Ballad,* p. 51.

12. Shepard, *Broadside Ballad,* p. 48.

13. Shepard, *Broadside Ballad,* p. 52.

14. Shepard, *Broadside Ballad,* pp. 53–54.

15. Norman Davies, *Europe: A History* (Oxford: Oxford University Press, 1996), p. 513.

16. Clair, *History of European Printing,* p. 274.

17. Clair, *History of European Printing,* p. 275.

18. Anthony Smith, *The Newspaper: An International History* (London: Thames and Hudson, 1979), p. 18.

19. Smith, *Newspaper,* p. 8.

20. As cited in Smith, *Newspaper,* p. 9.

21. Smith, *Newspaper,* p. 12.

22. Smith, *Newspaper,* p. 10.

23. Harold Herd, *The March of Journalism: The Story of the British Press from 1622 to the Present Day* (London: Allen and Unwin, 1952), p. 15.

24. As cited in Herd, *March of Journalism,* p. 24.

25. Herd, *March of Journalism,* pp. 33–36.

26. Clair, *History of European Printing,* p. 275.

27. Raymond Kuhn, *The Media in France* (London: Routledge, 1995), p. 16.

28. Herd, *March of Journalism,* p. 39.

29. Herd, *March of Journalism*, p. 47.

30. As cited in Stephen Copley, ed., *Literature and the Social Order in Eighteenth Century England* (Beckenham, UK: Croom Held, 1984), p. 30.

31. Herd, *March of Journalism*, pp. 53–54; William Bragg Ewald Jr., *Rogues, Royalty and Reporters: The Age of Queen Anne through Its Newspapers* (Westport, CT: Greenwood, 1978); Copely, *Literature and the Social Order.*

32. As cited in Herd, *March of Journalism*, p. 53.

33. Margaret Drabble, ed., *The Oxford Companion to English Literature*, 5th ed. (Oxford: Oxford University Press, 1985), pp. 512, 809.

34. As cited in Alison Adburgham, *Women in Print: Writing Women and Women's Magazines from the Restoration to the Accession of Victoria* (London: Allen and Unwin, 1972), p. 97.

35. Smith, *Newspaper*, pp. 63–65.

36. Smith, *Newspaper*, pp. 65–66.

37. Jacques Barzun, *From Dawn to Decadence: 500 Years of Western Cultural Life, 1500 to the Present* (New York: HarperCollins, 2000); Davies, *Europe*, pp. 679–82, 774–75.

38. Herd, *March of Journalism*, p. 161.

39. As cited in Herd, *March of Journalism*, p. 162.

40. Herd, *March of Journalism*, pp. 144–45; Stephens, pp. 237–38.

41. Smith, *Newspaper*, p. 112.

42. Smith, *Newspaper*, pp. 115–16.

43. John C. Merrill, *The Elite Press: Great Newspapers of the World* (New York: Pitman, 1968), pp. 95–102; Mark W. Hopkins, "Media, Party, and Society in Russia," in *Mass Communications: A World View*, ed. Alan Wells (Palo Alto, CA: National Press Books, 1974), pp. 42–72; see also Wilford Van Der Will, "Culture and the Organization of National Socialist Ideology 1933–1945," in *German Cultural Studies: An Introduction*, ed. Rob Burns (New York: Oxford University Press, 1995), pp. 101–45.

44. Graham Murdock and Peter Golding, "The Structure, Ownership and Control of the Press," in *Newspaper History: From the 17th Century to the Present Day*, ed. George Boyce, James Curran, and Pauline Wingate (New York: Sage, 1978), pp. 130–42.

45. Herd, *March of Journalism*, pp. 263–64.

46. Virginia Berridge, "Popular Sunday Papers and Mid-Victorian Society," in *Newspaper History: From the 17th Century to the Present Day*, ed. George Boyce, James Curran, and Pauline Wingate (New York: Sage, 1978), pp. 247–64; Herd, *March of Journalism*, p. 275.

47. Merrill, *Elite Press*, pp. 170–77.

48. Kuhn, *Media in France*, pp. 17–20.

49. Kuhn, *Media in France*, p. 29; Peter Humphreys, *Mass Media and Media Policy in Western Europe* (Manchester, UK: Manchester University Press, 1996), pp. 83–84.

50. Humphreys, *Mass Media and Media Policy*, p. 85; Merrill, *Elite Press*, pp. 67–70.

51. "The Hitler-Goebbels Press," in "Newspapers," in *Encyclopaedia Britannica* (Chicago: Benton, 1957), p. 350; Merrill, *Elite Press*, pp. 203, 211.

52. Humphreys, *Mass Media and Media Policy*, pp. 22, 81; "Under the German Republic," in "Newspapers," in *Encyclopaedia Britannica* (Chicago: Benton, 1957), p. 349.

53. Humphreys, *Mass Media and Media Policy,* p. 90; Merrill, *Elite Press,* pp. 226–32.

54. Merrill, *Elite Press,* pp. 56–59.

55. Merrill, *Elite Press,* pp. 59–67, 77–80, 178–86.

56. Hopkins, "Media, Party, and Society in Russia," pp. 42–56; Merrill, *Elite Press,* pp. 95–102.

Chapter 8

Newspapers in the Americas

David A. Copeland

On the eve of national elections in the United States in 1799, Thomas Jefferson wrote to fellow Republican James Madison, "The engine is the press."[1] Jefferson understood what political leaders and citizens of most countries in the Americas came to realize or had already discerned: The heart of news in any nation revolves around government and politics because those entities to a great degree dictate the necessities of daily life for everyone.[2] How much or how little of that news reaches the people has a bearing on the life of a nation or a culture. Consequently, Jefferson's and Madison's Republican Party flooded newspapers with information and changed the direction of the United States forever. Similarly, Juan Perón controlled newspaper content in Argentina in the 1970s, which, in turn, allowed him to consolidate his power.[3] For Perón—just as it had been for Jefferson and Madison more than a century and a half earlier—the engine to power was the press.

The use of information-dispersal tools—whether they be traditional printed newspapers, Incan quipus, or continuously updated online versions—has similarities in the Americas. They have served as a principal tool of sharing and storing knowledge. Those that produced them have often fought for independence from government control, gained it, lost it, sometimes regained it, and in some cases continue to battle to maintain autonomy. Other newspapers in the Americas have developed with no governmental interference. Newspapers have adapted to meet changing societal needs, too. Newspapers have and continue, in other words, to set the agenda for society[4] or to adapt to readers' needs and desires.[5] The information in newspapers, then, is, according to Mitchell Stephens, "what is on society's mind."[6] Or, to quote another observer, newspapers are "of all the means of enlightening a nation, the best and the most easily accomplished."[7]

Newspapers also have served other functions for society when the political system allows it: They have assumed vital roles in commercial and economic growth and development. Advertising revenue for Canadian newspapers of the 1890s, for example, produced two-thirds of monies made by newspapers, and by 1900 advertising threatened to take over almost all news space in some papers.[8] Similarly in the United States, newspapers offered a venue for expanding industry and business. At the same time, newspapers offered readers information on goods and services available and affected massive changes in American economic life, especially in rural America in the first third of the nineteenth century,[9] something newspaper advertising continues to do in the United States.

Newspapers have provided society with entertainment as well. From essays on any number of subjects in the eighteenth century, to sensational and exaggerated stories, serialization of novels, and introduction of comics in the nineteenth century, to the massive sports and feature sections, consumer reporting, and magazines of today's publications, newspapers have sought ways to fill the needs of people beyond the political and economic realms. As a result, the number of newspapers, especially in North America, has exploded, creating a consumer-driven product that reacts not only to advertising revenue, but also to the needs of those the papers serve. Printers, editors, publishers, and the corporations that now own newspapers in most of the Americas continue ultimately to see the role of the newspaper for society the same as British colonial American printers, who in 1770, claimed in flowery doggerel:

News'papers are the spring of knowledge,
The gen'ral source throughout the nation,
Of ev'ry modern conversation....
    A News-paper is like a feast,
Some dish there is for ev'ry guest;
Some large, some small, some strong, some tender,
For ev'ry stomach, stout or slender;
Those who roast beef and ale delight in,
Are pleas'd with trumpets, drums and fighting;
For those who are more puny made,
Are arts and sciences, and trade;
For fanciful and am'rous blood,
We have a soft poetic food;
For witty and satyric folks,
High-season'd, acid, BITTER JOKES;
And when we strive to please the mob,
A jest, a quarrel, or a job.
    If any gentleman wants a wife,
(A partner, as 'tis term'd, for life)
An advertisement does the thing,
And quickly brings the pretty thing.
    If you want health, consult our pages,
You shall be well, and live for ages....

Our services you can't express,
The good we do you hardly guess;
There's not a want of human kind,
But we a remedy can find.[10]

Those who use newspapers for sources of information have understood their purpose in much the same way.

To determine the function of newspapers in the Americas, this chapter will look at patterns of knowledge acceptance and use of newspapers that recur among societies and nations. It will observe how newspapers have served cultures through times of political and economic stress and during periods of social, political, and economic stability. It also will look at how newspapers have adapted and survived the introduction of competing media and changes in technology. What emerges are broad areas of use of and for newspapers. First, newspapers have served as tools for shaping thought, principally by those who control political and economic power. Second, newspapers have provided a forum for public discussion and debate and as such have allowed the public—not leaders solely—to provide guidance for nations. Third, newspapers have developed a watchdog mentality as a way to protect and inform the public of wrongdoing. This concept may be considered an outgrowth of the second function of newspapers, or it may be considered a simultaneous development. The watchdog function has expanded to include more than merely observation of government but of any aspect of society that has the potential to abuse the people. Fourth, newspapers have created a consumer-driven product that seeks to meet the needs of those it serves. As commercialism, the number of newspapers, and subscription numbers increased in the nineteenth century, newspapers found themselves competing for readers. In North America, at least, newspapers saturated the market so that readers could pick and choose which papers they read. Newspapers became commodities and sought input from readers for content. Newspapers expanded their content to entertain and sell. This function of newspapers, therefore—just as the watchdog function—is reciprocal; it is driven by those who use newspapers and those who produce them. In all of these areas, however, we must never lose sight of the fact that while many may use newspapers as a means of control, newspapers ultimately inform, and at all times and in all places, newspapers are not used purely to sway public opinion. The newspaper's information dispersal function ultimately, according to Stephens, helps in the coordination of society and in the socialization of its members.[11]

The countries of the Americas divide into two groups—those of Latin America and those of North America. Latin America encompasses South America and North America from Mexico to the Caribbean islands, countries that developed principally from colonization efforts of Spain, Portugal, and France and were so named because of the Latin foundation for those countries' languages. The United States and Canada, nations that trace most of their settlement to

Great Britain, are considered North America for this study. Exceptions to these colonization patterns exist, of course, but for this chapter these designations are used nonetheless.

In the Americas, the traditional newspaper form—that of regularly published text and graphics on a paper-based product that is distributed among social groups—is generally considered to have first developed and consequently evolved into a highly sophisticated information form in the United States and subsequently was copied by other nations in the Western Hemisphere. Indeed, the press in the United States has served as a prototype for other nations in the Americas and around the globe, but the first news sheets to come off of the printing press in the Western Hemisphere were in Spanish, not English. The first *hoja volante* was published in Mexico in 1542. Although not printed on a regular basis, these early news sheets provided Spaniards who were in the process of conquest in Latin America news of local events as well as reports from Europe. Similar sheets appeared in Peru late in the sixteenth century but were published on a more regular basis beginning in 1618.[12]

Even though the printing press was not available to people indigenous to the Americas until after European settlement, they, too, found it important to share information. For most of the native cultures of the Americas, oral transmission served as the principal means of information dispersal. At times, however, groups discovered it was necessary to find another way to share information or to save knowledge in a more lasting—or perhaps more official—way. These precursors to the more traditional newspaper included, for example, petroglyphs and pictographs, quipus, and wampum belts. The cultures that used these forms of recorded information systems did so for the same reasons as those who produced printed newspapers: They needed to share political, economic, and general societal information—or knowledge—that was of value to the social function of those for whom it was created. The oldest form of nonpaper written information dispersal in the Americas is the petroglyph, or writings on stone. Some of those found in California have layers of information painted or carved into rock in places so people would see the communication as they passed. Some of the information in each layer may have been identical, but the writings were made by successive generations who used the sites as places to disperse information. Much of this information dealt with alignment of the sun and planets, information that was vital to societies whose political hierarchy depended on religious holidays and festivals for proper public order.[13]

Closer in function to our traditional understanding of newspapers were the Incan quipus. The quipu was a series of colored cotton cords knotted in ways that transmitted messages, most of which dealt with numbers and the economics of Incan society.[14] According to Marcia Asher, the quipus were transmitted daily by runners and sent to Incan elites, informing them of materials available in storehouses, taxes, census records, and other information required to keep the highly structured Latin American society functioning. The messages encoded in quipus were clear, compact, and portable.[15] Some may also have dealt with literary content not specifically related to the economics of Incan culture.[16] Similarly, Native Americans who lived in the Eastern woodlands of North America used wampum belts as a means of carrying on official business and for recording history. The belts, composed of small shells or beads, were woven to convey information. Treaties were not ratified without them, and nations from the Iroquois to the Cherokee used the belts to send messages and to record history.[17] According to Michael K. Foster, the Iroquois saw wampum as the device for recording information, just as white settlers viewed printed material.[18] Just as the Incas used knots and colored string to convey messages, Native Americans in Eastern North America used colored shells woven into the wampum. The information in the wampum was then conveyed orally at meetings,[19] much as British colonials read newspapers orally at taverns in the eighteenth century.

So, Native Americans of both continents found it necessary to produce written documents that dealt with the political, economic, and literary functions of society before the introduction of European culture and news dispersal methods. Most Europeans, no doubt, paid little attention to Native American methods of sharing information and probably did not realize that quipus, for instance, were ways of recording information. Colonists who emigrated to the New World desired the same types of information and adopted European methods of news dispersal to serve the same function. As the European populations of the Americas grew and technology advanced, information dispersal grew and reached a wider audience. Its growth and influence, obviously, did not occur simultaneously in the Americas, but many of the characteristics have appeared and make analogy possible.

TOOLS FOR SHAPING THOUGHT

Whether done intentionally or unintentionally, newspapers effect change or reinforce ideas. The selection or omission of information and news placement are but two ways that printers, editors, and the companies that own newspapers have used their products to shape opinion. In the Americas, those in power realized immediately the potential newspapers had and sought ways to control them, making the use of newspapers central to political power in the Americas. Any number of means have been employed, including closure and suspension of publication, seizure of newspapers, control of newspaper personnel, economic controls, and content controls.[20] Generally, whenever those in power have sought to influence information dispersal, they have employed a variety of these controls.

Suspension of publication works best in authoritarian situations. The Massachusetts governing council banned *Publick Occurrences Both Forreign and Domestick,* the first newspaper of the British American colonies, after only one issue in 1690, declaring "their high Resentment and Disallowance of said Pamphlet and Order that the Same be Suppressed and called in."[21] The council objected to some of the subject matter that Benjamin Harris printed and invoked a 1686 parliamentary directive as its basis for shutting down the publication.[22] When the next newspaper was printed in the colonies, the words "Published by Authority" appeared in the nameplate. This meant that the information in the paper had prior approval of the colonial government, a form of content control that ensured that unless the paper submitted its contents to a government censor prior to publication, printing ceased. According to Robert Pierce, closure and suspension of newspapers in Latin America is a much more powerful tool than censorship of content. Censorship allows newspapers to continue publishing and to maintain an economic base. Suspension destroys the monetary framework needed to continue publication. The press will, according to this method of control, structure its content to avoid closure, and those in power will be able to formulate public opinion.[23] Similar efforts to exert political manipulation have occurred in the United States at various times.[24] In the twentieth century, the landmark Supreme Court case *Near v. Minnesota* in 1931 dealt with the right of government to suspend publication of newspapers considered to be nuisances. In the case of Jay Near's *Saturday Press*, its exposés of Minnesota government misappropriations were considered the annoyance.[25] Although such closures legally ended with the Court's decision, they were still a recourse in the United States to that point, and numerous other attempts to silence newspapers have occurred despite a broadening of the understanding of First Amendment rights, such as attacks on radical and underground publications during the Vietnam War era.[26] Canadians have resorted to an alternate press, as well.[27]

The seizure of newspapers—either offices or copies of papers—has not been as widely employed in North America as it has in Latin America as a way for those in power to shape the flow of information. Most governments in Latin American nations have employed the practice at one time or another. The seizure of newspapers in Brazil, Peru, Chile, and Argentina in the 1970s are prime examples.[28] Seizure is also a viable tool when groups are seeking power. New York printer James Rivington, who often supported British control of colonial America rather than independence, had his print shop mobbed twice in an effort to silence his views. The second time his press was demolished, and he fled to England. Those seeking power effectively eliminated opposing viewpoints, which is exactly what happens when the state assumes control of newspapers. When Fidel Castro took control of Cuba, he also took control of the island's newspapers and other media, effectively ending any voice but his regime's into media-based discussion. This same sort of control extends to Internet access for news as the Cuban government limits the ability to go online to almost all unless they have a purpose such as gathering medical information.[29]

Control of newspaper personnel is often tied closely with the economic interests of newspapers. Perhaps the best example in the United States was the age of patronage, which lasted, according the Culver Smith, from 1789 to 1875.

Patronage began in a period of crisis for the United States. Political leaders and ideologies vied for control of the young nation, and printers and editors began to align with one political party, producing a partisan press. The party in power supported certain newspapers by giving them patronage—that is, money to print official government documents. To reciprocate, the newspapers published articles and editorials that promoted their patron party's political ideology along with scathing attacks on the opposition. Patronage meant considerable income for the newspaperman, so it was unlikely that anything negative was ever said about the party granting favoritism. The editors of the newspapers generally agreed with the political ideology of their benefactors, but politicians also sought out willing printers and editors to fulfill these roles. The same privileges were granted on all levels in the United States, from the presidency to local councils.[30]

The U.S. government, the Federalist Party specifically, employed the Alien and Sedition Acts of 1798 to stop partisan attacks against it early in this period. The acts forbade anyone to write, utter, print, or publish false, scandalous, or malicious comments against the government. The acts were aimed directly at political opposition, particularly printers. About twenty-five people were arrested, with fourteen indictments handed down during the acts' duration.[31]

Peru instituted a similar law in 1969 with the "press statute" of President Juan Velasco. The law declared that any publisher could be jailed for a defamation of any citizen, but anything printed about political leaders was an aggravated libel. That same year, Brazil stationed censors in the offices of the *Jornal do Brasil* and jailed its editor, Alberto Dines, after the paper published articles on press censorship by the government. Dines and other Brazilian editors discovered that they would continue to face imprisonment and censors in their offices to control newspaper content if they continued to make comments on governmental economic policies and political actions.[32]

Economic pressure as a way to control the flow of information by those in power has always been more prevalent in Latin America. According to Silvio Waisbord, newspapers in Latin America have survived because of government subsidies and loans with few exceptions. Governments, not producers of commodities, are the principal advertisers. As a result, Waisbord says, the press never attained independence from the state. Power for the press in most cases in Latin America meant "proximity to, not distance from, the state." The resulting newspapers became "lapdog media," meaning those who fostered and promoted government positions solely.[33]

All restrictions on newspapers serve one function—content control. From the closure of *Publick Occurrences* to the injunctions filed against the *New York Times* and *Washington Post* by the Nixon administration in the United States to Perón's closing of *La Prensa* to stop attacks on his administration,[34] those in power often find it imperative to manipulate the flow of information. The same holds true, of course, with those seeking power. In the 1880s, for example, Canadians struggled with whether Britain or France would assume dominion. The largest papers in Canada were controlled by Anglophones who used the press to attack Catholicism and French Canadians. The success of these attacks ensured British dominion and led to further uses of newspapers to shape Canadian policy.[35] The same has happened in the United States during most times of political, economic, or social stress. Prior to the American Revolution, Americans who advocated separation from Great Britain used all means possible to manipulate and control what was printed. John Adams, for example, noted that the work of men such as agitator Samuel Adams and printer John Gill with the *Boston Gazette* was "a curious employment, cooking up paragraphs, articles, occurrences," to usurp British control of the American colonies.[36] Chile's *El Mercurio* did the same thing in 1973 as it backed a powerful and successful attempt to unseat the country's socialist government.[37]

As a function of newspapers in the Americas, the press as a tool for shaping thought by those in political power or those seeking to assume power does appear to be waning, particularly in Latin America where it has been a staple of government-media relations for two centuries. As long as society turns to newspapers for information and as long as authoritarian governments exist, however, those in power will continue to use the press for its own purposes in information dispersal.

FORUMS FOR PUBLIC DISCUSSION

The concept that a function of newspapers in the Americas could be to allow public dialogue on issues when one use of newspapers is the control of information circulation by those with or seeking political power seems contradictory. Yet, as newspapers developed, this is what has happened. Newspapers have served as the place where society discusses and debates issues. This idea of a place where open discussion could take place—the public sphere—was initially aligned closely with influencing political power, according to German sociologist Jürgen Habermas. As trade developed, a growing, working, and more influential middle class arose. People increasingly sought ways to insert themselves into public discussions. The best way to do that was with the newspaper,[38] and in eighteenth-century British colonial America, for example, printers readily opened their publications on any number of issues. As Benjamin Franklin said in his 1731 "Apology for Printers," when society has differing opinions, printers present the arguments of all "without regarding on which side they are of the Question in Dispute."[39] But the debate was not limited to the written word. Newspapers provided the catalyst for public deliberations in settings ranging from public gathering spots to homes, from public ceremonies and orations to private conversations.[40] The printed and disseminated word became a storehouse for all types of information that was of value, not just political news but information with any consequence for society, particularly commercial news.[41] Consequently, by 1800 in the United States, it was no accident that "Advertiser" was the most common name for a newspaper.[42]

Newspapers cannot easily become the information dispersal tool described earlier in authoritarian states. In the United States, public prints became the place where aristocratic planters, backcountry farmers, merchants, and politicians were bound together to discuss issues. And once an essay, letter, or comment was published, its interpretation and further comment were open to any who read it.[43] In addition, many disenfranchised elements of society found ways to participate in public debate.[44] Newspapers as forums for public discussion necessitate a more open political system, and, ironically, newspapers help to create such a system as much as the system allows for their use for open debate. Consequently, this function of newspapers rarely occurred in Latin America before the second half of the twentieth century and then only sporadically. According to Waisbord, none of the factors that created the tradition of participatory journalism that developed in North America in the eighteenth and nineteenth centuries ever existed in Latin America. Because of so much political instability caused by authoritarian military and civilian governments in Latin America, he says, basic democratic rights disappeared. As a result, newsrooms were controlled by government, and journalists were persecuted and killed if they ever opened their presses up for dialogue.[45] Still, some Latin America journalists found ways to create a forum for debate by using an alternative or underground press, which developed in Argentina, Brazil, and Peru in the 1960s and 1970s. By using simple duplicating methods and shunning opportunities to make money, these publications functioned in much the same way newspapers operated in British colonial America in the eighteenth century. They introduced ideas to the public in order to stimulate discussion among citizens in public venues.[46] Now, as Latin American authoritarian governments turn toward democracy, more people are writing letters to the editors and speaking out on political, social, and economic issues.[47]

In North America, newspapers began shaping issues and serving as a place for public debate almost from the beginning of their existence. Even though an authoritarian Massachusetts government shut down *Publick Occurrences* after a single issue and successfully controlled content of the colony's next paper for nearly two decades, the very nature of the British colonies in North America, which were an ocean away from those who made the majority of rules for them, made authoritarian rule practically impossible even though autocratic rule was attempted and successful in several cases. In the British American colonies, people quickly realized that having a single newspaper did not best serve the public's interest when controversial issues arose and debate was needed. Competition, most realized, allowed for more debate of important subjects. Inoculating people against smallpox was one such example. Inoculation was considered heathenistic and an unproven medical practice to many, so when its advocates began to promote the practice in a Boston newspaper in 1721, those opposing it started a newspaper. The public controversy raged for months in Boston and for decades in America.[48] A similar need for more public debate led to the trial of New York printer John Peter Zenger. Zenger's newspaper provided a forum for debate on corrupt political practices that could not have existed without a forum that provided space for opinions that opposed the ruling party's.[49] The sharing of opinions and knowledge became central to the United States and Canada, which is why most towns with populations of only a few hundred generally had newspapers by early in the nineteenth century.[50]

The use of newspapers to stimulate debate increased dramatically around 1765 as the colonies that eventually became the United States broke with Great Britain, fought the Revolution, and then worked to establish political and economic stability in the last decades of the eighteenth century and the first ones of the nineteenth century. Issues that affected the young nation swirled within the public sphere. In the earlier part of this period, those who had access to newspapers to stimulate debate were still the more elite of society, but their ideas were shared with a far wider range of people.[51] Isaiah Thomas, who wrote the first history of American printers and newspapers, concluded that newspapers "have become the vehicles of discussion, in which the principles of government, the interest of nations, the spirit and tendency of public measures... are all arraigned, tried, and decided.... By means of this powerful instrument, impressions on the public mind may be made with a celerity, and to an extent, of which cannot but give rise to the most important consequences in society. Never was there given to man a political engine of greater power."[52]

This public debate did not subside; in fact, it increased dramatically in the nineteenth century because of the proliferation of newspapers that provided increasing opportunities for participation within the public sphere for people in all walks of life in the United States. The number of papers printed grew from 35 in 1783 to 1,200 by 1833.[53] Newspaper circulation outdistanced the rest of the world in per capita readership, fulfilling a prophecy predicted by editor Noah Webster some forty years earlier. "In no other country on earth," Webster wrote, "not even in Great-Britain, are newspapers so generally circulated among the body of people, as in America."[54] In fact, by 1830, more than half of all American families subscribed to a newspaper.[55] The United States' public prints, as described by Alexis de Tocqueville, "drop the same thought into a thousand minds at the same moment."[56]

There can be little doubt that the public debate carried on in newspapers in the United States in the first third of the nineteenth century fueled participation in American politics and commerce, and what was in the papers, consequently, set the agenda for society's discussions. Newspapers grew at an enormous rate from 1783 to 1833, in excess of 3,300 percent. Voting rates for the early republic were low, with only 10 to 15 percent of eligible voters—white males—voting in 1775.[57] But newspapers continued to grow, prosper, and discuss the issues that directed public debate and opinion. Consequently, by 1829 about 50 percent of American households subscribed to a newspaper, and approximately 44 percent of eligible voters participated in the 1832 election, an increase of more than 190 percent over pre-Revolution numbers.[58] The correlation of the two—voting and newspaper subscription—is not coincidence, and, as Thomas C. Leonard notes, "reading the news ushered in American nationalism."[59] Newspapers as a forum for debate helped set political agenda in the United States at this time. After Andrew Jackson lost the 1824 presidential race despite defeating John Quincy Adams in popular votes, many turned to newspapers to ensure that the governmental power play that elected Adams in the House of Representatives would not be repeated. One newspaper declared that "public opinion will eventually be respected by the election of the General."[60] The public outcry intensified, and Jackson handily won the 1828 election. Jackson wisely read the papers and realized people wanted change. He allowed the voices that echoed in the papers to set the agenda, and he followed. "The recent demonstration of public sentiment inscribes on the list of Executive duties, in characters too legible to be overlooked, the task of reform," Jackson said in his 1829 inaugural address, in direct reference to public opinion as voiced in newspapers.[61]

But the use of newspapers by people in the United States as a means of entering, following, and shaping public debate had just begun. The introduction of penny papers and technological advances such as the rotary press soon meant that more newspapers were available than ever before. Daily circulation grew from about 200,000 to more than 1.5 million by 1860,[62] and penetration into society continued to grow into the twentieth century. By the end of World War II, newspaper market penetration reached 135 percent, meaning that more newspapers were sold each day than there were households in the United States. These figures continued through the 1960s.[63] Such a sizable press both opened doors for public dialogue and closed them. Debate for most citizens increasingly turned to smaller, local newspapers that focused on issues that affected individual communities, and people in all types of communities—even those who were institutionalized—felt a need to begin newspapers so that their voices could be heard.[64] Still, what happened nationally remained important to people, and the press found a way to allow the people to speak: through public opinion polls.

By the end of the nineteenth century, many Americans realized that the size and breadth of papers and what was happening in North America made it nearly impossible for most people to enter into public debate. Another means of allowing the voice of the people had to be arranged. James Bryce, in his 1895 book *The American Commonwealth*, said that a way had to be found to make the will of the majority of citizens ascertainable at all times, and there needed to be a way to inject that collective voice to the public debate.[65] The result—the public opinion poll—helped newspapers create what Michael Schudson calls "democracy through technology."[66] Through careful analysis, the thoughts of the public could be ascertained and reported in a collective voice, which became the work of pollsters such as George Gallup. Theoretically, polls statistically allowed everyone the opportunity to be heard and allowed newspapers to continue to serve as the place of public debate.[67]

In the twentieth century, then, newspapers, working as local and national publications, allowed individuals to continue to effect change through individual voices on the local level and through a collective voice in national public opinion polls. People could express themselves, and the public had the ability to hear what they were saying. Technology had provided for penetration of newspapers into every part of the nation. Individual participation, a hallmark of the eighteenth and nineteenth centuries, never disappeared. It refigured itself thanks to technological changes, so that even in the twenty-first century people still look to the press as a place for individual voices, be it one person or a collective of people with common traits.[68] This is especially true as newspapers make the move to online versions. In 1995, only about one hundred daily papers had Web versions, but by 2000, all did with most smaller papers doing the same.[69] The Internet also has allowed people everywhere access to a source for public expression. Anyone with a network hookup can obtain free server space for a Web page to promote opinions, and some Internet sites, such as Matt Drudge's *Drudge Report*, have gained international exposure and notoriety for their information. Others have begun to provide voices of dissent even in authoritarian countries where media are state controlled.[70]

THE WATCHDOG FUNCTION

The idea that newspapers function as a watchdog for wrongdoing may have its etymological origins in the events of the 1960s and 1970s in the United States, but the concept that newspapers report on injustices by government or any aspect of society that has some form of power over people has existed much longer and is employed in places other than North America.[71] The ability of the press to function as an investigator to uncover malfeasance is generally associated with democratic nations, but the desire to inform people of injustices can be found in authoritarian nations, too. To be a watchdog in such a setting, however, newspapers must often function outside of government's ability to regulate, much as the alternative underground press has done in some Latin American countries. The watchdog mentality developed as a way to protect and inform the public of government actions, but the concept now includes any type of reporting that protects people from abuse, such as muckraking.[72] Newspapers function in a watchdog capacity because of the roles of the press already discussed. When the press is used to shape thought by those in power or seeking to assume power, information may be manipulated or kept from the people. Uncovering abuses in such a system is a natural consequence. Being a watchdog for abuses is a natural outgrowth of the use of newspapers as a forum for public debate as well.

The idea that newspapers can serve in a watchdog function is based in the concept of press rights and freedoms, such as the First Amendment to the U.S.

Constitution. Press freedom has increasingly become a part of the constitutions of Latin American countries, too, and the separation of state and press to some degree must exist for newspapers to truly serve a watchdog function.[73] Still, newspapers began serving this function during periods of stricter censorship, charges of seditious libel, and threats of journalists' imprisonment in the Americas. The origins of the watchdog function may be disputed to some degree, however, because those who produced the information were working to achieve their own goals in many cases. The attacks of Zenger's *New-York Weekly Journal* on the governing administration of the colony of New York from 1733 to 1735 is one example. Zenger's imprisonment was the result of a political power play between the ruling administration of William Cosby and the opposing political faction of the colony. Even though Cosby's counterparts were seeking political power, they used the press to uncover corruption and abuse.[74] The same use of the press occurred in British America from 1765 to 1775. Again, those using the press had a political agenda, but they still used newspapers as a way to expose perceived governmental corruption and abuse. As printer John Holt said, "It was by means of News papers that we receiv'd & spread Notice of the tyrannical Designs formed against America and kindled a Spirit that has been sufficient to repel them."[75]

The early newspapers of North America paid correspondents for information and on rare occasions employed news writers,[76] but the rapid growth in the number of newspapers in the nineteenth century and the subsequent competition that accompanied the penny press made them a necessity. Newspapers needed reporters to dig up information, and enterprising newspaper people such as James Gordon Bennett introduced investigation into the mix.[77] Although investigative journalism of this period may not have always functioned as a voice for the powerless or as a guardian against governmental abuses, reporters quickly began to apply these principles. And often, it was not the mainstream press that championed the watchdog role. Ida B. Wells-Barnett's *Free Speech* in Memphis, Tennessee, became a leading voice in uncovering abuses in the political and legal system of the Southern United States. Her writings on the lynching of blacks in the late nineteenth century, *Southern Horrors: Lynch Law in All Its Phases* and *Red Record*, were widely reprinted in African American newspapers, and she wrote ceaselessly on social injustice, digging up facts to support her exposés.[78]

In the twentieth century, the watchdog function of the press came to fruition in North America. The press began actively to look to uncover corruption and abuses. Muckrakers, who operated mainly from around 1902–1912, revealed government corruption, tainted business practices, and abuse of workers. Investigative journalism reached its zenith in North America in the 1970s with the publication of the *Pentagon Papers* and the Watergate investigation that helped topple Richard Nixon from office. What may be even more amazing, however, is the amount of investigative journalism that was taking place in Latin America. At the same time the *Washington Post* was revealing the corrupt nature of the Nixon White House, newspapers in Brazil, Peru, and Mexico were doing similar reporting despite strong governmental controls. *O Estado de São Paulo* in Brazil combined muckraking and governmental watchdog activities to report on the failure of inspectors to keep contaminated milk from reaching the public and on the lavish lifestyles of politicians.[79] Despite varying amounts of governmental control, Latin American newspapers have increased their watchdog function in no small part because of Watergate, where reporters who expose corruption are commonly referred to as "the sons of Watergate," and "mini-Watergates" are being uncovered in many countries often at the risk of repercussions to reporters.[80] Exposing government corruption and exposing human rights violations are the main watchdog functions in Latin America, both of which were reported by the Argentine *Noticias* in a 1994 case involving the murder of Omar Carrasco, an army private. Official government reports first said the soldier deserted and subsequently died of natural causes. A second version claimed he was killed outside his barracks by a gang. *Noticias* continued to investigate, however, and revealed that Carrasco was beaten to death by a captain who did not like the soldier's smile.[81]

CONSUMER-DRIVEN PRODUCTS

The idea that newspapers and their content are consumer driven and consumable commodities has long been understood by those who have produced papers. The 1770 poem that proclaimed "A News-paper is like a feast/Some dish there is for ev'ry guest" captured the notion that newspapers contain information to meet the needs of those they serve. The newspaper may function as a tool for shaping thought, allowing public debate, and exposing wrongdoing, but it ultimately must reflect a specific audience and mirror a particular place to function as a societal necessity.[82] Newspapers have done so longer in North America than in Latin America, but, increasingly, Latin American papers are catering to societal diversity in their content because "it pleases customers."[83]

Technological changes in the nineteenth century spurred the consumer-driven application of newspapers even though newspapers served many of these functions earlier. The ability to produce thousands of copies per hour through new mechanical means coupled with low cost made newspapers more accessible than ever before in the nineteenth century. According to Leonard, newspapers became so popular in the United States in the 1800s because they fostered a sense of community among a wide sociological and geographic base.[84] Knowing the method of determining the specific occurrence of the summer solstice was imperative to a pre-Columbian California culture, hence how to determine it was inscribed in petroglyphs. Knowing as much as possible about French incursions into British America in the mid-1750s was imperative for life to survive as British colonials knew it, so newspapers focused almost their entire content on the war.[85] Knowing as much as possible about potential military coups' effects on everyday life in Brazil dominated conversation at various times in the 1950s and 1960s, therefore newspapers discussed those repercussions.[86]

But, Leonard says, newspapers achieved wide social acceptance for reasons beyond examples such as these, even though in each case society no doubt felt it needed the information to survive. He refers to a consumer-driven function of newspapers as "reporting from the bottom," which allows in some way for "everybody to be his or her own editor."[87] Newspapers assumed a consumable function because they gave something to all elements of society—"There's not a want of human kind/But we a remedy can find," according to the 1770 newspaper poem. By the last two decades of the nineteenth century, newspapers penetrated all economic and social levels of society in North America. But by the middle of the century, newspapers thrived as products designed to meet varied societal needs. A growing black press, which attacked slavery, found a market in the northern United States and Canada.[88] Nearly 200 religious newspapers, which dealt with issues peculiar to particular groups as well as secular subjects, were listed in the 1850 U.S. Census.[89] As a result, people could pick and choose which newspapers they wanted to read in many areas, allowing those people to be their own editors. And, people talked with one another about what they read, a vital social function.[90]

Increasingly, the newspapers' role as a consumable has turned its focus more toward what readers want, and, conversely, readers have long admitted they need newspapers. As early as 1750, New York printer James Parker noted that newspapers were something "we can't be without."[91] One hundred years later, a Canadian writer claimed that "the Canadian cannot get on without his newspaper any more than an American without his tobacco."[92] One hundred fifty years later, newspapers were considered the most credible of all Brazilian institutions.[93] In the eighteenth century, printers added poems and other writing to attract female readers. As leisure time grew in the nineteenth century, papers added novels by leading authors along with news of sports and entertainment. As newspapers began to face greater competition from other media in the twentieth century, they sought ways to meet the needs of those they served by asking the public what it wanted in the newspaper.[94] Increasingly in the last half of the twentieth century, many newspapers looked to those they serve to shape content. The concept of civic or community journalism is an attempt by newspapers—specifically those serving a local or regional public—to return the function of local newspapers more to the public forum function described earlier.

Though public opinion polls allow a collective voice to speak, the individual voice is consumed by the collective. Community journalism, however, differs because of the commodity function assumed by newspapers. Newspapers ask those they serve what they are most interested in through convenience surveys or call-ins, for example. The newspapers then sponsor public forums and cover them—not as things they have created—but as news events. The newspaper, according to Jay Rosen, functions as a partner with the public.[95] The concept is to make people feel as if what is occurring—the work of the newspaper and what is being addressed at the forum—is theirs.[96] In Latin America, some newspapers are attempting to empower the public through community journalism. "We get more and more letters to the editor and our phones are constantly ringing," Gustavo Gorriti of Panama's *La Prensa* said at the 1996 Civitas Panamericano conference in Buenos Aires. "In support of the development of a civil society, we need to explain the news, come close to the people, sustain the relationship, and be more committed."[97] As the U.S. population continues to diversify, many editors believe what individual communities want will be even more crucial. "How well do we understand our new communities?" Martin Baron, editor of the *Boston Globe*, asks. "Do their agendas include issues simply off the radar of the national media in the United States?"[98] Baron's questions are simply a reformation of the same questions asked by editors a century earlier when they wondered for whom they were writing and then began to observe and adapt their papers to their local constituencies.[99] By making what newspapers cover more relevant to the communities they serve and by actively enlisting input from those communities, newspapers are working to stave off decreasing circulation. But they also are making newspapers products that rely even more on the consumers who subscribe to them. Consumer-driven newspapers do not aim for all readers. Their function is to serve particular communities with common interests. Civic journalism is merely the latest tool to ensure success,[100] and newspapers are increasingly using the Internet to continue this function. Nearly every North American newspaper is online as are most major newspapers in Latin America.

The consumer-driven function of the press has another important function. Newspapers help fuel consumption of goods through advertising. Newspapers have always run advertisements, but the explosion of newspapers in the nineteenth century led to greater knowledge of products. The newspaper became the means for economic growth and development, and at least one enterprising advertiser called newspapers and the printing press "the engine of the world."[101] Newspapers' function as society's principal outlet for goods and services grew continually from the nineteenth century to the last quarter of the twentieth century. In Latin America, Jayme Zirotsky, president of the World Association of Newspapers, reports that in 1997, newspapers in Latin American countries generated more than $15 billion in advertising, capturing 30 percent of advertising revenue, and surpassing television as the region's principal advertiser.[102] In the United States, newspaper advertising accounted for 35 percent of all advertising revenue in 2000, an amount exceeding $70 billion and equal to that spent on television ads.[103]

CONCLUSION

Newspapers in the Americas have served similar functions, but those created on printing presses developed along different time lines in North and Latin America, due in no small part to political ideologies. Where authoritarian governments have long been the norm, newspapers have functioned principally as tools for shaping thought and controlling people. Where democracy has flourished, newspapers have been used for the same purpose but soon moved on to become avenues for public debate and discussion. This function expanded into a watchdog role as it became difficult for citizens to devote so much time to public dialogue. Technology helped push newspapers into their consumer-driven function along with a growth in capitalism, and technology and a move toward democratization in many states are quickly allowing the newspapers of Latin America to follow paths similar to those in North America.

Technology is also driving newspapers in the Americas as nearly all now provide some form of online product. This version of the newspaper is probably the most consumer-driven yet. Newspaper sites constantly poll readers about their opinions and wants for the site and offer links to advertisers and online services. Some offer the possibility of customizing content.[104] Online newspapers rarely serve the first function—being a tool for shaping thought by those in power—and they rarely earn publishers as much profit as print versions. The *Wall Street Journal* is the exception. It established an interactive version in 1996 and charged a subscription to use the service. By 1999, more than a quarter of a million subscribers were using the online version.[105]

In the Americas, newspapers have served a unique function. They have helped form and topple governments. They have provided people with a platform for debate. They have shaped themselves to meet society's needs. And they have adapted to changing technology whenever needed. Though newspapers may have to further target their audiences to remain viable, they will continue in the Americas because, as one wise printer noted more than two and one half centuries ago, "News'papers are the spring of knowledge/The gen'ral source throughout the nation/Of ev'ry modern conversation."

NOTES

1. Jefferson to Madison, 5 February 1799, cited in Paul L. Ford, *The Works of Thomas Jefferson* (New York: Putnam's, 1904–1905), p. 7:344.

2. Marvin Alisky, *Latin American Media: Guidance and Censorship* (Ames: Iowa State University Press, 1981), p. 3.

3. Alisky, *Latin American Media*, p. 2.

4. The seminal study on the agenda-setting role of media was Maxwell E. McCombs and Donald Shaw, "The Agenda-Setting Function of the Mass Media," *Public Opinion Quarterly* 36 (1972): 176–87.

5. For example, see Jack Fuller, *News Values: Ideas for an Information Age* (Chicago: University of Chicago Press, 1996), p. 69; Thomas C. Leonard, *News for All: America's Coming-of-Age with the Press* (New York: Oxford University Press, 1995), p. 117.

6. Mitchell Stephens, *A History of News: From the Drum to the Satellite* (New York: Viking, 1988), p. 9.

7. Julian Ursyn Niemcewicz, *Under Their Vine and Fig Tree: Travels through America in 1797–1799*, trans. and ed. Metchie J. E. Budka (Elizabeth, NJ: Grassmann, 1965), p. 55, cited in Richard N. Rosenfeld, *American Aurora: A Democratic-Republican Returns* (New York: St. Martin's, 1997), p. 62.

8. Paul Rutherford, *A Victorian Authority: The Daily Press in Late Nineteenth-Century Canada* (Toronto: University of Toronto Press, 1982), pp. 97, 104.

9. William J. Gilmore, *Reading Becomes a Necessity of Life: Material and Cultural Life in Rural New England, 1780–1835* (Knoxville: University of Tennessee Press, 1989), p. 57.

10. *Virginia Gazette* (Williamsburg, Purdie, and Dixon), 22 January 1770, p. 2; *New-York Gazette: or the Weekly Post-Boy*, 16 April 1770, p. 4; *New-York Journal; or the General Advertiser*, 19 April 1770, p. 3; *New-London Gazette*, 25 May 1770, p. 4; *Providence Gazette; and Country Journal*, 7 July 1770, p. 4. All or portions of this poem recurred at various times in U.S. newspapers. For example, see *Pennsylvania Packet* (Philadelphia), 22 September 1784.

11. Stephens, *History of News*, p. 67.

12. Al Hester, "Newspapers and Newspaper Prototypes in Spanish America, 1541–1750," *Journalism History* 6 (1979): 74–76.

13. Roderick L. Schmidt, "Swansea, a Multicultural Petroglyph Site in Inyo County, California," *The Epigraphic Society Occasional Papers* 21 (1993): 268–76. The earliest account of these California petroglyphs is Clifford Park Baldwin, *Archaeological Exploration and Survey in Southern Inyo County, California* (unpublished manuscript, Eastern California Museum, Independence, California, 1931). Other cultures used hieroglyphics and pictographs for similar purposes. See Alvin M. Josephy Jr., *500 Nations* (New York: Knopf, 1994), pp. 33, 78.

14. See Marcia Asher and Robert Asher, *Code of the Quipu: A Study in Media, Mathematics, and Culture* (Ann Arbor: University of Michigan Press, 1981; reprint, New York: Dover, 1997).

15. Marcia Asher, *Ethnomathematics: A Multicultural View of Mathematical Ideas* (Pacific Grove, Calif.: Brooks/Cole, 1991), p. 17.

16. Viviano Domenici and Davide Domenici, "Talking Knots of the Inka," *Archaeology* 49, no. 6 (1996): 50–56.

17. Rennard Strickland, *Fire and the Spirits: Cherokee Law from Clan to Court* (Norman: University of Oklahoma Press, 1975), p. 11.

18. Michael K. Foster, "Another Look at the Function of Wampum in Iroquois-White Councils," in *The History and Culture of Iroquois Diplomacy: An Interdisciplinary Guide to the Treaties of the Six Nations and Their League,* ed. Francis Jennings (Syracuse, NY: Syracuse University Press, 1995), p. 105.

19. "Treaty of Peace between the French, the Iroquois, and Other Nations," in *The History and Culture of Iroquois Diplomacy: An Interdisciplinary Guide to the Treaties of the Six Nations and Their League,* ed. Francis Jennings (Syracuse, NY: Syracuse University Press, 1995), pp. 137–40. For a brief but thorough discussion of the use of wampum for information exchange, see C.F. Smith, "Material Rhetoric: Wampum Records," at http://web.syr.edu/~cfsmith/congress/episodes/1789/comments/Cher/wampum. (February 2002).

20. Robert N. Pierce, *Keeping the Flame: Media and Government in Latin America* (New York: Hastings House, 1997), pp. 181–86, 192.

21. *By the Governour and Council* (Boston), 29 September 1690.

22. The decree states: "Forasmuch as great inconvenience may arise by liberty of printing within our said territory under your government you are to provide by all necessary orders that no person keep any printing-press for printing, nor that any book, pamphlet or other matter whatsoever be printed without your especial leave and license first obtained." See "Licensing of Printing Presses and Printing," in *Royal Instructions to British Colonial Governors, 1670–1776*, ed. Leonard W. Labaree (New York: Appleton-Century, 1935), p. 2:495.

23. Pierce, *Keeping the Flame*, pp. 181–82.

24. For example, see Ralph Frasca, "*The Helderberg Advocate:* A Public-Nuisance Prosecution a Century before *Near v. Minnesota*," *Journal of Supreme Court History* 26 (2001): 215–30.

25. *Near v. Minnesota* 283 U.S. 687 (1931). For more examples of government efforts to silence the press, see Jeffrey A. Smith, *Printers and Press Freedom: The Ideology of Early American Journalism* (New York: Oxford University Press, 1988); Donna Lee Dickerson, *The Course of Tolerance: Freedom of the Press in Nineteenth-Century America* (Westport, CT: Greenwood, 1990); Margaret A. Blanchard, *Revolutionary Sparks: Freedom of Expression in Modern America* (New York: Oxford University Press, 1992); William E. Porter, *Assault on the Media: The Nixon Years* (Ann Arbor: University of Michigan Press, 1976).

26. Blanchard, *Revolutionary Sparks*, pp. 352–54.

27. David R. Spencer, "Fact, Fiction, or Fantasy: Canada and the War to End All Wars," in *Newsworkers: Toward a History of the Rank and File*, ed. Hanno Hardt and Bonnie Brennan (Minneapolis: University of Minnesota Press, 1995), pp. 182–205.

28. Pierce, *Keeping the Flame*, pp. 184–85.

29. Emmanuelle Richard, "Cuba's Newest Information War: Keeping the Internet Revolution under Control," *Online Journalism Review*, 6 May 1998, at http://ojr.usc.edu/content/story.cfm?id = 238 (February 2002).

30. Culver H. Smith, *The Press, Politics, and Patronage: The American Government's Use of Newspapers, 1789–1875* (Athens: University of Georgia Press, 1977), pp. 17–23.

31. James Morton Smith, *Freedom's Fetters: The Alien and Sedition Laws and American Civil Liberties* (Ithaca, NY: Cornell University Press, 1956), pp. 185–87.

32. Alisky, *Latin American Media*, pp. 72–73, 108–9.

33. Silvio Waisbord, *Watchdog Journalism in South America: News, Accountability, and Democracy* (New York: Columbia University Press, 2000), pp. 16–17.

34. Waisbord, *Watchdog Journalism in South America*, p. 20.

35. Rutherford, *Victorian Authority*, p. 60.

36. John Adams, *The Works of John Adams, Second President of the United States: With a Life of the Author, Notes, and Illus. by His Grandson, Charles Francis Adams* (Boston, 1850–1856), p. 2:219, cited in Philip Davidson, *Propaganda and the American Revolution, 1763–1783* (Chapel Hill: University of North Carolina Press, 1941), p. 227.

37. Waisbord, *Watchdog Journalism in South America*, p. 19.

38. Jürgen Habermas, *The Structural Transformation of the Public Sphere: A Structural Transformation of Bourgeois Society,* trans. Thomas Burger and Frederick Lawrence (Cambridge: MIT Press, 1989), p. 29.

39. *Pennsylvania Gazette* (Philadelphia), 10 June 1731.

40. Richard D. Brown, *Knowledge Is Power: The Diffusion of Information in Early America, 1700–1865* (New York: Oxford University Press, 1989), p. 292; see also David Waldstreicher, *In the Midst of Perpetual Fetes: The Making of American Nationalism, 1776–1820* (Chapel Hill: University of North Carolina Press, 1997); David S. Shields, *Civil Tongues and Polite Letters in British America* (Chapel Hill: University of North Carolina Press, 1997). Brown also argues that oral tradition affected what happened within the print culture.

41. Gilmore, *Reading Becomes a Necessity of Life,* p. 26.

42. James W. Carey, "The Press and the Public Discourse," *Kettering Review* (Winter 1992): 16.

43. Saul Cornell, *The Other Founders: Anti-Federalism and the Dissenting Tradition in America, 1788–1828* (Chapel Hill: University of North Carolina Press, 1999), pp. 10, 22.

44. For example, see Mary Beth Norton, *Founding Mothers and Fathers: Gendered Power and the Forming of American Society* (New York: Knopf, 1996); Mary P. Ryan, *Civic Wars: Democracy and Public Life in the American City during the Nineteenth Century* (Berkeley: University of California Press, 1997); Gary B. Nash, *Forging Freedom: The Formation of Philadelphia's Black Community, 1720–1840* (Cambridge, MA: Harvard University Press, 1988); Carol Sue Humphrey, *The Press and the Young Republic, 1783–1883* (Westport, CT: Greenwood, 1996), pp. 141–43.

45. Waisbord, *Watchdog Journalism in South America,* pp. 22–23.

46. Waisbord, *Watchdog Journalism in South America,* pp. 28–31. Similar uses of the alternative press occurred in North America in the twentieth century. See Blanchard, *Revolutionary Sparks;* Spencer, "Fact, Fiction, or Fantasy."

47. Pierce, *Keeping the Flame,* pp. 213–14.

48. David A. Copeland, *Colonial American Newspapers: Character and Content* (Newark: University of Delaware Press, 1997), pp. 180–82.

49. David Copeland, "The Zenger Trial," *Media Studies Journal* (Spring–Summer 2000): 2–7.

50. Anthony Smith, *The Newspaper: An International History* (London: Thames and Hudson, 1979), p. 91, cited in Hannah Barker and Simon Burrows, eds., *Press, Politics and the Public Sphere in Europe and North America 1760–1820* (Cambridge, England: Cambridge University Press, 2002).

51. See David A. Copeland, "America, 1750–1820," in *Press, Politics, and the Public Sphere in Europe and North America, 1760–1820,* ed. Hannah Barker and Simon Burrows (Cambridge: Cambridge University Press, 2002), pp. 140–58; Saul Cornell, *The Other Founders: Anti-Federalism and the Dissenting Tradition in America, 1788–1828* (Chapel Hill: University of North Carolina Press, 1999); Waldstreicher, *In the Midst of Perpetual Fetes.*

52. Thomas, *History of Printing in America,* p. 19. Thomas is cited directly from Samuel Miller, *A Brief Retrospect of the Eighteenth Century* (New York: T. and J. Swords, 1803), pp. 2:251–255.

53. Humphrey, *Press of the Young Republic,* p. 155.

54. *American Minerva* (New York), 9 December 1793.

55. Gilmore, *Reading Becomes a Necessity of Life,* pp. 193–94.

56. Alexis de Tocqueville, *Democracy in America,* ed. Richard D. Heffner (New York: Mentor, 1956), p. 202.

57. Michael Schudson, "Was There Ever a Public Sphere? If So, When? Reflections on the American Case," *Habermas and the Public Sphere,* ed. Craig Calhoun (Cambridge, MA: MIT Press, 1992), p. 149.

58. Gilmore, *Reading Becomes a Necessity of Life,* pp. 193–94; Walter Dean Burnham, *The Current Crisis in American Politics* (New York: Oxford University Press, 1982), p. 129.

59. Leonard, *News for All,* p. 3.

60. *Aurora* (Philadelphia), 2 February 1825.

61. Andrew Jackson, *The Correspondence of Andrew Jackson,* ed. John Spencer Bassett (Washington, DC: Carnegie Institution of Washington, 1926–1935), p. 4:19.

62. William David Sloan and James D. Startt, *The Media in America,* 4th ed. (Northport, AL: Vision, 1999), p. 123.

63. Wilson Dizard Jr., *Old Media New Media: Mass Communications in the Information Age,* 3rd ed. (New York: Longman, 2000), p. 157.

64. For example, see Constance Ledoux Book and David Ezell, "Freedom of Speech and Institutional Control: Patient Publications at Central State Hospital, 1934–1978," *Georgia Historical Review* 85 (2001): 106–26; Russell Baird, *The Penal Press* (Evanston, IL: Northwestern University Press, 1967).

65. James Bryce, *The American Commonwealth,* 3rd ed. (New York: Macmillan, 1895), 2:258.

66. Michael Schudson, *The Good Citizen: A History of American Civic Life* (Cambridge, MA: Harvard University Press, 1999), p. 223. See pages 223–28 for a discussion of the role of polling as part of public debate. For a complete discussion of the role of public opinion polling as a means of ascertaining thought, see Theodore L. Glasser and Charles T. Salmon, eds., *Public Opinion and the Communication of Consent* (New York: Guilford, 1995).

67. Glasser and Salmon, *Public Opinion and the Communication of Consent,* p. 444.

68. Not all people agree that polling allows for public debate and for the will of the people to direct policy. For some general comments about how polling limits, not enhances, public debate, see James W. Carey, "The Press and the Public Discourse," *Kettering Review* (Winter 1992): 9–22.

69. Dizard, *Old Media, New Media,* p. 162.

70. Richard, "Cuba's Newest Information War."

71. See Julianne Schultz, *Reviving the Fourth Estate: Democracy, Accountability, and the Fourth Estate* (Cambridge: Cambridge University Press, 1998).

72. Waisbord, *Watchdog Journalism in South America,* p. xix.

73. Waisbord, *Watchdog Journalism in South America,* p. 5.

74. For example, see *New-York Weekly Journal,* 17 December 1733, and 7 October 1734. In the first of these papers, a potential alliance with France—Britain's enemy—was described in detail. In the second, the *Journal* reported a rigged election. Both were considered to be the work of the Cosby administration.

75. John Holt to Samuel Adams, 29 January 1776, cited in Arthur M. Schlesinger, *Prelude to Independence: The Newspaper War on Britain, 1764–1776* (New York: Random House, 1958), p. 284.

76. See David Copeland, "'Join, or Die': America's Newspapers in the French and Indian War," *Journalism History* 24 (1998): 117.

77. Stephens, *History of News,* p. 242.

78. Pamela Newkirk, "Ida B. Wells-Barnett: Journalism as a Weapon against Racial Bigotry," *Media Studies Journal* (Spring–Summer 2000): 26–31.

79. Pierce, *Keeping the Flame,* p. 216.

80. Waisbord, *Watchdog Journalism in South America,* p. 170; Pierce, *Keeping the Flame,* p. 215.

81. Waisbord, *Watchdog Journalism in South America,* pp. 32, 37–38.

82. Fuller, *News Values,* p. 69.

83. Pierce, *Keeping the Flame,* p. 213.

84. Leonard, *News for All,* p. xiii.

85. Copeland, "'Join, or Die,'" p. 116.

86. Alfred Stephan, *The Military in Politics: Changing Patterns in Brazil* (Princeton, NJ: Princeton University Press, 1971).

87. Thomas C. Leonard, *The Power of the Press: The Birth of American Political Reporting* (New York: Oxford University Press, 1986), pp. 137–65; Leonard, *News for All,* p. 117.

88. See Bernell Tripp, *Origins of the Black Press: New York, 1827–1847* (Northport, AL: Vision, 1992); Jane Rhodes, *Mary Ann Shadd Cary: The Black Press and Protest in the Nineteenth Century* (Bloomington: University of Indiana Press, 1998).

89. Frank Luther Mott, *A History of American Magazines, 1741–1850* (Cambridge, MA: Harvard University Press, 1966), p. 342.

90. Leonard, *News for All,* p. 136.

91. *New-York Gazette,* 22 January 1750.

92. Cited in Rutherford, *Victorian Authority,* p. 3.

93. Robert U. Brown, "Latin Press Thriving: Report," *Editor and Publisher,* 8 March 1997, p. 12.

94. Charles E. Swanson, "Midcity Daily: What the People Think a Newspapers Should Be," *Journalism Quarterly* 26 (1949): 172–80.

95. Jay Rosen, "Making Journalism More Public," *Communication* 12 (1991): 14. Numerous articles and books have been published on the function and practice of community or civic journalism. For example, see Jay Rosen, *Getting the Connections Right: Public Journalism and the Troubles of the Press* (New York: Twentieth Century Fund, 1996); Jock Lauterer, *Community Journalism: The Personal Approach* (Ames: Iowa State University Press, 1995).

96. Paul Malamud, "Civic Journalism: An Antidote to Apathy?" *Issues of Democracy* 1, no. 8 (1996): 30.

97. Cited in Valerie Kruetzer, "Media Said to Have Crucial Role in Building Community," *Civitas*, 30 September 1996, at http:www.civnet.org/civitas/panam/dispatch/dis1.htm (February 2002).

98. Martin Baron, "Covering a New America: How Multicultural Communities Are Shaping the Future of Journalism" (paper presented at the Association for Education in Journalism and Mass Communication Annual Convention, Washington, DC, August 7, 2001).

99. William Allen White, *Autobiography of William Allen White*, ed. Sally Foreman Griffith (Lawrence: University of Kansas Press, 1990), p. 143.

100. Fuller, *News Values*, pp. 69–70.

101. Daniel Frohman, *Hints to Advertisers* (1869), cited in Frank Presbrey, *The History and Development of Advertising* (Garden City, NY: Doubleday, 1929), p. 256.

102. Brown, "Latin Press Thriving," p. 13.

103. The Veronis, Suhler and Associates, "Communications Industry Forecast 1999–2003," in *Media/Impact: An Introduction into Mass Media*, 5th ed., Shirley Biagi (Belmont, CA: Wadsworth, 2001), pp. 228, 239.

104. See Nicholas Negroponte, *Being Digital* (New York: Knopf, 1995).

105. Dizard, *Old Media, New Media*, p. 165.

Chapter 9

Newspapers in the Twentieth Century

Agnes Hooper Gottlieb

November 22, 1963, is a day that looms large in the collective memory of the American people. And while its significance in the long and complicated history of the United States is probably minimal, it is a day of extreme importance in the story of newspapers in the twentieth century. On the afternoon that President John F. Kennedy was shot in a motorcade that was winding its way through the streets of Dallas, the American people laid to rest finally the notion that newspapers were the purveyor in information for the nation. Indeed, final editions of newspapers on the West Coast reflected the American tragedy and some newspapers on the East Coast published special editions. Forty years later, those papers are collector's items. But on the day of the event, their impact was insignificant. It was television's coming-out party. Technology assured that within minutes of the shooting, the people around the world were alerted.[1] Americans by the millions sat glued to their televisions, watching the story of a beloved president and the fairy-tale existence of his Camelot fall apart. Two days later, the drama accelerated when the man arrested for the assassination was himself gunned down on live television. Not only America, but the entire technologically advanced world was hooked.

In the years since the Kennedy assassination, other international events captured the attention of an international audience—the explosion of the *Challenger* space shuttle, the death of Princess Diana of England, the airplane crash that claimed the life of President Kennedy's charming son—but none could match the global reaction most recently to the twenty-first century's cataclysmic event: the terrorist destruction of New York City's World Trade Center. In each of these events, newspapers were extraneous, the conveyor of in-depth, yet oftentimes out-of-date, information nearly twenty-four hours removed from the event itself.

After the Kennedy assassination, the admonition to newspapers was clear, or at least it should have been: They had no choice but to change to stay competitive in the information and communication market that now included both the audio and the visual. But trying to make an institution as unwieldy as the fourth estate rethink its purpose and its direction was never easy. And while the American newspaper was only one component—dominant though it was—of the global perspective, its struggle to maintain supremacy and hold off competition in an increasingly technological world market was a central theme throughout the twentieth century.

Initially, newspapers perceived a threat to readership from the radio, then concern centered on the movies and their related newsreels. After World War II, the threat appeared in the form of television. Finally, in the last decade of the century, traditional newspapers were challenged by the Internet. Each of these new technologies should have provided an opportunity to newspapers to re-examine their purpose and rearticulate their goals, but in reality the emersion of a new technology usually just forced newspapers to attempt to fend off the challenge with little introspection.

As a result, newspapers at the end of the twentieth century continued to be an endangered species. Indeed, they even looked almost identical to newspapers at the beginning of the century. The *New York Times*'s front page in 1901 chronicling the shooting of President William McKinley varies little in form and content from a paper produced 100 years later. There is some comfort in that. Yes, the development of color in 1982 in *USA Today* ultimately prompted all American newspapers and many international papers to make the transition. But color aside, what newspapers perceived as news, how they covered it, and what it looked like in the newspaper changed little during the century. While technological advances swirled around them, newspapers held a steady course.

The most obvious change in Western newspapers came not from how news was gathered and presented, but how news was written within the newsroom and how news was printed in the composing room. The tap-tap of typewriters and clatter of wire service Teletypes gave way in the 1970s and 1980s to a more silent newsroom where reporters worked on computer, and wire service copy was delivered directly into computers. And while the twentieth century itself was marked indelibly as the most technologically transforming era in the history of the world, for newspapers the century was a story of missed opportunities and the slow erosion of a reading public. Former British Prime Minister Margaret Thatcher states the problem succinctly: "Television has changed everything."[2] And media mogul Rupert Murdoch observed in 1985, "Newspapers are under threat all over the world from electronic competition, and in many countries there is a decline of readership. The greatest asset newspapers have is the habit factor."[3]

In many countries, that habit was dying as the television generation came of age. The *St. Petersburg Times,* published in the retirement Mecca of the United

States, is one of the most well-read and absorbed papers in the United States. But throughout the developed world, newspaper circulation has been in decline for decades. France's circulation crested in 1950, Australia in 1956, Great Britain in 1957, the United States in 1971, and Japan in 1981.[4] It was a phenomenon that was apparent throughout the world. In China, 93.5 percent of the residents of Beijing watch television every day, but only 64 percent read newspapers. And in the rural outreaches of China, the country's 3,000 television stations are king. In rural and poor nations of Africa, where a reading culture is not predominant, radio reigns supreme. In Tanzania, for example, the cost of a newspaper is about 25 cents, while half the residents live on less than a dollar a day.[5] The poor in the nation prefer to eat, rather than read.

By the end of the twentieth century, the world's newspaper capitals, based on the number of newspapers and their quality, included New York, London, Paris, Moscow, Amsterdam, Copenhagen, Stockholm, Brussels, Rome, Hamburg, Vienna, Zurich, Beijing, Tokyo, Cairo, Johannesburg, Toronto, Melbourne, Havana, Mexico City, Rio de Janeiro, Buenos Aires, and Bogotá.[6] And while the world's shift away from communism at the end of the century did much to further the cause of press freedom around the globe, freedom of the press, considered sacrosanct in the United States and other democracies, was a much debated and often controversial topic.

The century was punctuated not only by harsh criticism of the press and related news media, but the readers themselves, the consumers of news through various media, also carried part of the blame. "As if by instinct, human beings seek to satisfy a basic need to know. And just as persistently, the power-hungry hoard the news or connive to control its flow. The particulars of this tug-of-war change, but the dynamic doesn't."[7] News organizations wrestled with the need to cover important, but dry, world events, but peppered their newspapers with sensationalistic drivel that audiences loved.

This chapter looks at the trends in the newspaper industry during the twentieth century and explores some of the reasons why, despite the industry's rosy predictions of continued health, readers are looking elsewhere for the information they need.

THE TWENTIETH CENTURY IN PERSPECTIVE

The story of newspapers in the twentieth century is very much the stories of the emergence of electronic technologies that threatened newspapers, the ongoing debate about press freedom, and the globalization of news. As the renowned columnist Walter Lippmann observed in 1941, man was "learning to see with his mind vast portions of the world that he could never see, touch, smell, hear, or remember. Gradually he makes for himself a trustworthy picture inside his head of the world beyond his reach."[8] Of course, this newfound capability was linked to the continuing reliance on electronic technologies. When the twentieth century dawned, newspapers around the globe were flourishing in their golden age. In the United States and the West, newspapers were increasingly relying on new technologies to routinize how they gathered news and what that news looked like when it was presented in print.

The first major technological advance in the gathering of news actually had occurred some sixty years before with the invention of the telegraph in the nineteenth century. This invention fostered the establishment of international news agencies to aid in the dissemination of distant news stories, which in turn contributed to the globalization of news. Reuters, Agence France-Presse, the Associated Press, and others became powerful forces in the distribution of news to many countries of the world during the twentieth century. In 1931, one pundit predicted, inaccurately it appears through hindsight, "These international highways to better understanding should bring peoples the knowledge that alone can make the world an enlightened neighborhood of nations."[9] The use of undersea cables gave way to satellite and internet technologies, which did much to spread the Western perspective of news to all the world's continents and perpetuate the Western dominance of the flow of news. This has not been without criticism. During the 1980s, debate raged around the world, especially through the forum of the United Nations, against the "communication domination by the West." The New World Information Order, as envisioned and supported by developing nations, proposed information sharing to make the press in the developing world "partners rather than...helpless consumers."[10] This issue was unresolved at the end of the century.

While the story of technology very much characterizes the story of newspapers around the world during the twentieth century, there were numerous trends that affected both news and readership. By the end of the century, there were 8,391 daily newspapers in the world, with a combined circulation of 548 million, a circulation total of 96 per 1,000 inhabitants.[11] The number of daily newspapers around the world actually peaked at 8,445 in 1985 while the combined circulation crested in 1992 at 575 million. Thus, the story at the end of the twentieth century was of an institution in decline. And while the number of newspapers actually increased again during the 1990s, readership figures and circulation per 1,000 inhabitants never returned to the peak levels in 1980. What caused the downward spiral at the end of the century? Did that spiral signal the ultimate demise of newspapers? Before we can consider what the statistics mean, we need to consider what trends molded and affected newspapers and their readers during the century.

More than any other century in the history of newspapers, the twentieth century was marked by trends that affected readership. Sometimes the trends were technologically driven, sometimes they were the result of social phenomena, and sometimes they were driven by world events. A prime example of the changing nature of newspaper readership was the rise and fall of the afternoon newspaper in the United States during the twentieth century. It was a trend affected by technology, society, and world events. When the century dawned, afternoon newspapers were an established, but relatively young, phenomenon. The reading public liked the habit of passing an evening at home with newspaper in hand. Wide-scale electrification of America had made reading at night feasible. The country was becoming more urban. Workers began commuting from suburban outposts into nearby cities, often on public transportation. This daily commute made it possible, and indeed desirable, to read to pass the time. The afternoon newspapers were easily distributed in urban centers to commuters heading home from work. They contained up-to-date information about sporting events that had occurred during the daytime, financial listings, and news of the day. Newspapers were the primary conveyance of all this information.

The downward spiral began slowly after World War II. During the 1950s, television emerged as a favorite evening activity. From a mere 8,000 television sets in the United States in 1945 to 55 million sets around the country by 1960, the broadcast medium exploded.[12] The term "prime time" in fact referred to the precious hours after dinner that previously had been spent with evening newspaper in hand. In addition, increased traffic congestion in urban areas meant that newspaper delivery trucks had difficulty getting the afternoon newspaper to its destination at newsstands and news deliverers' homes. The ability to play sports in the evening under lights meant that sports fans no longer needed to get the day's scores at 6 P.M. Television news was especially effective in its coverage of the Vietnam War, which was sometimes referred to as America's first television war. The uncensored footage that exposed the American people for the first time to the true horrors of war has been credited by some, especially the military, with contributing to the United States' failure in Vietnam. No one factor killed the afternoon newspaper, but all of these factors converged to ensure the demise of the afternoon or evening newspaper.

This trend coincided with and affected the downsizing of newspapers in urban areas. Throughout the United States, cities slowly lost the competitive newspaper spirit and often were streamlined into one-newspaper towns in places like Newark, New Jersey, and Baltimore, Maryland. New York City went from nine major dailies in 1947 to just three in 1990, and circulation slipped from 10.1 million to 3.5 million. But, just as city papers closed, newspapers took advantage of an increasingly suburban population. While city newspapers folded, suburban newspapers were launched.

For the century that was the most violent since people started keeping track of such things, it is not surprising that circulation trends were affected by war. This phenomenon started in England with the Crimean War and in the United States with the Civil War. New York newspapers spent big to cover that war and reaped the return in terms of soaring circulations. Newspapers were the only game in town—that is, the only way to follow war developments of battles that were happening far away. Coverage of the Great War, as it was called at the time, was not much different. The reporters were more professional, better trained, and adept at new technologies, like the typewriter and the telephone, which were unheard of during the Civil War. From 1914, audiences exhibited a hearty appetite for war news and newspapers responded by increasing their pages.[13]

That trend continued throughout the century. While World War II saw the emergence of radio as a vehicle for disseminating war news, newspapers of the world were still seen as the primary conveyor of news. In fact, World War II coverage around the world cemented the importance of the global citizen with knowledge of foreign news. "As the world has been drawn closer together in the physical realm, political schisms at any point have taken on importance all around the globe. Foreign news is less 'foreign' in its influence on people's lives."[14] The violence of war translated throughout the century into higher circulations around the globe. "[W]ar is cruel, bloody and destructive.... Its reporting, however, makes brilliant news: it offers excitement, anxiety and horror and sometimes exultation or despair."[15] Unfortunately, it was not just the violence of war, but violence in general that often translated into higher readerships.

Sometimes, in fact, it has been called "jazz journalism," but it is really just another snazzy word for sensationalism. One trend that carried throughout the century and pervaded newspapers around the world was readers' love affair with violence, the bizarre, the outlandish, the sexy, and, indeed, the sensational. The old saying held true: "When dog bites man, that's not news, but when man bites dog, that is." Readers might complain that the press is too sensational, but editors know that outrageous, screaming headlines sell newspapers.

The trend toward sensationalism was not new. Nineteenth-century editors regularly lamented the dependence on the sensational, while mainstream editors at the beginning of the twentieth century sharply criticized the recent emergence of a brand of newspaper writing, dubbed "yellow journalism," which was more concerned with making a splash than sticking to the facts. In England, the trend was called "gutter journalism," but whatever the term, it was indeed an international trend.

Historians generally agree that publisher William Randolph Hearst's *New York Journal* fueled the growth of yellow journalism in the final years of the nineteenth century when he threw restraint into the wind in his circulation battle with Joseph Pulitzer's *New York World*. The term "yellow journalism" is traced to the little cartoon urchin the *Yellow Kid*, whose antics were published in both papers and symbolized the devil-may-care attitude toward newspaper ethics and restraint.

Throughout the twentieth century, the definition of what was news broadened to explore the private lives, including sexual and personal habits, of politicians, athletes, royalty, and movie stars around the world. Anyone was fair game, including former U.S. President Bill Clinton, who nearly was booted from office because of his sexual escapades in the Oval Office with a White House intern. It was a century when pop artist Andy Warhol suggested that everyone should have fifteen minutes of fame and the roll was legion with people who did: Barney Clark, Megan Marshak, Donna Rice, Christina Crawford, Ivana Trump, Dodi Al Fayed, and others.

Tabloid newspapers were especially susceptible to charges of sensationalism, from the British dailies' constant hounding of Princess Diana and her reputed lovers, to the famed *New York Daily News* headline when President Gerald Ford failed to relieve the city's financial crisis in the October 30, 1975, edition: "Ford to City: Drop Dead." London was especially noted for its popular but trashy tabloids that tracked down scandals wherever they could be found. The public might have been quick to criticize the excesses of the tabloid press, but readers ate it up. Circulation among the scandal sheets was always high. The weekly *News of the World* topped the British charts, for example, with a circulation of 4.4 million.[16] The lines between news and entertainment blurred; the term "infotainment" came in vogue. The venerable dean of the American news media, Walter Cronkite, blamed the confusion over the fact that broadcast news organizations shifted from money-losing divisions of a network to profit centers some time in the 1980s.[17] How broadcast went, print surely followed.

Just as newspapers in the twentieth century were accused of sensational and tabloid tactics, they also were recognized for their crusading fervor and sense of social responsibility. Indeed, the model most emulated and imitated was the social responsibility model of many American newspapers. From the beginning of the century, reform writers focused on problems in the United States, especially where urban sprawl and political corruption deprived residents of a safe environment. These writers were dubbed the muckrakers by then President Theodore Roosevelt, who meant the reference derogatorily when he compared them to the man who raked the muck in the allegory *Pilgrim's Progress*. The writers were not dissuaded by his distain. Muckraking flourished in the United States and took many forms, from writers like Ida Tarbell who focused on the great monopoly Standard Oil to the municipal housekeepers who wrote about threats to the health and life of women and children in the cities.

While the spirit of reform writing ebbed somewhat with the coming of international unrest and the Great War, newspapers in the United States continued to embrace their status as the "fourth estate," a reference to media's power alongside the legislative, the executive, and the judicial branches of government. Newspapers lobbied for decades and eventually gained access to a plethora of government records through the Freedom of Information Act, which was passed and signed into law in 1966.

The watchdog role of the press was highlighted in the late 1960s when newspapers and broadcast outlets, critical of U.S. involvement in the Vietnam War, waged what amounted to a publicity campaign by exposing to the American public the realities of war. Then, in 1972 the American press once again challenged government authority in what has come to be known as the Watergate scandal. There, two reporters for the *Washington Post* exposed a pattern of government wrongdoing and ultimately toppled the administration of President Richard Nixon, who resigned in disgrace in 1974. Since that time, newspapers and broadcast media continued in the spirit that the fundamental tenet of press freedom is that the people have a right to know. That social responsibility aspect of the press was one of the four generally recognized press theories that flourished during the century.

For the press in the developing world, the century was marked by a series of bad news headlines: "Famine in Ethiopia"; "Tyrannical Ravings in Uganda"; "Earthquakes in Mexico City, Nicaragua and Costa Rica." How and when the international press chooses what to cover has caused harsh criticism, especially among developing nations. As nations turned to industrial technology and as even remote areas of the globe were touched by communication advances, the world's people became increasingly interested in news. How the news was conveyed varied throughout the developing world. For many of the most remote and poorest nations, radio was the medium of choice. It was relatively inexpensive, accessible to those who were illiterate, and easily beamed to even the most rural of communities. Still, not all the world's citizens are convinced of the need to know what is happening. In Tanzania, where the middle class relies on television and newspapers, "the vast majority of Tanzanians are completely out of the picture. In the general elections last October, some rural folk were asked to register to vote for president and members of parliament. 'I know who the president is,' said a peasant. 'It is Nyerere, of course!' he said, meaning Tanzania's former president, who died the year before but had retired from the presidency in 1985."[18]

While television and radio came of age during the century, newspapers in the developing world increased in power, readership, and circulation. In some places, like Tanzania and Nigeria, newspapers were seen as the vehicles of the rich. "For Nigeria's ordinary people, print is problematic for several reasons: incessant cover price increases, low purchasing power, the low level of formal education."[19]

Initiatives by international organizations especially after World War II focused on the education of journalists in developing nations and a critique of how these countries were covered by Western journalists. Both of these contributed to an introspective period of self-study in which Western newspapers and broadcast outlets carefully scrutinized the patronizing, often negative way developing nations were covered. As developing nations achieved better access to Western technologies, an increase in the numbers of newspapers and their circulations soon followed. The UN Educational, Scientific, and Cultural Organization's statistics note that in 1970 there were 2,681 daily newspapers in developing countries. That figure increased to 4,419 by 1996, more than half the daily newspapers in the world, with a circulation of 272 million, again nearly half of the world's newspaper circulation. And the challenges to the developing nations' press were great. More than in Western nations, where citizens tend to have the habit of reading, press in developing nations must convince people with oral traditions, who naturally gravitate toward television and radio, of the subtle benefits of reading a newspaper.

Press freedom, one of the recurring themes throughout the century, has fluctuated greatly with first the rise and then the fall of communism in Eastern Europe. By the end of the twentieth century, the great experiment had toppled in
most countries that had embraced communism. Most dramatically, the breakup
of the Soviet Union gave new life to Russia's newspapers. For as far back as
Henry VIII in England, world leaders recognized that a strong, independent
press posed a constant threat to their power. Thus, most of the century in the
Communist world translated into a period of stringent press control. Indeed, in
the countries that remained Communist, that control has continued. "The Chinese Media, all under government control, are expected to be the mouthpieces
of the Communist Party and the government."[20] This presents a problem for
the Chinese press, because while they are forced to be the mouthpiece of government, they also are expected to entertain. The media in China must straddle
this dual role.

In fact, many attribute the fall of communism in the Soviet bloc in a large
part to the role the media played as mouthpieces of government. "The citizens
in these countries lost whatever faith they may have once had in the system because they could see that reality didn't correspond with what they were told
about reality," one writer muses.[21] Since the fall of communism in 1989, however, the road to press freedom has been rocky. Western journalists, especially
Americans, assumed the new found press freedom in the Soviet bloc would
translate into an imitation of the "objectivity model" they themselves avowed.
"For some of the post communist political leaders, freedom of the press did not
necessarily mean objectivity. Sometimes their view of freedom of speech meant
freedom of speech for themselves, not for their opponents."[22] The growth of the
press in Poland after the fall, for example, was informed by the hundreds of
underground informal newsletters that flourished surreptitiously during the
1980s. While these were printed on mimeograph machines and circulated by
hand, some of them successfully transformed into respected mass circulations
newspapers during the 1990s.

The story is not entirely rosy, however. In Serbia, for example, efforts to
loosen state control on the press were met with many casualties. "Journalists
continue to be harassed, jailed, and killed. News outlets are peremptorily shut
down. Valiant attempts to break away from state-controlled news media are
met with repressive laws that censor, fabricate charges of criminal libel, or block
legitimate applications for broadcast frequencies."[23]

Newspapers also grappled throughout the century with social, economic, and
technical developments that some perceived as threats to their readership. The
dawn of the twentieth century also saw the rudimentary beginnings of an international radio industry. Its initial impact on newspapers and their readers
was unclear. The end of the same century was punctuated by a fear that the Internet and the trend toward online newspapers could be signaling the death
knell for newspapers as we have known them for centuries. That fear appears at
this time to be premature, but the attempt by newspapers to ensure their

presence in the Internet revolution was reminiscent of the scramble by publishers when radio appeared.

The loss of readers translates directly into a loss of advertising dollars, and
newspapers were already stinging from a decline in their share of ad revenue
even before the Internet emerged as a major distraction, and indeed, serious
competitor. In North America, newspapers' ad revenue share dropped from 41
percent in 1985 to 37 percent in 1998, while the share in Europe fell from 44
percent to 38 percent. While that still represents an enormous chunk of ad dollars, given the competing media, which include magazines, television, radio, and
the Internet, newspaper publishers understood that the Internet was a medium
on the upswing whose full potential as a competitor was unclear as the century
ended. Perhaps its potential for most serious damage is in the area of classified
advertising. The World Association of Newspapers notes that "[p]rojections of
explosive growth in the online audience have led some to an impending sense
of doom for the future of print advertising."[24]

Newspapers have been relatively quick to provide both print and online publication of consumer classified ads in an effort to maintain the backbone of their
advertising dollars. The World Association of Newspapers notes that newspapers around the world have actually benefited from the U.S. experience by setting an aggressive tone for advertising their sites. While U.S. sites like Yahoo
and Netscape provide entry portals for Internet users, in Europe national newspapers have taken the lead in this area. Still, the profitability of online journalism has yet to be proven.[25] Despite the streamlined costs of production and
distribution, newspapers have been thwarted by the Internet practice of giving
away for free what costs money in print.

As one observer notes, "Imagine a library that carries the equivalent of 4,925
daily newspapers from all over the globe. Stop imagining: it's here."[26] Newspapers, unwilling to be left behind, are intricately involved in this second communication revolution that involves the convergence of media. What remains
to be seen is whether they can adapt to the new technologies or adapt the new
technologies to fit their needs. Whatever the case, the story of newspapers
around the world does not end with the twentieth century. There is more to un-
fold and much more to be written.

NOTES

1. Bernard Moore, *Workers in World News* (Oxford: Pergamon, 1969), p. 16.

2. Specifically, Thatcher is referring to the coverage of war by the media. She is cited
in Miles Hudson and John Stanier, *War and the Media* (New York: New York University Press, 1998), p. 303.

3. Cited in Peter J. S. Dunnett, *The World Newspaper Industry* (New York: Croom
Helm, 1988), p. 1.

4. Dunnett, *World Newspaper Industry*, p. 2.

5. Adam Lusekelo, "Tanzania: Poverty and the Press," *World Press Review Online*, at http://www.worldpress.org/specials/press/tanzania.htm (October 10, 2002).

6. John C. Merrill, *Global Journalism: A Survey of the World's Mass Media* (New York: Longman, 1983), p. 38.

7. "Hungry for News," *World Press Review Online*, at http://www.worldpress.org/specials/press/front.htm (October 10, 2002).

8. Walter Lippmann, "The Pictures inside Our Heads," an excerpt from *Public Opinion*, cited in George L. Bird and Frederic E. Merwin, *The Newspaper and Society* (New York: Prentice-Hall, 1942), p. 4.

9. Charles Hodges, "How World Press Horizons Have Broadened," excerpt from *The Background of International Relations* (1931), cited in Bird and Merwin, *Newspaper and Society*, p. 242.

10. Merrill, *Global Journalism*, p. 51.

11. World press statistics can be found at http://www.uis.unesco.org/statsen/statistics/yearbook/tables/CultAndCom/Table_IV_S_1.html (October 10, 2002).

12. Michael Emery and Edwin Emery, *The Press and America: An Interpretive History of the Mass Media* (Boston: Allyn and Bacon, 1996), p. 376.

13. Frank Luther Mott, *American Journalism: A History, 1690–1960* (New York: MacMillan, 1962), p. 632.

14. International Press Institute, *The Flow of News* (New York: Arno, 1972), p. 7.

15. Hudson and Stanier, *War and the Media*, p. xii.

16. Brian McNair, *The Sociology of Journalism* (New York: Arnold, 1998), p. 107.

17. McNair, *Sociology of Journalism*, p. 121.

18. Adam Lusekelo, "Tanzania: Poverty and the Press," *World Press Review Online*, at http://www.worldpress.org/specials/press/tanzania.htm (October 10, 2002).

19. Babafemi Ojudu, "Getting the News in Nigeria," *World Press Review Online*, at http://www.worldpress.org/specials/press/nigeria.htm (October 10, 2002).

20. Xiong Lei, "China: TV Dominates Information Sources," *World Press Review Online*, at http://www.worldpress.org/specials/press/china.htm (October 10, 2002).

21. Owen V. Johnson, "Power from the People: News Media in and about East Central Europe," *Media Studies Journal* (Fall 1999): 190.

22. Johnson, "Power from the People," p. 198.

23. Jerome Aumente, "Struggles for Independent Journalism: Ten Years of Learning and Teaching, from Poland to Yugoslavia," *Media Studies Journal* (Fall 1999): 167.

24. World Association of Newspapers, *Strength in Numbers: The Challenges for Newspaper Advertising*

25. John V. Pavlik, *Journalism and New Media* (New York: Columbia University Press, 2001), p. 149.

26. Pavlik, *Journalism and New Media*, p. 28.

Chapter 10

American Daily Newspaper Evolution: Past, Present . . . and Future?

Donald L. Shaw and Charles McKenzie

Of all the participants in the news business, none is remotely as committed to covering news as the country's daily papers.

—Leonard Downie Jr. and
Robert G. Kaiser,
"Shoptalk," *Editor and
Publisher,* 18 February 2002, p. 30

One cannot predict a medium's future by looking in a rearview mirror. Still, a look back can tell the type of historical terrain newspapers have traversed and allow you to make guesses about the direction American daily newspapers may take in the future. Newspapers are not just about communication, but are also about community. For more than 300 years, daily and weekly newspapers have been an important part of community life in the United States, and newspapers are likely to remain important in one form or another throughout the twenty-first century. The normative role of newspapers—setting a community agenda—remains essential, but the ways in which the newspapers fulfill this function are in constant transition.[1]

All media are about relationships. We are connected with community by means of our contact with media, including other people, who also are a form of media after all. Communication scholar Keith Stamm argues that children are a "medium of connection" between families and the school system. Similarly, news media connect us to the communities to which we belong, or want to belong. Likewise, the World Wide Web is not just a medium about information but about relationships—a way for individuals to connect with other individuals. Audiences have historically connected with their community by means of newspaper agendas.

Obviously, audiences learn priorities from reading local newspapers. Not as obviously, audiences who are committed to newspapers use newspapers as a surrogate for the community. Audiences who collectively or individually adopt the newspaper agenda of issues as their own, meld with their local community. Sharing media agendas means that different types of people—men versus women, old versus young, rich versus poor—become more focused on the same public issues, suggesting that one function of news media is to draw disparate individuals around selected public issues. That role has been important for American newspapers since our colonial beginning and is likely to remain so in the twenty-first century.

Since 1975, the United States has lost 280 daily newspapers. The 1990s have seen U.S. daily and Sunday circulation decline 1 percent per year. According to the National Newspaper Association, "[a] straight line formula shows that if the 1961 to 1988 trend continues, the year 2078, at the latest, would see the end of daily newspaper reading in the United States. Using the 29 studies available from 1961 to 1997 pushes the predicted drop-dead date out to 2098. In either case, that marks the year when there will be no more daily newspaper readers."[2]

But the future is more than numbers. History suggests newspapers do more than write about a community. In modern times, newspapers have proven important platforms to examine the performance of contemporary institutions, such as the *Washington Post* investigations of the incidents surrounding the Watergate break-in during the administration of President Richard Nixon in the early 1970s. Newspapers reflect the community dynamic, and the future of newspapers is linked to the future of communities. This chapter concentrates on daily newspapers, rather than weekly newspapers, which have an even closer relationship to their local communities.

COMMUNITY MELDING: NEWSPAPERS AND HISTORICAL CONFLICT

Newspapers place community issues on the agenda. Newspapers promote and reflect communities in transition and provide a platform on which community agendas contend for the next level of social development. As part of social evolution, communities could meld around new issues as they emerge, and newspapers are the main medium for local community melding. In the United States, newspapers have evolved with social communities since the 1704 founding of the successful Boston *News-Letter* and have helped readers deal with the local issues of the communities in which they are published. The *New York Times* prides itself on printing all the news that is fit to print, but, as importantly, the *Times, Washington Post, Chicago Tribune, Los Angeles Times,* and several other newspapers serve the normative role of establishing news agendas for both their communities and the nation—and for the television networks and national magazines.

Newspapers set priorities, from front-page headlines to the smallest stories on the last page. This normative function of newspapers has been clear for three centuries, certainly since the early eighteenth century. From roughly 1700 to 1720, printing spread in the colonies. Boston's John Campbell worked with printer Bartholomew Green to publish the *News-Letter,* a newspaper with the running banner "Published by Authority." By the 1720s, however, James Franklin, brother of the far more famous Benjamin Franklin, challenged authorities with stories that were published without authority. Like the emerging Whig editors in London, he used journalistic allegories to criticize government. About 1734, New York printer John Peter Zenger was charged with seditious libel for allegories published—although not written by him—in his *New York Weekly Journal.* The 1735 not-guilty jury verdict suggested that truth might be an acceptable libel defense, a sort of blending of views resulting from three decades of conflict over freedom versus control of public discourse, although colonial legislatures still took a dim view of press criticism. Not until the 1798 Alien and Sedition Acts was truth recognized, if imperfectly and uncertainly prosecuted, as a libel defense at the federal level.

The years from the 1740s to 1760s represented a synthesis of the agendas of authority represented by Campbell and the agendas of protest of the Franklin and Zenger years. In this period, the colonials established better connections with each other via improved mails, with the help of former editors Benjamin Franklin and William Parks, and the economic power of the colonies in the British mercantilist system began to consolidate and grow. Scholar Richard L. Merritt argues that eighteenth-century newspapers reflected the emergence of an American community as news stories reflected an identity independent from England.[3] For example, after the 1750s, journalists used words such as "South Carolina" more than "England" and "governor" more than "king." Later, southern newspapers reflected a region whose beliefs isolated itself from most of the Western world, which had already abandoned slavery.

After 1760, colonials such as propagandist Samuel Adams and journalists such as Isaiah Thomas of Boston's *Massachusetts' Spy* and Benjamin Edes and John Gill's *Boston Gazette* took positions that helped lead the public, gradually, from seeking more political and economic freedom to full independence, the revolution in hearts and minds required for independence, according to historian Arthur Meier Schlesinger Sr.[4] On the other side, editors like New York's James Rivington of the *Gazetteer* and John Mein of the *Boston Chronicle* sought to present a balanced agenda but failed because of a lack of public support, and they eventually fled to British safety.

Revolutionary fighting ended in 1781, with the formal peace treaty signed in 1783, and after a period under the Articles of Confederation, the states joined in union: the United States. The political rhetoric flew fiercely from 1780 to 1800. Federalist editor John Fenno of the *Gazette of the United States* and William Cobbett of the *Porcupine's Gazette* gave little quarter to those who sought to retain more power and authority with the states. Antifederalist editors Philip Freneau of the *National Gazette* and Benjamin Franklin Bache, grandson of Benjamin Franklin, challenged the idea of an overly strong federal union, sometimes with language that even criticized George Washington, the winning general of the Revolution and first president.

Once issues of national freedom—then states' freedom—were ironed out, small groups turned their eyes toward human freedom. In 1827, John B. Russwurm and Samuel Cornish started the first African American newspaper, the short-lived *Freedom's Journal* in New York. In 1831, William Lloyd Garrison, a white abolitionist, published the *Liberator*. In addition to its antislavery writings, the paper included advertisements from black businesses, feature stories, wedding announcements, and church and social group news. The weekly created a community around race. When Cornish started the *Colored American* (1836) and Frederick Douglass began the *North Star* (1847), support for the *Liberator* waned. By the 1850s, there were more than twenty newspapers that focused on antislavery. In 1905, the *Chicago Defender* debuted, later including Langston Hughes's famous "James B. Semple" column. The African American newspaper tradition was followed by African American magazines like W. E. B. Du Bois's the *Crisis* and John Johnson's *Negro Digest* and *Ebony* as well as other forms of media. Other minority groups formed their own tradition. In 1808, a Spanish-language newspaper formed in New Orleans, and even Benjamin Franklin helped found the continent's first non-English newspaper, *Philadelphische Zeitung* in German. Just a year after the debut of *Freedom's Journal*, Elias Boudinot created the first Native American newspaper, the *Cherokee Phoenix*.

In the middle of the nineteenth century, female journalists started writing about civil rights not only for African Americans, but also for women. Elizabeth Cady Stanton wrote for suffrage newspapers the *Lily* and the *Revolution*. Later, *St. Cloud Visitor/Democrat* (Minnesota) founder Jane Grey Swisshelm was such a champion for women's and slaves' rights that her press was destroyed. When reporter Nellie Bly was cutting her journalistic teeth, the rare women journalists, or "girl reporters," as they were called, were usually relegated to the society or arts and entertainment pages. Bly wrote exposé after exposé until she reached Joseph Pulitzer's *New York World*, where her own international celebrity status was soon displayed as prominently as her stories' headlines. She once went undercover in an insane asylum, and in 1889 she sailed around the world in seventy-two days, her own version of Jules Verne's tale *Around the World in 80 Days*, reporting from each romantic stop. These groundbreaking women reporters set the tone for future crusading reporters such as Alice Stone Blackwell for women's right to vote, Ida B. Wells against lynching, Ida Tarbell about Standard Oil Co., Margaret Sanger for birth control, and Gloria Steinem for feminism. With civil unrest bubbling in the cities, newspapers had shown that they could adapt to social change. It would be irresponsible to say that newspapers led the fight for equal rights or to posit that publishers reached out to untapped market fragments for purely altruistic reasons, but once these social issues were championed by newspapers, they found their way onto national and community agendas. These narrow-cast newspapers paved the way for special-interest magazines and other media to come. Historically, newspapers have been an important part of community building. Then, as now, newspapers provided an arena in which public agendas could compete, and new political ideas could emerge.

The work of German philosopher and historian George Hegel suggests a historical pattern in which an idea takes root (thesis) but attracts a challenger (antithesis) and the two ideas evolve through competition. The new idea that emerges (the synthesis) represents the new thesis, and then the process repeats until the end of time. Part of a romantic philosophical and historical challenge to the fixed, orderly Newtonian world, Hegel sees this thesis-antithesis-synthesis cycle as representing a kind of progress in human society. With Hegel, social systems have a life of their own. One can hypothesize this dynamic in newspaper history of the eighteenth century, and today's media history as well. One can sketch the 1700s something like what Figure 10.1 shows.

There is another side to change: stability. While Hegel examines social change in terms of conflict, twentieth-century sociologist Talcott Parsons sees social change in terms of stability and endurance. If we substitute newspapers for Parsons's society, newspapers minimize disruptive forces (magazines, television, Internet, conglomerations, and societal change) on a day-to-day basis because conservative audience and journalistic patterns, particularly shared norms and news values, resist sweeping changes. For example, the popularity of television news did not mean the death of newspapers, as some media futurists predicted. Instead, newspapers evolved, like society.

Scholar Harold Lasswell writes that the press performs the functions of surveillance, correlation of the parts of society, and transmission of the social

Figure 10.1
1700–1800—Public Issues of Place

John Campbell   J. Franklin, J.P. Zenger

"Published by authority"   v.   Challenge to Authority

    Trade and improved   v.   Independence seeking

    postal connections   ↓

    Federalist Newspapers   v. Anti-federalist Newspapers

Alien and Sedition Acts (1798-1801)

inheritance of the community. Contemporary social research demonstrates that newspaper readers do seem to pull together as a result of sharing a common public agenda, almost as if that is an unstated function of newspapers. Still, newspapers, like other institutions, struggle to thrive and even survive, regardless of their ability to highlight community issues and work as an evolutionary force in a larger society that is faced with media choices every day.

ECONOMIC ADAPTATION: NEWSPAPERS AND MEDIA COMPETITION

Challenges to newspapers—legal, political, or commercial—are nothing new. Clearly, newspapers' historical adaptations also have helped them to compete with new forms of media and have forced newspapers to alter content or approaches to gathering and presenting news. One can argue that newspapers were the predominant medium from about 1700 to 1870, when magazines, with the spread of railroads, could achieve national circulation for news and advertising. By the end of the nineteenth century, newspapers responded to differences in audiences, a process begun with the penny press in the 1830s, and adapted news and comment to fit readers from the working class to the elite business, political, and cultural classes. With Edward Lawrence Godkin, founder of the *Nation* (1866), one could see that journalists had secured a normative role as interpreter of modern life, a role played throughout the twentieth century and into the present one.

The 1844 telegraph, soon used by the Associated Press, brought news of events to readers within hours or days, not months as in the previous century. Publishers and editors experimented with evolving technologies. The 1887 Linotype, invented by German Ottmar Mergenthaler, eliminated the need to select type letter by letter by hand, thereby cutting production time significantly. The telephone enabled reporters to call in facts from the police station or elsewhere. The rewrite man (and woman) appeared. Other developments, such as the camera, color, and typographical innovations, allowed Pulitzer and William Randolph Hearst to publish, respectively, the *New York World* and *New York Journal* for an audience of working-class people and immigrants not yet ready to graduate to the more expensive magazines. Newspapers engaged in a new journalism to meet the competition from magazines. The daily press achieved the highest circulation up to that point in history, reaching more than a million on some days during the period of the 1898 Spanish-American War. Confronted with special interest magazines, newspapers sought more profitable market niches. It was not to be the last time newspapers adjusted to the news competition.

Journalism historian Frank Luther Mott's five-volume history of magazines shows that there was an explosion of magazines in the late nineteenth century.[5] The twentieth century saw the growth of powerful national mass magazines, such as *Time* (1923), *Reader's Digest* (1925), and others that reached millions to help shape the culture. From 1870 to 1940, magazines like *Life* (1936) and *Look* (1937) powerfully competed with newspapers, which adapted to the challenge of magazines. Unlike newspapers, these national magazines did not focus on local news. They fit almost every conceivable interest or demographic group—women, socialists, African Americans, baseball enthusiasts, and film buffs—in all the special interest classes—with that word construed broadly—into which humans fit. As media grew aware of fragmented audiences, newspapers, like magazines, created sections to reach out to these previously unrecognized demographic sectors. Newspapers systematized, adding regular beats for different sports, women, and professions and offering more feature content such as entertainment reviews, panel cartoons like the *Yellow Kid,* crossword puzzles, and advice and gossip columns.

By the end of the 1930s, Americans told the new public opinion surveyors, like George Gallup, the Crossley Company, and others, that they used radio as their major news medium. Newspapers sought more depth and objectivity. The *New York Times* reflected an increase in the use of bylines, which represented an increase of journalistic professionalism, which might also have been a reflection of the growing numbers of university schools and departments of journalism. The same decade saw Northwestern University professor Curtis MacDougall publish *Interpretative Reporting,* the first journalism textbook with "interpretive" in the title. In *Discovering the News,* sociologist Michael Schudson argues that modern models of newspaper objectivity are an outgrowth of this period in which the contemporary social sciences suggested that journalists could achieve more professional levels. In the 1940s, the Commission on Freedom of the Press encouraged continuation of the trend toward depth by the news media, especially print media.[6]

Television, like radio, spread rapidly in the United States and by the late 1950s audiences used television as the major source of national and international news. In the early 1960s, Columbia Broadcasting System (CBS) offered a longer regular evening newscast. Newspapers, as usual, evolved to adjust to the loss of newspaper readers during the prime-time hours in a variety of ways. One causality, over time, was the afternoon newspaper. In 1960, afternoon papers (1,763) outnumbered morning papers (312), but by 2000, the morning papers pulled ahead (776 to 727). This probably reflected changes in the workplace—for example, the decline of blue-collar workers—and not just media competition. In the last forty years of the millennium, the total daily circulation dropped 3.1 million, according to the National Newspaper Association, a figure more staggering when considering that the population increased 102 million during that time.

Newspapers in the 1950s engaged in a period of self-discovery to determine what newspapers could contribute to the news differently from radio and television. Newspapers in the decades after 1950 used more color, photographs, and experimental typography. Sunday newspapers, in time, began to take on the qualities of a good in-depth magazine. The *New York Times* created the op-ed page in 1970, which was widely imitated over time, and used color in 1997 for the first time since its 1851 founding.

Due to the allure of television, audiences for network radio and commercial films shrank while newspaper circulation remained relatively steady. In the 1950s, televisions spread rapidly to nearly all homes. Some newspapers experimented with new journalism, an approach associated with magazine writers Gay Talese and Tom Wolfe, in which detailed observations and quotes are assembled to portray a rich picture of events, something almost like fiction and, indeed, Wolf called it the new fiction. Mike Royko of the *Chicago Daily News* and then the *Chicago Tribune* continued to reach millions with columns and details that showed the power of newspapers to reach audiences uniquely, as Scripps-Howard columnist Ernie Pyle had demonstrated during World War II. In the era of broadcasting great Edward R. Murrow, Pyle showed print retained a unique power to capture emotion and a sense of small-town community.

In the early 1960s, all mass media turned their eyes toward Vietnam. David Halberstam of the *New York Times* and Neil Sheehan of the Associated Press began to raise questions about the goals of the far-off war in Vietnam, legitimizing issues later displayed on television. As early as 1963, John F. Kennedy told *New York Times* publisher Arthur Ochs Sulzberger, "I wish like hell that you'd get Halberstam out of there." *Washington Post* editor Benjamin C. Bradlee, in his memoir *A Good Life,* said Vietnam changed how news media saw their role in society: "The best newspapers were still involved in the pursuit of truth with conscience.... But at the bottom of the barrel, the stain of the tabloids was spreading with the help of television into what could be called 'kerosene journalism.' In this genre of journalism, reporters pour kerosene on whatever smoke they can find, before they determine what's smoking and why."[7]

In a 1965 CBS broadcast, Morley Safer and his crew reported on the burning of the village of Cam Ne. As families ate their dinner, television sets served images of marines using cigarette lighters to ignite thatched huts. In February 1968, an army major told Associated Press reporter Peter Arnett: "It became necessary to destroy the town to save it." Less than three weeks later, in his "We Are Mired in Stalemate" broadcast, *CBS Evening News* anchor Walter Cronkite said America should "negotiate, not as victors, but as an honorable people who lived up to their pledge to defend democracy and did the best they could." One viewer, President Lyndon Johnson, is said to have told aides, "If I've lost Cronkite, I've lost middle America." Newspapers and television reflected reality from different perspectives, and they supplemented each other.

In the early 1970s, newspapers continued to shape the national agenda. The *Washington Post*'s Bob Woodward and Carl Bernstein wrote a series about the 1972 Watergate break-in of the Democratic campaign headquarters. This break-in, orchestrated by men hired by Republican supporters, gradually gained public attention, despite the initial lack of attention by other newspapers. The power of newspapers to set the national agenda was very clear. After newspapers and, finally, television news spotlighted the controversy, the televised Watergate hearings overwhelmed public attention. Then, like today, newspapers served as public issue scouts for other media.

Figure 10.2 sketches a version of this competition. The news media, such as magazines, radio, television, and the World Wide Web, have taken their toll by attracting away audiences. The number of daily newspapers shrank from nearly 3,000 in the era of World War I, if foreign language newspapers are included, to about 1,480 today. Average weekday readership has shrunk from 81 percent in 1964 to 50 percent in 2001. Total daily circulation peaked in 1973 (63.1 million), and in 2000 it was at the lowest level (55.8 million) since 1954, according to the National Newspaper Association.

The 1980s, an age of the World Wide Web, mobile phones, and more personal media, have seen newspapers, like radio, television, film, and magazines, again confront the challenges of new media. Taking advantage of satellite technology, which enables a newspaper to send pages to various national locations for printing, Al Neuharth of the Gannett group inspired and founded *USA Today* in 1982. The paper lost approximately $1 billion dollars before becoming profitable in recent years, justifying Neuharth's faith in the concept of a newspaper for Americans both on the move in airports, hotels, and at home. Many newspapers frankly imitated *USA Today* with engaging photographs, graphics, and tight, focused writing. By early 2002, *USA Today* clearly was a national newspaper. Its circulation of 1.7 million—just 65,000 short of the *Wall Street Journal*—was 50 percent higher than the third biggest newspaper.[8]

Figure 10.2
Newspapers and Media Competition

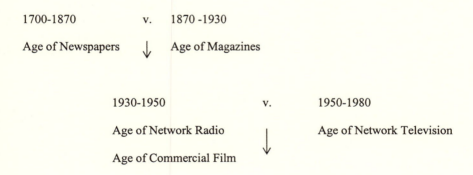

1700-1870   v.   1870 -1930

Age of Newspapers   ↓   Age of Magazines

          1930-1950   v.   1950-1980

          Age of Network Radio   ↓   Age of Network Television

          Age of Commercial Film   ↓

                    1990-Present

                    Age of World Wide Web

Many newspapers created online editions, so that news became available on a twenty-four-hour cycle. The *Dallas Morning News*'s online edition set off a media frenzy when it reported that Timothy McVeigh allegedly admitted his guilt in the Oklahoma City bombing, for which he was executed in 2001. Nearly every American daily newspaper and many weeklies have online editions, sometimes promoting them in the published editions. Since the 1990s, the Internet has enabled individuals to pursue personal and group interests outside traditional civic boundaries, with news and chat rooms, and newspapers—like magazines, radio, and television—have turned to more consumer-oriented stories that provide information and direction to individuals, not just members of a local or national community or members of special interest groups.

Many traditional newspapers provide the e-mail address for the bylined reporter of major news stories and encourage a dialogue between writer and reader, which sometimes occurs. Some newspapers are experimenting with joint gathering, processing, or distributing news—the industry term is convergence—as ways to enrich the news process. Starting in 1992, when there was a relaxation of federal regulatory laws, newspapers were able to own other media outlets in the same market. This led to an increase in the already powerful consolidation movement.

For the past twenty years, some newspapers have experimented with public journalism, an approach that uses interviews, public opinion surveys, and other methods to determine what audiences want to know. This helps editors plan stories, especially campaign stories. Journalism schools such as the University of South Florida are educating students to produce online, print, and video packages in a single course.

Newspapers do more than compete with newer media. Newspapers reflect the social challenges of different periods and find ways to present issues in their own special way. In the years 1700–1870, newspapers were the predominant news medium, although magazines and books were important, and the major social conflicts of the period evolved around issues that had to be resolved in a particular place, such as winning the Revolutionary War and ejecting slavery from the South. The Declaration of Independence and the Constitution were designed to fit a particular place. Newspapers remain rooted to tradition and place as they compete in the Internet age. A more detailed picture of newspaper evolution within the context of social and political change as well as media competition is briefly sketched in the Appendix.

NEWSPAPERS AND EVOLVING COMMUNITIES IN THE TWENTY-FIRST CENTURY

In the social upheaval of the 1960s, Parsons reevaluates his views about a stable society, arguing that change alters the social equilibrium. Change to newspapers occurs when internal strains, such as professionalization, increasing concern for the bottom line, conglomeration, or external strains, such as literacy, immigration, social reform, urbanization, and new media competition, throw the system out of balance, forcing newspapers to adapt. The new equilibrium is noticeably different, but no less stable—for a while at least. According to Parsons, societies always change from simple to complex, but the society strives to stay in equilibrium because the new parts are integrated with one another. That is likely true of newspapers and other publications. We saw this in the eighteenth century. The Internet, the graying of America, the information glut, and today's other forces will not stop the newspaper's historic pendulum. Instead, these forces will be absorbed, creating a new equilibrium, as we might also argue from Hegel.

Newspapers in an Era of Declining Authority

As there has been a decline in public acceptance of institutions and authority, there has been a decline in the power of journalists to shape the public agenda. Newspapers historically have developed beats around major institutions in a community, such as the courts, city councils, and police and fire departments, all part of the official ruling structure of a society. *New York Times* columnist Arthur Krock regularly had dinner with high Washington officials in the 1930s, and in 1951 he earned acclaim for an exclusive interview with President Harry Truman. While Hearst and Pulitzer were reaching out to the masses, the *Baltimore Sun*'s H. L. Mencken and the *Nation*'s Edwin Godkin held the attention of the nation's elite for decades. Even earlier, Horace Greeley helped shape the mind of Americans, perhaps even Abraham Lincoln's, on such public issues as slavery and morality. Benjamin Franklin, a statesman and public servant who wanted to be remembered as a printer, was among the most prominent of citizens in the 1700s.

In the twentieth century, U.S. presidents sought audiences with journalist and columnist Walter Lippmann, a valuable source of information and perspective. Since his 1974 death, no print journalist—not even the *New York Times*'s William Safire—has achieved the same kind of power. Although the role of print journalism has declined in the shadow of widely used broadcast news, even the ubiquity and communicative power of television has not given the popular news anchors the same type of influence Lippmann wielded with both leaders *and* the public. Lippmann was a public intellectual, important for how he contextualized events, not just for the news he covered. Newspapers now compete in a world in which journalists' normative role of rank ordering information is in decline and a world in which information, regardless of its source, is competing for audience attention. It really will be a test of John Milton's 1644 *Areopagitica* in which truth and falsehood battle. Newspapers need to compete for audiences in a world of new communities, many built around media agendas and some communities existing mainly in space.

Online newspapers are not simply digital versions of their print predecessors. Websites show different readership patterns for news on an Internet newspaper versus the same news in the published paper. The published version represents the judgment of editors and journalists in terms of headlines and so forth while the Internet gives editorial power to the audience in terms of which information to select.

Content

Newspapers are likely to continue to serve local communities directly, but they also will publish menus of information outlets that provide more depth, such as websites, magazines, or other evolving sources. News will provide an orientation to public affairs topics, allowing audiences to swim at different levels from sailing across the surface to diving deep. The content will reflect audience interests more than has been true in the past, when newspaper editors' judgments were more readily accepted by the audience. The current experiments with public journalism demonstrate an effort to reach audiences via use of public opinion surveys, among other methods, to determine what readers want politicians to talk about and act on. Agendas will clash in the twenty-first century, as they have in earlier eras, and newspapers will provide the community agenda to compete for public attention.

Process of Information Gathering

Clearly, newspapers have benefited from an evolution of technologies that improved their ability to gain news through telegraph and telephone, for example, and to distribute it by way of railroads, trucks, and satellites. News organizations will continue to experiment with ways of gathering, processing, and sharing information, such as the current convergence of Media General in Tampa, where a newspaper shares a newsroom with both a television station and an online news site. Reporters are likely to be more cross trained in the future. Newspapers will continue to experiment with branding their product and providing ways via the Internet or data disks to give information options, for a price, to those who need greater depth.

Presentation and Connections

The *USA Today* approach of shorter stories with graphic and visual aids that enable readers to absorb information is likely to remain a model for the future, especially as newspapers become guides for readers to pursue other information sources in greater depth. About a fourth of the approximately 8,000 daily newspapers in the world have Web editions, a development that is likely to continue and expand. Even as newspapers will continue to be scooped up in corporate conglomerates that include a variety of media outlets, newspapers will develop ways to connect audiences with a variety of communities, from local to international, via chat groups or other options.

Audiences

Because newspapers tend to attract older audiences, that is, longtime citizens with roots and social investments in their community, the graying of America seems to bode well for the medium. Social scientist Philip Meyer finds that older age groups are more likely to read the newspaper than younger age groups, but scholar Robert L. Stevenson concludes that although older people do read newspapers more, each generation has brought a declining number of older readers.[9] As the younger groups have aged, their newspaper reading habits have remained consistent. The graying of America suggests that newspapers are starting a twenty- to thirty-year period in which they will confront a declining base of loyal readers. There is a kind of quarter-century grace period for newspapers to experiment with ways to secure their position with present audiences and reinvent themselves to attract new audiences.

These reinvented newspapers must serve as conduits for a variety of informational levels in order to attract audiences across all ages. We know the Internet also makes newspapers more accessible to younger audiences as, for example, college students stay in touch with their hometowns via the Web version of the hometown paper. In times of crisis, major news media, such as the wire services, initially are likely to seek out the Web editions of newspapers closest to the news event, as happened during the 1999 school shootings in Columbine, Colorado. Reporters not only look back but also forward. By localizing far away events, such as civil unrest, droughts, terrorists attacks, and national issues, such as AIDS, Y2K, and the war in Afghanistan, newspapers have helped community members start planning proactive solutions to future community crises.

What will newspapers be like as the new century evolves? No one knows. Hegel argues that human society is in evolution and that as social positions develop society will be challenged by other positions, with a synthesis eventually evolving that reflects the best of both. Newspapers represent something of this evolution over time, and the new century is likely to find newspapers to be as highly adaptive to social changes as they have been for the past three centuries. In the twenty-first century, newspapers necessarily will reinvent themselves to fit with their communities in competition with other media. One can make guesses about general directions newspapers will evolve in terms of content, news gathering techniques, presentation styles, modes of connection with audiences, and audience changes themselves, but they are only informed guesses.

Communities cannot survive without agenda renewal, and they cannot thrive without civic-minded and committed media. If newspapers do not survive, it will be because some other medium serves that vital community agenda function. Television and radio stretch like telephone wires to the distant world;

magazines are like the coffee shop where we meet our friends for discussions; and the Internet is pulling us together into a world audience with a common nervous system. So far, we have evolved with newspapers, and it does not seem likely that the need for the agenda setters of local place—newspapers—will be lessened in this new century. Newspapers will adapt and survive so long as we value our local community and the people who live there. After all, even as we e-mail our friends around the world, we are aware of our next door neighbor whom we see mowing the lawn, whose dog is barking, and from whom we may need to borrow a cup of sugar now and then. The new century is not likely to change that.

NOTES

1. Special thanks to Glel Feighery and Graham Fields for their help in researching this chapter.

2. Stu Tolley, "The Abyss That Is Destroying Daily Newspaper Reading," Newspaper Association of America (2001), at http://216.182.209.78/preview.cfm?AID=1593 (viewed March 2002).

3. Richard L. Merritt, *Symbols of American Community, 1735–1775* (New Haven, CT: Yale University Press, 1966).

4. Arthur Meier Schlesinger Sr., *Prelude to Independence: The Newspaper War on Britain, 1764–1776* (New York: Vintage, 1965).

5. Frank Luther Mott, *A History of American Magazines* (Cambridge, MA: Harvard University Press, 1938).

6. Michael Schudson, *Discovering the News: A Social History of American Newspapers* (New York: Basic, 1978).

7. Benjamin C. Bradlee, *A Good Life: Newspapering and Other Adventures* (New York: Simon and Schuster, 1995).

8. Audit Bureau of Circulations, 26 February 2002.

9. Robert L. Stevenson, "The Disappearing Newspaper Reader," *Newspaper Research Journal* 15, no. 3 (1994): 22–31.

Chapter 11

Conclusion

Shannon E. Martin

At the close of the twentieth century, there were many news industry analysts and advisors who wondered if the newspaper would survive into the next century. Readership studies indicated declining interest in newsprint products. Newspaper groups seemed to be buying up all the independent publishers, and then in turn were bought by even larger media groups. Corporation revenues were reported to be a in slump, though profits remained substantial. Inside the newsroom, reporters and editors saw their staff numbers declining.

As the information resources explosion continued to expand, many newspaper publishers wrestled with fundamental questions about budget allocations. Whether to invest in data warehousing or to continue the maintenance of hundred-year-old back file archives or "morgues," whether to stay with newsprint publishing or to move entirely into a digital delivery environment, or whether to welcome corporate ownership and management or to remain as an independent entity as long as possible—these are just a few of the problems faced by most newspapers around the world.

Those outside the industry management, too, worried and wondered about the evident devaluing of newspapers as a cultural necessity. For example, even the ways in which we chose to save or discard newspapers was cause for comment and concern. In Nicholson Baker's *New Yorker* article "Deadline: An Author's Desperate Bid to Save America's Past,"[1] he includes photographs of microfilmed newspaper pages with comparative color photographs of the original pages published in 1902, along with a black and white photograph of the Historic Newspaper Archives in Rahway, New Jersey, showing stacks of bound newspaper volumes in disarray.

The story itself is about the dismantling of both private and public library collections of original copies of newspapers for several reasons. Sometimes the archives are disbanded because the cost of housing and maintaining them is greater than the libraries want to bear, and sometimes it is because archivists believe that the newspapers themselves are a bacterial contaminant to other parts of the library collection. Baker reports at length on the problems with the microfilm copies of these hundreds of thousands of newspaper pages and of the loss to researchers that will probably result. "We're at a bizarre moment in history, when you can have the real thing [century-old newspapers] for considerably less than it would cost to buy a set of crummy black-and-white snapshots of it, which you can't look at without the help of a machine."[2] The story is both wrenching and all too familiar to those who are now doing research involving these increasingly rare artifacts.

Similar attention to the fate of original newspapers kept in both private and public archives, and the research losses that are likely when these bound volumes are destroyed, is given in a *San Francisco Chronicle* article by Kevin Fagan. "The dilemma of how to save America's disappearing newspaper history has become nettlesome at best and desperate at worst for historians and librarians across the country, and they are now casting around for solutions."[3]

The stability of the newsprint format has provided historians for centuries with the opportunity to see firsthand what had been reported and read by generations of subscribers. When these treasure troves of historical research are no longer available—because newspapers do not exist, because the archives are not maintained, or because the format of newsprint does not continue—has the important social function of the newspaper disappeared as well?

There are those who have been wondering out loud about the loss of cultural memory when newsprint newspapers are no longer available,[4] while others have bemoaned the glut of paper records that require storing and maintaining.[5] There also are varying opinions about the move many newspapers are making from newsprint publications to digital delivery of the news.[6] Some practitioners believe that the loss of paper copies and the time required for newsprint publication infuse a shallowness in the news product when it is delivered only to a cyber reader clicking from link to link. There are concerns, too, about partnering with broadcast affiliates, and cross-over news bulletins from reporters who work at a print news desk but who also tell the story more immediately to broadcast viewers and online visitors.[7] Some believe that the speed of story generation that is typical of a broadcast or online news release dilutes the quality of the news product when stories move so directly from the reporters' notes to the web page display or broadcaster's prompter.

Every downturn in a country's economy affects the news organizations' advertising revenue or government tax supports, and that in turn affects the news product, from the newsroom to the subscriber, from the legal practitioner to the academic scholar. And even when the economy improves, at least in the United States, there is much speculation that newspapers had better get used to a leaner budget as a permanent condition rather than a temporary setback.[8] It is no wonder that many inside and outside the newspaper industry speculate about the demise of newspapers. Occasionally, the discussions move to visions of a chaotic world *without* newspapers to chronicle the day's events, give thoughtful voice to social struggles, and provide a cohesive community identity. Infrequently, the discussion turns to visions of a world without newsprint newspapers, but that has some other delivery format that reports on the day's events, provides a forum for thoughtful comment, and engages an entire community in problem-solving and self-governance. The preceding chapters here should have made clear that newspapers, as defined by twentieth-century historians, media analysts, and in some instances by community law, have a long-held place in societies around the world. But how that history helps us prepare for, shape, or predict the future is still not clear.

The questions about the life expectancy of newspapers, as we know them at the beginning of the twenty-first century, depend on a conception of the nature of newspapers. And this is something like the questions about the nature of humans. Though humans could be characterized as featherless bipeds with broad nails, it might be more useful to the discussion of our history and progress if we described humans as rational animals. While the first description—featherless biped—aims only at identifying characteristics that belong to humans, the second—rational animal—tries to point to the human essence. Similarly, we might want to reconsider how we describe and define a newspaper. Apparently, there is some ambiguity about the term "newspaper" and what it means, because so many historians have had to write so many pages defining the essence and edges of their subject, as noted in Chapter 1. There also is evidence of the term's ambiguity. There is the simple but recurring fact that researchers find on so many occasions when news-containing or broadsheet-like artifacts that do not precisely fit the Eric W. Allen and Otto Groth definitions are still referred to as newspapers of some sort. This suggests intuitive blurring of the definitional outlines.

The long histories of and much attention given to newspapers reported in the preceding chapters only emphasize the fact that newspapers are important to many societies in a variety of ways. As we saw in these chapters, newspapers have played a crucial role in the development of many cultures. And while the accessibility, portability, and reproducibility of the newspaper format was certainly part of its social usefulness, the format alone does not account for its success. If the format were the most important condition for newspaper success, the variations of that format would never have taken hold in the ways that we have noted and surely would not have carried the conceptual name tag as well.

For example, in Arab cultures newspapers were used by colonial powers to distribute the government agenda. But when the local writers and publishers were in control of the newspapers, they became vehicles for national identity-building. Though the press continued to be an arm of the government, the face of that government was Arab. Where the press was locally owned, it represented local interests rather than those beyond the border. The ownership and organization of the media is still the focus of attention and debate among those countries that have mixed government and private proprietors. But all of these countries continue to be concerned with the notion that the newspapers are a vital and integral part of the society.

Similarly, the African and Pacific Rim cultures valued newspapers for identity-building and strategic government interaction. In the case of several African nations, the newspapers were militant voices against government regimes, and in other nations, the newspapers were political instruments of the authoritarian leaders, and in still other examples, the newspaper's role was one of leadership toward better social order, taking direct cues from no one already in power. The Pacific Rim countries were quite a different set of examples in that the newspapers were much less agents of change and much more liaisons of social order. The relative isolation of these many island nations promoted the use of newspapers as tools of companionship, education, and entertainment. While there were clearly political issues at play on the pages of the newspapers and among the agenda of publishers, the relative stability of government organizations prompted newspapers to fill a different role in that region.

The newspapers of Eastern Asia exemplify nearly all of the social functions discovered in our historical survey. With high readership among the general population in some cases, and a very narrow but powerful readership in other cases, the newspapers served as both government agent and purveyor of new ideas, cultural educator, and voice of the people. The extreme difficulty in producing a news product that requires so many individual and delicately rendered characters, rather than the simpler, several-dozen-letter alphabet, was overcome to meet the need of cultures that wanted both to promote themselves and to provide a forum for national education among their population. Whether publicly or privately owned, the newspapers of this region had enormous tasks in simply putting out a print news product that could be produced daily and rendered legibly. Though the governments from one country to another varied radically, the political and cultural uses of the newspapers were clearly evident and similar. The newspaper provided a cultural bonding agent and when a neighboring nation invaded, the newspapers were a reflection and conduit of the new regime's style.

Though not specifically described in this book, the continental areas of central Asia and eastern Europe experienced many of the cultural developments in their newspapers also found in Asia, with the exception of a simpler writing alphabet by which to make newspaper production easier. In the case of India and its neighbors, colonialism gave way to the need for promoting cultural identity, and the newspapers reflected and bolstered these changes. The nations of the Soviet Union, too, benefited from a less complicated writing system but a much more volatile political environment of city states and warring neighbors. Newspapers, when they could flourish, were enthusiastically embraced as a part of the community. Huge stores of these newspapers, however, have been lost in the frequent burning and looting of national libraries. The Sarajevo National Library destruction, witnessed by news media from around the world in August 1992, is a striking example of the value and loss a community feels when the archive of newspapers and books is extinguished. These newspapers' histories now, in many instances, are relegated to speculation and fractured references.

Newspapers in Europe, too, served many social functions. Their origination may have been simply to keep a particular group of traders informed about goods and services, or they may have been the bully pulpit of Caesars and kings. But in all cases, the important components were the authority of the news items, the ease and low cost of production, the stability and transportability of the format, and the popular hunger to know the news. Though many of these elements were part of the newspapers of the colonial Americas, there also is evidence that native cultures had news products of their own that were not dependent on the development of a transportable writing surface. Because the cultures moved from place to place, the "newspaper" could remain immobile, as in the case of newspaper rocks where travelers could add their news, much in the way that early newspapers provided blank space for handwritten notes as the issues were passed among readers. But even in these examples found among the Western regions, the format was inexpensive, stable, and easy enough to inscribe.

The need for news and the format stability, portability, accessibility, and inexpensiveness of the news product have all made the newspaper a practical venue for nearly every culture. And where most of these elements could be replicated or brought together, something like a newspaper was born. While the label "newspaper" has come to represent a particular format in the twentieth century, it is really the combination of elements—snapshots of news that are easy to have and contemplate, but also easily tossed aside—that are the components society finds most useful. Apart from the form, however, is the content of the newspaper, which varies from society to society as each one calls on the paper to provide leadership, education, public opinion, entertainment, or cultural identity.

Those industry captains who are able to continue to bring these elements together in a commercially viable package, whether it is actually called a newspaper, are the leaders of a successful news market for every age and every culture. Whether the present-day newspaper industry can adjust or hold onto the news product market is yet to be seen, but it is clear that societies around the world have always sought, and will continue to need, news that is convenient to handle and inexpensive to produce and disperse. The larger question, however, that should trouble every community member is: If the modern news industry does not fill the social function of newspapers, how will we move ahead together?

What is a newspaper, and how do we as a society—any society—want to think about and maintain its functionality? The minimized or diminishing availability of competent news products is worth everyone's attention because the knowledge of the news is so much a part of so many cultural successes, whether the social members are power brokers, historians, lawyers, nosey neighbors, or just the casual information gatherer. How we continue to use and treat newspapers, per se, may not be a cultural imperative, but these questions applied to the larger issues of news handling and its value apparently do matter. It is important, then, that we understand the essence of newspapers, the uses we have for newspapers as part of any society's organization, and those social functions of newspapers that have served many cultures for many centuries.

NOTES

1. Nicholson Baker, "Deadline: The Author's Desperate Bid to Save America's Past," *New Yorker*, 24 July 2000, pp. 42–61.

2. Baker, "Deadline," p. 61.

3. Kevin Fagan, "Battling to Preserve the Remnants of History: Newspaper Archives Expensive and Complex," *San Francisco Chronicle*, 2 November 2000, p. A17.

4. For example, see Shannon E. Martin and Kathleen Hansen, *Newspapers of Record in a Digital Age* (Westport, CT: Praeger, 1998), pp. 126–30.

5. Margo Nash, "In the Paperless Era, the Problem Is Too Much Paper," *New York Times*, 3 September 2000, p. 7.

6. Mike Wendland, "Reading the News in the Inkless World of Cyberspace," *New York Times*, 25 May 2000, p. G15; William Glaberson, "In San Jose, Knight-Ridder Tests a Newspaper Frontier," *New York Times*, 7 February 1994, p. D1.

7. David Barboza, "Tribune Is Laboratory for Newsroom of the Future," *New York Times*, 15 March 2000, p. A21; Laurence Zuckerman, "Don't Stop the Presses! Newspapers Balk at Scooping Themselves on Their Own Web Sites," *New York Times*, 6 January 1997, p. D1.

8. Lucia Moses, "The Jobs Are Gone for Good: Even When the Economy Recovers, Many Newspapers That Have Gone on a Lean Diet Won't Be Bulking up Again," *Editor and Publisher*, 4 March 2002, pp. 10–14.

Appendix

History of Newspapers

1690—First American newspaper, *Publick Occurrences, both Foreign and Domestick*, published in Boston.

1704—Boston *News Letter* (Campbell) first weekly. First classified ads. Benjamin Franklin born.

1721—The *New England Courant* by James Franklin (older brother of Benjamin, who fakes satiric "Dogood" letters to paper).

1729—The *Pennsylvania Gazette* by Benjamin Franklin. Becomes largest and highest-circulation newspaper in the colonies.

1734—John Peter Zenger (*N.Y. Weekly Journal*) arrested and charged with seditious libel. Zenger acquitted in 1735 because truth a defense against libel.

U.S. History

1692—Salem witch trials.

1693—College of William and Mary.

1700—Boston has largest population (7,000).

1720—Philadelphia becomes second largest city (10,000).

1726—Religious revivalism.

1730—English colonies hold estimated 655,000.

1741—Alaska founded (Bering).

1749—Ohio surveyed.

1752—Benjamin Franklin's electricity experiments. First general hospital.

1754–1763—French and Indian War.

1760—Colonial population reaches 1.5 million.

1769—Steam engine (Watts).

1770—Boston Massacre.

History of Other Media

1640—*The Whole Book of Psalmes,* the first book published in North America.

1702—Cotton Mather's books published.

1730—First art exhibition in U.S.

1732—*Poor Richard's Almanac* (Franklin).

1741—In Philadelphia, *American Magazine* (Bradford) published days before *General Magazine* (Franklin), the first two magazines.

1767—*The Prince of Parthia,* first professional U.S. play produced.

1774—*Royal American* (Thomas) has anti-English propaganda.

1775—Thomas Paine attacks English in *Pennsylvania Magazine.* "Yankee Doodle."

1776—Thomas Paine's pamphlets *Common Sense* and *The American Crisis.*

1779—*Connecticut Courant* produces *Children's Magazine.*
(continued on next page)

History of Newspapers

1754—"Join, or Die," first editorial cartoon runs in Benjamin Franklin's *Pennsylvania Gazette.*

1765—Stamp Act passed.

1770—Paul Revere's engraving of the massacre appears in Samuel Adam's *Boston Gazette.*

1775—First picture of an event (publisher James Rivington hanged in effigy) runs in *N.Y. Gazetteer.*

1776—*Massachusetts Spy* publishes account of first battle of the revolution. Within weeks of its signing, newspapers across the nation reprint the Declaration of Independence.

1783—*Pennsylvania Evening Post,* first daily newspaper.

1787—*Federalist Papers* appear in N.Y.

1790—Benjamin Franklin Bache starts the *Aurora,* becomes fiercely partisan.

1791—First Amendment protects freedom of the press.

1800—About 200 newspapers printed in U.S.

1808—*El Misisipi,* first Spanish-language newspaper, begins in New Orleans.

1812—Antiwar editor James M. Lingan (*Federal*

U.S. History

1773—Boston Tea Party.

1774—First Continental Congress.

1775—Benjamin Franklin becomes first postmaster.

1776—Declaration of Independence (July 4). French send aid to U.S.

1779—Spain declares war on Britain.

1883—Treaty of Paris.

1784—Bifocals (Franklin).

1789—President George Washington elected. Constitution ratified. First state university (UNC).

1790—Cotton mill. American Industrial Revolution begins.

1791—Washington, DC; Bill of Rights adopted.

1794—Postal Act aids magazines.

1798–1800—Alien and Sedition Acts. 5.3 million people in U.S.

1804—Meriwether Lewis and William Clark expedition.

1810—N.Y. is biggest city.

1812—War of 1812.

1819—Spain gives Florida to U.S.

1820—Missouri Compromise.

1823—Monroe Doctrine.

History of Other Media

1783—*American Spelling Book.*

1786—Philip Freneau poems.

1787—*America Magazine* (Webster).

1789—*The Power of Sympathy,* first U.S. novel.

1791—*Rights of Man* (Paine).

1792—*Ladies' Magazine* (Hale), the first women's magazine. *Vindication of the Rights of Woman* (Wollstonecraft).

1800—Library of Congress.

1806—Webster's dictionary.

1807—Washington Irving starts satirical magazine.

1811—*Niles' Weekly Register,* first news magazine.

1820—Steam-driven cylinder press.

1821—*Saturday Evening Post.*

1823—*Kiplinger Washington Letter.*

1827—*Birds of America* (Audubon).

1828—*Ladies' Magazine, American Dictionary* (Webster).

1830s—Edgar Allen Poe, Ralph Waldo Emerson, and Nathaniel Hawthorne dominate literary scene.

1830—*Ladies' Book* (Godey).

1831—*Spirit of the Times,* first large sporting magazine.

History of Newspapers

Republican) killed in Baltimore jail.

1820s—Washington press corps forms as Congress becomes beat.

1827—*Freedom's Journal* (Russwurm and Cornish) becomes first successful African American newspaper.

1828—*Cherokee Phoenix* (Boudinot), first Native American newspaper.

1829—W. C. Bryant edits *N.Y. Evening Post.*

1830s—Midwest frontier newspapers. Abolitionist using more illustrations. Carrier pigeons carry news.

1831—*The Liberator* (Garrison).

1833—*N.Y. Sun* (Day) and its newsboys start penny press era. *Sun* shuns traditional news for human interest and humor.

1835—*N.Y. Herald* includes sections (money, sports, society news, and reviews) and extras.

1836—*The Colored American* (Cornish).

1837—Elijah Lovejoy (*St. Louis Observer*) killed fending off destruction of his fourth press.

1840s—Partisan press reemerges.

1841—*N.Y. Tribune* (Greeley). Tribune has high moral tone and first

U.S. History

1826—First American railroad completed.

1828—First passenger railroad.

1830s—Pony Express carries news.

1830—U.S. population 12.8 million.

1831—Alexis de Tocqueville visits U.S. Nat Turner revolt. Better reaper.

1833—Newspapers and magazines are 90 percent of all mail. Anti-slavery Society starts. Oberlin College first coeducational college.

1835—Colt pistol.

1836—The Alamo. Republic of Texas.

1837—Mount Holyoke first women's college.

1838—Trail of Tears kills 4,000.

1839—*Amistad* slave mutiny.

1840s—Mass political campaigning begins. America has gone from republic to modern democracy. Underground Railroad. Baseball organized.

1843—Westward migration. Sojourner Truth speaks out.

1845—Irish potato famine brings immigrants to U.S.

1846—Mexican War. Smithsonian Institution. Sewing machine (Howe).

History of Other Media

1833—*The Knickerbocker.*

1835—Alexis de Tocqueville's *Democracy in America.* Mark Twain born.

1836—Samuel Morse develops the telegraph. *Nature* (Emerson).

1837—Daguerreotype (Niepce and Daguerre).

1840s—Steamships and railroads carry the news.

1841—Edgar Allan Poe edits *Graham's Magazine.*

1844—Samuel Morse telegraphs message from Supreme Court to Baltimore. *The Raven* (Poe).

1845—John L. O'Sullivan writes of "manifest destiny" in the *United States Magazine and Democratic Review.* Henry Thoreau at Walden Pond.

1848—"Oh! Susannah" (Foster).

1849—*Civil Disobedience* (Thoreau).

1851—*Moby Dick* (Melville).

1852—*Uncle Tom's Cabin* (Stowe).

1855—*Frank Leslie's Illustrated Newspaper, Leaves of Grass* (Whitman).

1857—*Harper's Weekly.*

1859—*Origin of the Species* (Darwin). *On Liberty* (Mill).

1860—Dime novel.

1862—Matthew Brady and Alexander Gardner photograph Civil War. "The Battle Hymn of the Republic" (Howe).

(continued on next page)

History of Newspapers

female reporter
(Fuller).

1844—Edgar Allan Poe
writes for *N.Y. Sun.*
Baltimore Patriot uses
telegraph just hours after
invention.

1845—Walt Whitman
edits *Brooklyn Daily*
Eagle.

1846—Journalists cover
foreign war for first time;
editors get news before
government does.

1847—*The North Star*
(aka *Frederick Douglass's*
Paper).

1849—First wire service
(Associated Press) supplies
foreign news.

1850—First woman to
cover Congress
(Swisshelm).

1851—*N.Y. Times*
(Raymond and Jones).

1856—New Orleans
Daily Creole, first African
American daily.

1861—Reporters head
into field to seek news and
regularly use summary
leads in case telegraph
goes down. Newspapers
use several decks of
headlines. Columnists,
mostly women,
emerge.

1865—Unprecedented
coverage of Abraham
Lincoln's assassination.

1871—Halftone method
developed.

1872—James Gordon
Bennett Jr. takes control of
the *N.Y. Herald,* largest
paper in the world. Henry

U.S. History

1848—Gold discovered
in California.

1849—Harriet Tubman
escapes. Women's rights
groups emerge.

1850—Amelia Bloomer
wears trousers.

1854—Republican
Party.

1855—Western Union.
Kindergarten.

1856—Abolitionist
John Brown kills five.

1859—Harper's Ferry.

1860—South Carolina
secedes.

1861—Ten states
secede. U.S. Civil War.

1862—Homestead Act.
Federal income tax.

1863—Emancipation
Proclamation. Gettysburg
Address.

1865—Abraham
Lincoln assassination.

1867—Reconstruction.
Ku Klux Klan.

1868—Andrew Johnson
impeachment.

1869—Transcontinental
railroad. Black Friday
stock market panic.

1871—Great Chicago
Fire.

1872—Ulysses S. Grant
defeats Horace Greeley in
presidential race. U.S.
becoming global power.

1879—Light bulb
(Edison).

1880—U.S. population
50 million.

1881—James Garfield
assassinated.

History of Other Media

1865—*The Nation*
(Godkin), opinion
magazine.

1867—Typewriter.

1868—*Overland*
Monthly (San Francisco).

1870s—Herman
Melville, Mark Twain,
Francis Harte, and Louisa
May Alcott dominate
literary scene. "Greatest
Show on Earth."

1876—Telephone (Bell).

1877—Phonograph
(Edison).

1878—William Gilbert
and Arthur Sullivan's
operetta *HMS Pinafore.*
Telephone books.

1880s—Major
metropolitan museums
symphonies, opera houses.

1884—*Huckleberry*
Finn (Twain).

1887—Baseball cards.

1888—Kodak's Box
Camera. *National*
Geographic.

1889—Edward Bok edits
Ladies' Home Journal.

1890s—Magazine
illustrations growing.
Guglielmo Marconi's
wireless experiments.

1891—International
Copyright Law.

1892—Thomas Edison
develops kinetoscope.

1895—Radio
telegraphy.

1896—Lumière
brothers develop motion
picture camera.

1898—American
impressionists.

History of Newspapers

Stanley writes of finding Dr. Livingstone.

1880s—Halftones and Linotype used regularly.

1881—*Los Angeles Times.*

1883—Joseph Pulitzer starts first "New Journalism" movement with *N.Y. World.* Charles Dana's *N.Y. Sun* uses better writing and reporting and more human interest pieces.

1889—*Wall Street Journal* (Dow).

1890—15 English-language dailies in N.Y. City.

1890s—William Randolph Hearst raids *N.Y. Sun* and *N.Y. World* staff. Ida B. Wells attacks southern lynchings.

1894—Williams Jennings Bryan edits *Omaha World-Herald.*

1895—William Randolph Hearst and *N.Y. World* print yellow journalism as *Yellow Kid* appears in both *World* and *N.Y. Journal.*

1896—Adolph Ochs buys *N.Y. Times,* rejects yellow journalism.

1897—*The Sun* (Church): "Yes Virginia, there is a Santa Claus."

1898—William Randolph Hearst blames Spanish for USS *Maine* attack.

1900—*N.Y. World* uses large headlines, scandalous stories, and shocking photographs.

U.S. History

1882—Anti-Chinese sentiment.

1883—Standard time zones. Brooklyn Bridge.

1886—Haymarket Strike, labor unrest in Chicago. Statue of Liberty.

1888—Trolley line.

1889—Antitrust law. Oklahoma taken from Native Americans.

1890s—Progressive Era. Growth of baseball, basketball, and conservation.

1890—Average of 75 lynchings per year through 1930.

1892—Ellis Island opens.

1894—Labor Day holiday.

1895—Safety razor (Gillette).

1896—"Separate but Equal" ruled legal.

1897—First subway. Klondike gold rush. Library of Congress finished.

1898—USS *Maine* explodes in Havana harbor. N.Y. City second largest city in world.

1900—Since 1850, U.S. population triples to 76 million. Life expectancy: 47.

1903—First flight (Wrights). Ford Motor Company.

1906—Roosevelt coins "muckraker." Federal Pure Food and Drug Act. San Francisco earthquake.

History of Other Media

1899—Ragtime (Joplin). Interpretation of dreams (Freud).

1900—Muckraking in magazines (*McClure's* and *Collier's*). Kodak "Brownie" introduced for $1. Flowering of realism in literature (Crane, Whitman, London, and Sinclair).

1903—*The Great Train Robbery,* first edited film. *Ladies Home Journal* first to hit one million circulation. *McClure's* Ida Tarbell targets Standard Oil.

1904—Ivy Lee becomes public relations counselor.

1905—Nickelodeons.

1906—*The Jungle* (Sinclair). First sound broadcast (Fessenden).

1907—Guglielmo Marconi links England and U.S. The newspaper trade publications *N. Y. Journalist* and *Editor and Publisher* merge.

1909—Broadcast school (Herrold).

1910—*The Crisis* (Du Bois).

1912—Journalists use Speed Graphic camera. Universal Pictures. Neon sign.

1913—*Billboard.* Mack Sennet makes movie comedies.

1914—World War I propaganda invades U.S. media.

1915—Three-hour *Birth of a Nation* (Griffith).

1917—Radio improvements taken over
(continued on next page)

History of Newspapers

Approximately 1,000 foreign-language newspapers in the U.S.

1902—Chicago boasts seven dailies, including two of William Randolph Hearst's.

1904—Managing editor Carr Van Anda joins the *N.Y. Times.*

1905—*Chicago Defender* (Abbott), an African American newspaper later home to Langston Hughes's "James B. Semple." Frank Gannett buys first paper.

1907—First transatlantic Guglielmo Marconi message goes to *N.Y. Times.*

1908—*The Christian Science Monitor* (Eddy) offers analysis.

1910—2,200 English-language dailies in U.S. By 1930, morning papers down 22 percent. Union heads bomb *L.A. Times,* 21 die.

1913—First crossword (*N.Y. World*).

1917—War coverage censored through espionage and sedition acts. John Reed visits Russia. First Pulitzer Prizes awarded.

1918—*Stars and Stripes.*

1919—*N.Y. Daily News.* The Associated Negro Press (Barnett).

U.S. History

1907—Immigration peaks at 1.2 million. Washing machine. Mother's Day.

1908—Ford sells 15 million Model Ts by 1926. William Taft's "Dollar Diplomacy."

1909—NAACP. Instant coffee.

1910—Boy Scouts of America.

1912—Progressive Party. *Titanic* sinks.

1913—Panama Canal. Assembly line. Department of Labor. Federal Reserve.

1914—Federal Trade Commission created. World War I in Europe begins.

1915—German U-boat sinks *Lusitania.*

1916—Albert Einstein publishes Theory of Relativity.

1917—U.S. enters World War I. Committee on Public Information formed (Creel).

1918—Racial tension grows.

1919—Prohibition and gangsters. "Red Scare" and labor strikes sweep nation. Oliver Wendell Holmes writes "Clear and Present Danger" ruling.

1920—U.S. urban population more than rural population. Consumer boom. Women get right to vote. Harlem Renaissance. Prohibition. League of Nations.

History of Other Media

by government until 1920. First jazz band recording.

1919—Charles Chaplin, Douglas Fairbanks, D. W. Griffith, and Mary Pickford form United Artists.

1920s—Radio grows with AT&T, General Electric, and Westinghouse. Liberal magazines (*Nation* and *New Republic*) defend civil liberties. P.R. grows. Stars in Hollywood (Valentino, Arbuckle, and Bow) and in sports (Ruth, Rockne, Dempsey, and Jones).

1921—Number of radio sets grows 1,200 percent.

1922—*Reader's Digest. Better Homes and Gardens. Public Opinion* (Lippmann). *The Wasteland* (Eliot). *Ulysses* (Joyce). Will H. Hays oversees the MPPDA.

1923—Iconoscope tube (Zworykin). *Crystallizing Public Opinion* (Bernays). *Time* (Luce) starts modern news magazines.

1924—"Rhapsody in Blue" (Gershwin).

1925—*Chicago Tribune* radio station WGN broadcasts Scopes "Monkey" trial arguments of William Bryan and Clarence Darrow. *The New Yorker,* sophisticated literary magazine born.

1926—RCA starts NBC. Network radio lures advertisers.

1927—Rose Bowl is first coast-to-coast broadcast.

History of Newspapers

1920s—Early wave of chain consolidation. N.Y.'s *Globe* and *World* defend civil liberties. Tabloids create jazz journalism and war in N.Y. through 1927. H. L. Mencken and advice columnist Dorothy Dix rise to fame.

1922—*Brooklyn Daily Eagle* editor Hans von Kaltenborn moves to radio.

1924—*Daily News* becomes largest newspaper. Grantland Rice writes of Notre Dame's "Four Horsemen of the Apocalypse."

1928—*Daily News* sneaks photographer into Ruth Snyder's execution.

1929—With *Tarzan* and *Dick Tracy*, action stories appear in comics.

1930—Sensational gossip columnist Walter Winchell stolen away to William Randolph Hearst's *Mirror*. Louella Parsons's gossip column reaches one in four American homes.

1932—Arthur Krock becomes *N.Y. Times*'s Washington bureau chief.

1933—Newspapers fight with radio over Associate Press news access. Eleanor Roosevelt holds press conferences for female journalists.

U.S. History

1921—Age of isolationism. Nicola Sacco–Bartolomeo Vanzetti trial.

1922—Benito Mussolini and fascists take over government in Italy. Soviet Union established.

1923—Teapot Dome scandal exposed.

1925—Scopes "Monkey" trial in Tennessee.

1927—Pilot Charles Lindbergh crosses Atlantic.

1928—Ruth Snyder executed; celebrity trials emerge.

1929—Wall Street crash creates economic crisis.

1930—Jet engine.

1931—"Star-Spangled Banner" becomes official national anthem.

1932—Lindbergh baby kidnapped.

1933—Holocaust begins. Federal Communications Commission and New Deal start. "Dust Bowl." Prohibition repealed.

1935—Social Security. Around-the-world phone call.

1936—Jesse Owens wins four gold medals.

1938—40-hour work week. Child labor laws. Minimum wage.

1939—World War II begins when Germany invades Poland. Russia invades Finland.

History of Other Media

CBS born. Al Jolson's *The Jazz Singer*, first talkie. *Movietone* newsreels. Philo Farnsworth demonstrates television.

1928—*Mickey Mouse* and CBS.

1929—Auto radios. Eddie Bernays stages "Torches of Freedom" march to promote smoking.

1930s—Weekly movie attendance peaks at 90 million. Mae West, W. C. Fields, and Groucho Marx emerge. Golden age of radio and soap operas start national advertising industry. Comics target kids. Sinclair Lewis and Eugene O'Neil first Americans to win Nobel Prize for Literature.

1931—Radio news commentary (Kaltenborn, Thomas, and Winchell).

1933—Franklin D. Roosevelt's Fireside Chats on radio. FM radio. *Newsweek*. *King Kong*.

1935—Radio sponsorship.

1936–*Life* magazine and *March of Time* newsreels.

1937—Half of homes can hear *Hindenburg* blimp explosion.

1938—Modern newscast (CBS). *War of the Worlds*. Paperbacks.

1939—Paperback books. *Gone with the Wind*. *Wizard of Oz*.

1940—*Fantasia*. Paul Harvey on radio.

(continued on next page)

History of Newspapers

1936—John Steinbeck's *San Francisco News* stories of "Okies," which later become *The Grapes of Wrath.*

1937—Ernest Hemingway covers Spanish Civil War.

1938—Herb Caen starts *San Francisco Examiner's* "three dot" column.

1940—Gilbert Seldes publishes *In Fact,* first journalism review.

1942—Popular Scripps-Howard columnist Ernie Pyle covers everyday GI.

1945—Ernie Pyle killed by Japanese sniper in Pacific.

1947—Harvard produces *Nieman Reports,* a journalism review.

1948—Art Buchwald writes first column for *N.Y. Herald Tribune. Chicago Daily Tribune* prints "DEWEY DEFEATS TRUMAN."

1950—1,772 dailies.

1954—Radios outnumber newspapers.

1955—Anne Landers's advice column.

1956—National Press Club admits first African American member (Prattis).

1960—1,763 dailies.

1961—*Columbia Journalism Review.*

U.S. History

1941—U.S. enters World War II. Selective Service System lengthens service to 18 months.

1942—Atomic Age begins.

1943—Jitterbug dance.

1945—Atomic bombs dropped. Japan surrenders.

1946—Cold War. Bikini.

1947—Hutchins Commission urges social responsibility among media.

1948—Israel gains independence.

1949—People's Republic of China.

1950—Korean War. Women outnumber men. McCarthyism.

1952—AFL-CIO.

1953—DNA. Department of Health, Education, and Welfare.

1954—Civil rights movement. Segregation unconstitutional.

1956—Birth control pills. Martin Luther King Jr. leads bus boycott.

1957—Soviets launch *Sputnik.*

1960—John F. Kennedy–Richard Nixon debates on television. U.S. sends first troops to Vietnam.

1961—Berlin Wall. Cosmonaut in orbit.

1962—John Glenn orbits Earth. Cuban missile crisis.

History of Other Media

1941—Commercial broadcasting okayed by Federal Communications Commission. Franklin D. Roosevelt reaches 90 million on radio. *Citizen Kane.*

1942—Margaret Bourke-White photographs war. Office of War Information (propaganda).

1944—NBC newscast.

1945—Edward R. Murrow on radio reports from Buchenwald. *Ebony* (Johnson).

1947—Transistor.

1948—Ed Sullivan. NBC's John Cameron Swayze invents sign-offs. 15-minute newscasts. Federal Communication Commission freezes licenses. Disc Jockey era begins on radio.

1949–Network television.

1951—First commercial computer.

1952–*Today Show* (NBC).

1953—Marilyn Monroe on *Playboy's* first cover (Hefner). *TV Guide* (Annenberg).

1954—Color television. Elvis Presley. Rock 'n Roll.

1955—*National Review* (Buckley).

1956—NBC's *Huntley-Brinkley Report* makes first anchor/stars.

1957—Quiz show scandals.

1960s—CBS's *Harvest of Shame.* Modern 30-second commercials. Icons

History of Newspapers

1962—Russell Baker becomes editorial-page columnist for *N.Y. Times*. Tom Wolfe joins *N.Y. Herald Tribune*.

1965—*N.Y. Times's* David Halberstam reports critically from Vietnam. Saigon street execution photographed (Adams). Erma Bombeck starts column in Dayton.

1966—Use of hot-metal composing machines peaks.

1967—Newspapers computerize. First news ombudsman. Average weekday newspaper readership 76 percent.

1968—Journalism reviews grow in popularity.

1969—Seymour Hersch reveals My Lai massacre.

1970s—Offset printing. Terminals replace typewriters, and photos stored digitally.

1970—*N.Y. Times* starts op-ed page. 1,748 dailies.

1971—*Pentagon Papers* decision.

1972—At *Washington Post*, Benjamin C. Bradlee steers Bob Woodward and Carl Bernstein's Watergate coverage. The pair, *Washington Post* columnist David S. Broder,

U.S. History

1963—John F. Kennedy assassinated.

1965—Inflation jumps 10 percent in next 15 years. Hippies gathering in San Francisco.

1967—Antiwar and racial tension erupts. Six-Day War.

1968—Tet offensive in Vietnam. Martin Luther King Jr. and Robert Kennedy assassinated. *Apollo 8* orbits Moon.

1969—Woodstock. Neil Armstrong lands on Moon. Household income doubles over next 10 years. War demonstrations increase.

1970—U.S. population 203 million. More than a third of all workers are women.

1972—Watergate scandal.

1973—OPEC quadruples oil prices. *Roe v. Wade*.

1974—Richard Nixon resigns.

1975—U.S. withdrawn from Vietnam.

1978—Approximately 900 commit mass suicide in Guyana.

1979—Iran hostage situation. Gas shortage. High inflation.

1981—AIDS virus diagnosed. First woman U.S. Supreme Court justice (O'Connor). U.S.

History of Other Media

Marshall McLuhan and Howard Cosell. Magazines reject *Silent Spring* (Carson). *I.F. Stone's Weekly* attacks cover-ups and conservatives.

1961—Edward Murrow leaves television.

1962—First African American network television reporter (Goode).

1963—24-hour news coverage of John F. Kennedy's assassination. CBS and NBC move to 30-minute newscasts. *Show* magazine prints Gloria Steinem's "A Bunny's Tale" about *Playboy*.

1964—Negative political ad attacks Barry Goldwater. Beatles and Rolling Stones.

1965—Color television. Satellites send messages across Atlantic. Second "New Journalism" movement (Talese, Wolfe, Didion, Capote, Mailer, and Thompson).

1966—Fred Friendly quits when CBS broadcasts *I Love Lucy* rerun instead of Senate Vietnam hearing. *In Cold Blood* (Capote).

1967—Belva Davis (San Francisco's KPIX) becomes first African American female anchor. *Rolling Stone* (Wenner).

1968—Walter Cronkite's antiwar "We Are Mired in Stalemate" broadcast. CBS's *60*

(continued on next page)

History of Newspapers

and *Chicago Daily News* columnist Mike Royko win Pulitzer Prizes.

1974—George F. Will joins *Washington Post.*

1975—*Wall Street Journal* publishes via satellite.

1976—Don Bolles (*Arizona Republic*) killed by Mafia car bomb.

1978—Competing Chicago columnists Gene Siskel and Roger Ebert join forces on television.

1980—*Washington Post* prints Janet Cooke's "Jimmy's World," which is proven a hoax. She returns her Pulitzer Prize in 1981. 1,745 dailies.

1982—*USA Today,* national daily. Openly gay, AIDS-infected reporter (Shilts) covers disease for *San Francisco Chronicle.*

1985—Associate Press's Terry Anderson held captive nearly seven years in Lebanon.

1987—Average weekday newspaper readership 65 percent.

1990—There are 15 fewer daily newspapers (1,611) compared to 1989.

1994—Top 20 chains own a third of all dailies. The 20 largest chains own a third of all dailies.

1996—*N.Y. Times* joins almost 700 newspapers already online.

U.S. History

hostages released from Iran. Military buildup. Recession. Aid to Contras.

1983—Strategic Defense Initiative. U.S. invades Grenada.

1984—Ronald Reagan proposes $180 bill. Deficit. U.S. becomes debtor nation. Rainbow Coalition (Jackson).

1985—Mikhail Gorbachev announces perestroika and glasnost.

1986—Iran-gate scandal. Chernobyl. U.S. attacks Libya. *Challenger* explosion.

1989—Fall of Berlin Wall and communism in Eastern Europe. Tiananmen Square. U.S. invades Panama. *Exxon Valdez* disaster.

1990—U.S. population nears 250 million.

1991—Breakup of Soviet Union. Gulf War. L.A. Police Department beats Rodney King, leads to 1992 riots.

1992—U.S. has $3 trillion debt. Ross Perot gets 19 percent of vote.

1993—World Trade Center bombed. Waco, Texas, siege.

1994—Nancy Kerrigan clubbed. O. J. Simpson flees.

1995—O. J. Simpson acquitted. Oklahoma City bombing.

1996—Royal divorces. Unabomber arrested.

1997—Princess Diana dies.

History of Other Media

Minutes. MPAA ratings introduced for movies.

1970s—Specialized magazines.

1970—PBS. Garry Trudeau starts *Doonesbury.*

1972—*Pong,* first video game. *Playboy* sells more than 7 million per month. Gloria Steinem founds *Ms.* ABC sportscaster Jim McKay covers Summer Olympics hostage crisis.

1974—*People.*

1975—"Family Hour" adopted. *MacNeil/Lehrer Report.* HBO.

1976—ABC offers Barbara Walters $1 million.

1977—*Star Wars.*

1978—Love Canal.

1979—Cable television takes off. News groups form on Internet. Three Mile Island.

1980—VCR. CNN (Turner). Sony Walkman. *Dallas*'s worldwide viewers 300 million.

1981—IBM launches personal computer.

1982—Digital music (compact discs). *Thriller* (Jackson).

1983—*The Day After,* a television film about nuclear fallout, airs. Cell phone networks.

1984—Michael Eisner takes over Disney. Computer is *Time*'s Man of the Year. Desktop publishing. *M*A*S*H* finale draws 122 million.

History of Newspapers

1997—*N.Y. Times* uses color. Average weekday newspaper readership is 58 percent.

1998—Newspaper sites proliferate on the Internet.

2000—Gannett chain's total circulation (7.3 million) almost more than next two largest chains' combined.

U.S. History

1998—Bill Clinton impeachment. Microsoft antitrust filed.

1999—Columbine school shooting. Y2K Bug.

History of Other Media

1985—Musicians unite for Live Aid and "We are the World."

1986—Oprah Winfrey becomes first African American to host national television talk show.

1987—Television evangelist scandals.

1990s—"CNN effect." Rush Limbaugh, Howard Stern, and Don Imus on radio. Direct marketing.

1990—Children's Television Act.

1991—Internet opens. CNN's Bernard Shaw covers bombing of Baghdad ("the center of Hell") live.

1992—MTV covers presidential campaign, registers 100,000 young voters. Grunge music.

1994—Yahoo!

1995—O. J. Simpson trial televised.

1996—Telecommunications Act sends companies scrambling to buy new stations. *Newsweek*'s Joe Klein publishes *Primary Colors* under "Anonymous."

1998—*Drudge Report* breaks Bill Clinton sex scandal. *Titanic.*

1999—Explosion of teen-oriented pop.

2000s—Oprah Winfrey's book club.

Index

List of Contributors

Tamara Kay Baldwin is a professor of communication at Southeast Missouri State University in Cape Girardeau. She earned her master's degree from Southeast Missouri State University, and her doctorate from Southern Illinois University at Carbondale. Her research publications focus on women in early British media history.

W. Joseph Campbell is an assistant professor at American University's School of Communication. He earned his doctorate in mass communication at the University of North Carolina, Chapel Hill, in 1997. Campbell is the author of two books, *The Emergent Independent Press in Benin and Côte d'Ivoire* (1998) and *Yellow Journalism: Puncturing the Myths, Defining the Legacies* (2001). His work also has appeared in *American Journalism, Editor and Publisher,* and *American Journalism Review.*

David A. Copeland is the author of *Debating the Issues in Colonial Newspapers: Primary Documents on Events of the Period* (2000), *Colonial American Newspapers: Character and Content* (1997), *Benjamin Keach and the Development of Baptist Traditions in Seventeenth-Century England* (2001), and more than forty-five book chapters, articles, and papers on the press and early America and religion and the press. A past president of the American Journalism Historians Association, he was named the Carnegie Foundation Virginia Professor of the Year in 1998. He received his Ph.D. in mass communication from the University of North Carolina and is the A. J. Fletcher Professor of Communication at Elon University.

Ralph Frasca is an associate professor of mass communication at Marymount University in Arlington, Virginia. He has authored many journal articles and book chapters about media history. He is a former newspaper reporter and editor. He earned his Ph.D. in mass communication from the University of Iowa.

Agnes Hooper Gottlieb is a professor of communication and the dean of freshman studies at Seton Hall University. She is the author of *Women Journalists and the Municipal Housekeeping Movement, 1868–1914* (2001) and coauthor of *1,000 Years, 1,000 People: Ranking the Men and Women Who Shaped the Millennium* (1998). She also is the author of numerous articles and book chapters about journalism history, specially focusing on women in journalism.

Bradley Hamm is an associate professor and associate dean for the School of Communications at Elon University. He earned his undergraduate degree at Catawba College (North Carolina), his master's degree at University of South Carolina, and his doctorate at University of North Carolina. His research has been published in *American Journalism, International Journal of Public Opinion Research, Egyptian Journal of Public Opinion Research,* and *Journalism Studies.* He has taught as a visiting professor in Osaka, Japan, and Nanjing, China.

Rod Kirkpatrick, the director of Journalism Programs at the University of Queensland, earned his bachelor's degree at Canberra College of Advanced Education in 1976 and his doctorate in history at the University of Queensland in 1995. He is the author of *Sworn to No Master: A History of the Provincial Press in Queensland to 1930* (1984) and *Country Conscience: A History of the New South Wales Provincial Press, 1841–1995* (2000).

Shannon E. Martin is a member of the faculty at the University of Maine, Orono. She earned her master's degree at Indiana University, Bloomington, and her doctorate at University of North Carolina, Chapel Hill. Her books include *Bits, Bytes and Big Brother: Federal Information Control in a Technological Age* (1995) and, with Kathleen A. Hansen, *Newspapers of Record in a Digital Age: From Hot Type to Hot Link* (1998).

Charles McKenzie earned his undergraduate and master's degree from the University of South Florida. He has written for the *Tampa Tribune, Rolling Stone,* Poynter.org, and the *Observer* (West Palm Beach, Florida). He also coedited *Mass Media Reader* (2000), a college textbook. He is now a Park Ph.D. Fellow at the University of North Carolina.

William A. Rugh holds a Ph.D. from Columbia University and has taught at the Fletcher School. During his thirty years as a U.S. foreign service officer, he was assigned to six Arab countries and was ambassador to Yemen and to the United Arab Emirates. His publications include a book on Arab media, *The Arab Press: News Media and Political Process in the Arab World* (1979, 1987), and numerous articles in journals and newspapers. Since 1995, he has been the president of America-Mideast Educational and Training Services, Inc., located in Washington, DC.

Donald L. Shaw earned his undergraduate and master's degrees at the University of North Carolina and his doctorate at the University of Wisconsin. He is the coauthor, with Maxwell E. McCombs, of *The Emergence of American Political Issues: The Agenda Setting Function of the Press* (1977). He is a Kenan Professor in the School of Journalism and Mass Communication at the University of North Carolina.